Chilton's

RABBIT/ SCIROCCO

1975-78

REPAIR & TUNE-UP GUIDE

ALL MODELS
including DIESEL

Managing Editor KERRY A. FREEMAN, S.A.E.
Senior Editor RICHARD J. RIVELE

President WILLIAM A. BARBOUR
Executive Vice President RICHARD H. GROVES
Vice President and General Manager JOHN P. KUSHNERICK

CHILTON BOOK COMPANY
Radnor, Pennsylvania
19089

Library of Congress Cataloging in Publication Data

Chilton Book Company. Automotive Editorial Dept.
   Chilton's Repair and tune up guide, VW Rabbit/Scirocco,
1975–1978.

   Includes index.
   1. Rabbit automobile.   2. Scirocco automobile.
I. Title.
TL215.R2C47   1978   629.28'7'22   78-7169
ISBN 0-8019-6736-8 pbk.

The Chilton Book Company expresses its appreciation to Volkswagen
of America, Inc., Englewood Cliffs, New Jersey 07632 for its assistance
in the research for this book.

Although the information in this guide is based on industry sources and
is as complete as possible at the time of publication, the possibility
exists that the manufacturer made later changes which could not be
included here. While striving for total accuracy, Chilton Book Company cannot assume responsibility for any errors, changes, or omis-
sions that may occur in the compilation of this data.

SAFETY NOTICE

Proper service and repair procedures are vital to the safe, reliable
operation of all motor vehicles, as well as the personal safety of those
performing repairs. This book outlines procedures for servicing and
repairing vehicles using safe, effective methods. The procedures
contain many NOTES, CAUTIONS and WARNINGS which should be
followed along with standard safety procedures to eliminate the
possibility of personal injury or improper service which could damage
the vehicle or compromise its safety.

It is important to note that repair procedures and techniques, tools
and parts for servicing motor vehicles, as well as the skill and experience
of the individual performing the work vary widely. It is not possible to
anticipate all of the conceivable ways or conditions under which vehicles
may be serviced, or to provide cautions as to all of the possible hazards
that may result. Standard and accepted safety precautions and equipment should be used when handling toxic or flammable fluids, and safety
goggles or other protection should be used during cutting, grinding,
chiseling, prying, or any other process that can cause material removal
or projectiles.

Some procedures require the use of tools specially designed for a
specific purpose. Before substituting another tool or procedure, you
must be completely satisfied that neither your personal safety, nor the
performance of the vehicle will be endangered.

Contents

1 General Information and Maintenance 1

How to use this book, 1
Tools and Equipment, 2
Routine maintenance and lubrication, 4

2 Tune-Up and Troubleshooting 20

Tune-Up Procedures and Specifications, 20
Troubleshooting, 33

3 Engine and Engine Rebuilding 53

Engine Electrical System and Specifications, 53
Engine Service Procedures and Specifications, 59
Engine Rebuilding, 79

4 Emission Controls and Fuel System 97

Emission Control System and Service, 97
Fuel System and Carburetor Adjustments, 103

5 Chassis Electrical 120

Heater, Radio, Windshield Wipers, Instrument Panel, Light Bulbs and Fuses, 120

6 Clutch and Transaxle 128

Manual Transaxle, 128
Clutch, 132
Automatic Transmission, 134

7 Suspension and Steering 137

Front Suspension, 137
Rear Suspension, 140
Steering, 145

8 Brakes 150

Brake System Service and Specifications, 150

9 Body 164

Aligning Hoods and Doors, 164
Repairing Scratches, Dents and Rust Holes, 166

Appendix 175

Index 179

Quick Reference Specifications

For quick and easy reference, complete this page with the most commonly used specifications for your vehicle. The specifications can be found in Chapters 1 through 3 or on the tune-up decal under the hood of the vehicle.

TUNE-UP

Firing Order _____

Spark Plugs:

   Type _____

   Gap (in.) _____

Point Gap (in.) _____

Dwell Angle (°) _____

Ignition Timing (°) _____

   Vacuum (Connected/Disconnected) _____

Valve Clearance (in.)

   Intake _____   **Exhaust** _____

CAPACITIES

Engine Oil (qts)

   With Filter Change _____

   Without Filter Change _____

Cooling System (qts) _____

Manual Transmission (pts) _____

   Type _____

Automatic Transmission (pts) _____

   Type _____

Differential (pts) _____

   Type _____

COMMONLY FORGOTTEN PART NUMBERS

Use these spaces to record the part numbers of frequently replaced parts.

PCV VALVE   **OIL FILTER**   **AIR FILTER**

Manufacturer _____   **Manufacturer** _____   **Manufacturer** _____

Part No. _____   **Part No.** _____   **Part No.** _____

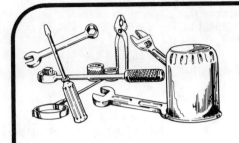

General Information and Maintenance

HOW TO USE THIS BOOK

Chilton's Repair and Tune-Up Guide for the Rabbit/Scirocco is intended to teach you more about the inner workings of your automobile and save you money in its upkeep. The first two chapters will be the most used, since they contain maintenance and tune-up information and procedures. The following chapters concern themselves with the more complex systems of the Rabbit or Scirocco. Operating systems from engine through brakes are covered to the extent that we feel the average do-it-yourselfer should get involved. Chilton's *Rabbit/Scirocco* won't explain rebuilding the transaxle for the simple reason that the expertise required and the investment in special VW tools make this task uneconomical. We will tell you how to change your own brake pads and shoes, replace points and plugs, and many more jobs that will save you money, give you personal satisfaction, and help you avoid problems.

Before loosening any bolts, read through the entire procedure. This will give you the overall view of what tools and supplies will be required. There is nothing more frustrating than having to walk to the bus stop on Monday morning because you were short one metric bolt during your Sunday af-ternoon repair. So read ahead and plan ahead.

The sections begin with a brief discussion of the system and what it involves, followed by adjustments, maintenance, removal and installation procedures and repair or over-haul procedures. When repair is considered to be out of your league, we tell you how to remove the part and then how to install the new or rebuilt replacement. In this way you at least save the labor costs. Backyard repair of such components as the alternator are just not practical.

Two basic mechanic's rules should be mentioned here. One, whenever the leftside of the car is referred to, it is meant to specify the driver's side of the car. Conversely, the right-side of the car means the passenger's side of the car. Second, most screws and bolts are removed by turning counterclockwise and tightened by turning clockwise. Safety is always the most important rule. Constantly be aware of the dangers involved in working on an automobile and take the proper precautions. Use jackstands when working under a raised vehicle. Don't smoke or allow an exposed flame to come near the battery or any part of the fuel system. Always use the proper tool and use it correctly; bruised knuckles and skinned fingers aren't a mechanic's standard equipment Always take your time and have patience; once you have some experience and gain confidence, working on your car will become an enjoyable hobby.

TOOLS AND EQUIPMENT

It would be impossible to catalog each tool that you would need to perform each or any operation in this book. It would also not be wise for the amateur to rush out and buy an expensive set of tools on the theory that he may need one of them at some time. The best approach is to proceed slowly, gathering together a good quality set of those tools that are used most frequently. Don't be misled by the low cost of bargain tools. It is far better to spend a little more for better quality. Forged wrenches, 10 or 12 point sockets and fine tooth ratchets are by far preferable to their less expensive counterparts. As any good mechanic can tell you, there are few worse experiences than trying to work on a car or truck with bad tools. Your monetary savings will be far outweighed by frustration and mangled knuckles.

Begin accumulating those tools that are used most frequently; those associated with routine maintenance and tune-up.

You will find that almost every nut and bolt on your car is metric. In addition to the normal assortment of screwdrivers and pliers you should have the following tools for routine maintenance jobs:

1. Metric wrenches—sockets and combination open-end/box wrenches to at least 18 mm; note that many parts of the car also use allen head bolts.
2. Jackstands—for support;
3. Band wrench—for oil filters;
4. Oil filler spout—for pouring oil;
5. Grease gun—for chassis lubrication;
6. Hydrometer—for checking the battery;
7. A container for draining oil;
8. Many rags for wiping up the inevitable mess.

In addition to the above items there are several others that are not absolutely necessary, but handy to have around. These include oil dry, a transmission funnel and the usual supply of lubricants, antifreeze, and fluids, although these can be purchased as needed. This is a basic list for routine maintenance, but only your personal needs and desire can accurately determine your list of tools.

The second list of tools is for tune-ups. While the tools involved here are slightly more sophisticated, they need not be outrageously expensive. There are several inexpensive tach/dwell meters on the market that are every bit as good for the average mechanic as a $100.00 professional model. Just be sure that it goes to at least 1,200–1,500 rpm on the tach scale and that it works on 4, 6 or 8 cylinder engines. A basic list of tune-up equipment could include:

1. Tach-dwell meter;
2. Spark plug wrench;
3. Timing light (a DC light that works from the car's battery is best, although an AC light that plugs into 110 V house current will suffice at some sacrifice in brightness);

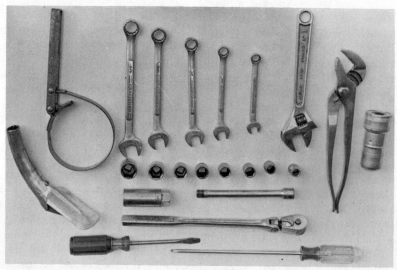

A basic assortment of hand tools will handle most maintenance jobs

4. Wire spark plug gauge;

5. Set of feeler blades.

6. Valve adjusting tools (VW 10-208 and 10-209. You'll need these if you plan on adjusting the valves, and they can be ordered through a VW dealer.

Here again, be guided by your own needs. A feeler blade will set the point gap as easily as a dwell meter will read well, but slightly less accurately. And since you will need a tachometer anyway . . . well, make your own decision.

SERIAL NUMBER IDENTIFICATION

Safety Compliance Sticker and Vehicle Identification Plate

The Safety Compliance sticker will be found on the crossmember under the hood, just above the grille, or on the left door jam. It is your assurance that the vehicle complies with all Federal Motor Vehicle Safety Standards (FMVSS) in effect at the time of manufacture. It also shows the month and year of manufacture and the chassis number. The chassis number is perforated to prevent transferral to another vehicle.

Vehicle identification plate location (arrow)

Chassis Number

The chassis number is located on the driver's side windshield pillar (Scirocco) and riveted to the drivers side of the dash (Rabbit) and is visible through the windshield. The chassis number is also on the right suspension strut mounting and the vehicle identification plate.

The Scirocco chassis number is on the driver's side windshield pillar

The Rabbit chassis number is on the driver's side instrument panel

Chassis number location

Engine Number

The engine number is stamped on the front of the engine block between the fuel pump and the distributor.

Engine number location

Engine Codes

Year	Engine Code	Description
1975	FC	1.5 liter, manual transmission and Zenith 32/32-2B2 carburetor
	FG	1.5 liter, automatic transmission and Zenith 32/32-2B2 carburetor
1976	FN	1.6 liter, manual or automatic transmission and Zenith 32/32-2B2 carburetor
	EF	1.6 liter with CIS fuel injection
1977	EE	1.6 liter with CIS fuel injection
	CK	1.5 liter Diesel
1978	FX	1.6 liter with Solex 34 PICT-5 carburetor
	EH	1.6 liter with CIS fuel injection
	CK	1.6 liter diesel

Manual Transmission

The manual transmission type number is located on a pad near the left side driveshaft. The code letters and date of manufacture are stamped on a pad at the lower center of the bell housing next to the starter.

Automatic Transmission

The automatic transmission type number is stamped into the center of the case near the dipstick. The code letter and date of manufacture are stamped on a pad on the upper center portion of the bell housing.

ROUTINE MAINTENANCE

Air Cleaner

The air filter is a key part of the engine. A restrictive, dirty element will cause a reduction in fuel economy and performance and an increase in exhaust emissions. The air filter should be cleaned or replaced according to the maintenance interval chart in this chapter.

SERVICE

1. Unsnap the cover retaining clips and remove the cover. The filter will probably come off with the cover.

2. Lift out the paper filter element. If it is very dirty and you cannot see light through it, discard the filter.

3. Wipe out the housing and replace the element.

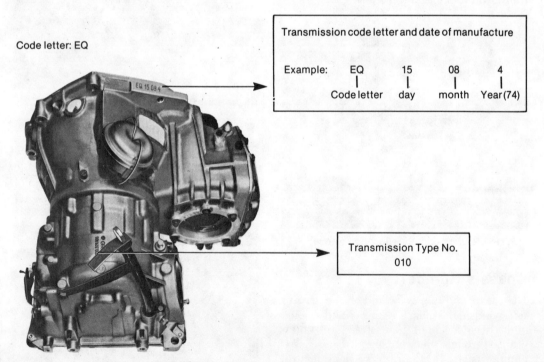

Code letter: EQ

Transmission code letter and date of manufacture

Example:

EQ	15	08	4
Code letter	day	month	Year (74)

Transmission Type No.
010

Automatic transmission code location

MANUAL TRANSMISSION TYPE NO. 020

Code letter: GC

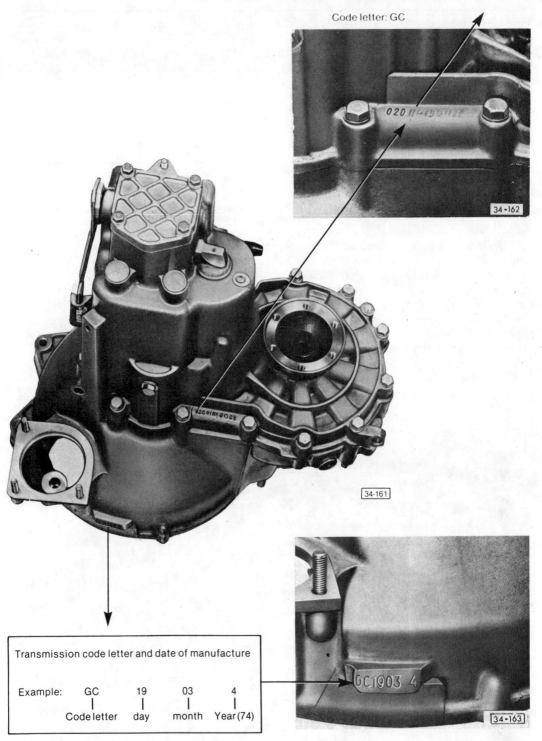

Transmission code letter and date of manufacture

Example: GC   19   03   4
             | | | |
         Code letter   day   month   Year (74)

Manual transmission code location

Maintenance Interval Chart

(thousands) miles	7.5	15	22.5	30	37.5	45	52.5	60	67.5	75	82.5	90
or months	6	12	18	24	30	36	42	48	54	60	66	72
Oil Change & General Maintenance	●	●	●	●	●	●	●	●	●	●	●	●
Tune up & Emission Control		●		●		●		●		●		●
Vehicle Maintenance		●		●		●		●		●		●

Crankcase Ventilation Valve

A PCV valve is installed in the hose between air cleaner and rocker cover on 1975–77 models. 1978 models have no valve. Blow-by gasses are routed from the camshaft cover to the air cleaner. Check the hoses at every tune-up for clogging or deterioration and clean or replace them as necessary. A clogged ventilation hose will cause excessive crankcase pressure and result in oil leaks. Keep the lines clean. Clean the crankcase ventilation valve when specified in the maintenance interval chart in this chapter.

Evaporative Canister

This system contains and disposes of raw fuel vapors from the fuel tank and carburetor. The charcoal canister connecting lines and fuel tank filler cap should be checked visually and discarded and replaced when specified in the maintenance interval chart in this chapter.

The air filter on the gasoline engine is on the right side fender

On the Rabbit diesel remove the hose from rocker cover to allow room

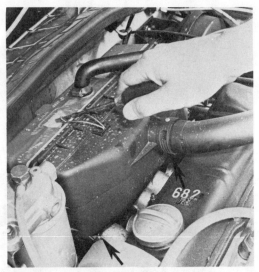

Unsnap the clips from the filter housing. There are also 2 on the bottom

Belts

CHECKING TENSION, ADJUSTING, AND REPLACEMENT

Check the belt tension every 3 months or 3000 miles. Push in on the drive belt about midway between the crankshaft pulley and the alternator. If the belt deflects more than $9/16$ in. or less than $3/8$ in., it's too loose or too tight. If the belt is frayed or cracked, replace it. Adjust belt tension as follows:

NOTE: *The alternator, A/C and air pump belts are adjusted the same way.*

1. Loosen both nuts on the bracket.
2. When replacing the belt, pry the alter-

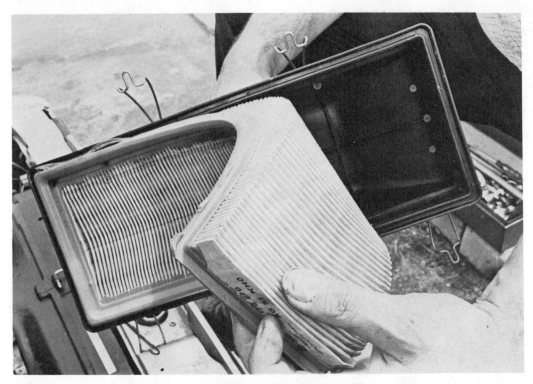

Remove the filter element from the housing

Filter showing slight dirt can be cleaned and re-used. If the filter is very dirty, install a new one

The crankcase ventilation valve should be cleaned at the specified interval

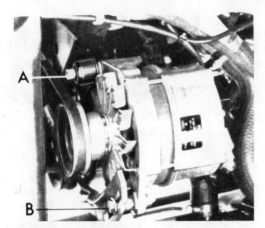

Alternator mounting bolts

Check the belt deflection (arrow)

nator toward the engine and slip the belt from the pulleys.

3. Carefully pry the alternator out with a bar, such as a ratchet handle or broom handle, and then tighten the alternator bracket nuts.

4. Recheck the tension.

The alternator drive belt also operates the water pump. It is good insurance to carry an extra belt in the trunk.

Air Conditioning

NOTE: *"Exercise" the A/C system at least once a week by running it for several minutes. This prevents seals from drying out from lack of lubrication.*

This book contains no repair or maintenance procedures for the air conditioning system other than checking drive belt ten-

sion and checking the refrigerant level. It is recommended that any repairs be left to the experts, whose personnel are well aware of the hazards and who have the proper equipment.

CAUTION: *The compressed refrigerant used in the air conditioning system expands into the atmosphere at a temperature of −21.7°F or lower. This will freeze any surface, including your eyes, that it contacts. In addition, the refrigerant decomposes into a poisonous gas in the presence of flame. Do not open or disconnect any part of the air conditioning system.*

SIGHT GLASS CHECK (REFRIGERANT LEVEL)

You can safely make a few simple checks to determine if your air conditioning system needs service. The tests work best if the temperature is warm (about 70°F).

1. Place the automatic transmission in Park or the manual transmission in Neutral. Set the parking brake.

2. Run the engine at a fast idle (about 1,500 rpm) either with the help of a friend, or by temporarily readjusting the idle speed screw.

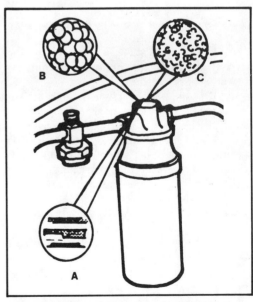

Oil streaks (A), constant bubbles (B) or foam (C) indicate there is not enough refrigerant in the system. Occasional bubbles during initial operation is normal. A clear sight glass indicates a proper charge of refrigerant or no refrigerant at all, which can be determined by the presence of cold air at the outlets in the car. If the glass is clouded with a milky white substance, have the receiver/drier checked professionally

3. Set the controls for maximum cold with the lower on high.

4. Locate the sight glass in one or the system lines and wipe it clean. Usually it is on the left alongside the top of the radiator.

5. If you see bubbles, the system must be recharged. Very likely there is a leak at some point.

6. If there are no bubbles and air coming from the vents is warm, the system needs a complete charge. If there are no bubbles and the vent air is cold, the system is ok.

7. You are probably making these tests because you think there is something wrong. As a further check, check the temperature of the 2 lines going to the belt driven compressor. If they are both the same temperature, the system is empty.

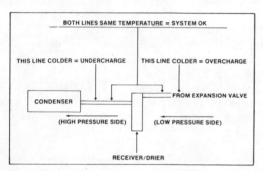

Checking refrigerant charge by line temperature

8. Have an assistant in the car turn the fan control on and off to operate the compressor clutch. Watch the sight glass.

9. If bubbles appear when the clutch is disengaged and disappear when it is engaged, the system is properly charged.

10. If the refrigerant takes more than 45 seconds to bubble when the clutch is disengaged, the system is overcharged. This usually causes poor cooling at low speeds.

CAUTION: *If it is determined that the system has a leak, it should be corrected as soon as possible. Leaks may allow moisture to enter and cause a very expensive rust problem.*

Fluid Level Checks
ENGINE OIL

Engine oil level should be checked weekly as a matter of course. Always check the oil with the car on level ground and after the engine has been shut off for about five minutes. The oil dipstick is located on the front side of the engine.

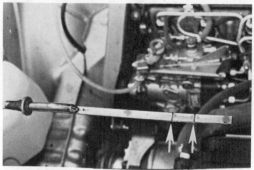

There is approximately ½ quart between the minimum and maximum marks on the oil dipstick

1. Remove the dipstick and wipe it clean.
2. Reinsert the dipstick.
3. Remove the dipstick again. The oil level should be between the two marks. The difference between the marks is one quart.
4. Add oil through the capped opening on the top of the valve cover. Select oil of the proper viscosity from the chart later in this chapter.

Add oil through the capped opening

Manual Transmission

Up to transmission number 06 054, check the oil level at the oil control plug. Remove the plug with a 5 mm allen wrench and insert your finger. The level should be even with the top of the hole. If not, add SAE 80 or 90 gear oil through the filler plug with a bulb syringe or oil squirt can.

Manual transaxle up to Number 06054—(A) filler, (B) drain plug

Later transmissions (beginning with number 07 054), the oil level is checked and filled at the oil control plug (arrow). Beginning with 1976 models, the transmission is lifetime filled at the factory.

Check the manual transmission fluid level at the oil plug (arrow) on later transmissions

Automatic Transmission

The automatic transmission dipstick is located at the right-side of the engine compartment near the battery. Use the following procedure when checking the fluid level:

1. Idle the engine for a few minutes with the selector in Neutral. Apply the parking brake.

2. Remove the dipstick, wipe it clean, reinsert it, and withdraw it again.

3. The fluid level should be within the two marks. Top up with Dexron® automatic transmission fluid. Bear in mind that the difference between the two marks is less than one pint. Use a long-necked funnel to add

Automatic transmission dipstick location

the fluid. Fluid should be drained and replaced at the specified interval in the maintenance interval chart in this chapter to drain/replace the fluid, see, "Automatic Transmission" in Chapter 6.

Automatic Transaxle Final Drive

The final drive uses SAE 80 or 90 gear oil. The filler plug is located on the left-side of the unit directly behind the axle driveshaft. Check and add oil in the same manner as the manual transaxle.

Brake Master Cylinder

The brake fluid reservoir is located on the left-side of the engine compartment at the firewall. Brake fluid level should be maintained at the MAX line on the reservoir. Level can be checked visually without removing the cap on this translucent unit. If necessary, top up with a brand name hydraulic fluid which bears the DOT 3 or 4 marking. This information will be stamped on the can.

Coolant

Make it a habit to periodically check the coolant level in the radiator. Ideally, this should be performed when the engine is cold. When checking the coolant level on a warm or hot engine, turn the cap to the first catch to permit pressure to be released from the system. Turn the cap off counterclockwise. A gauge plate inside the radiator aids in level checking—the coolant should be maintained at the bottom of the plate. Use only a quality

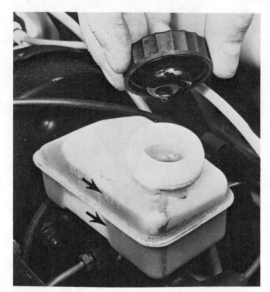

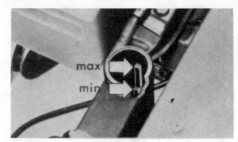

A gauge in the radiator neck makes checking coolant level easier

Arrows indicate the maximum/minimum marks on the see-through brake master cylinder reservoir. Fluid is added through the capped opening

If the car is equipped with a radiator overflow tank, check the level on the side of the tank and add coolant here

ethylene glycol antifreeze to refill or top up the cooling system.

The cooling system should be drained, cleaned, and refilled according to the maintenance interval in this chapter. There is a petcock at the bottom of the radiator and a drain plug on the engine block to facilitate drain-

Capacities

Year	Engine Displacement Cu in. (cc)	Engine Crankcase (qts) With Filter	Engine Crankcase (qts) Without Filter	Transmission (pts) Manual	Transmission (pts) Automatic	Drive Axle (pts)	Gasoline Tank (gals)	Cooling System (pts)
1975	89.7 (1,471)	3.7	3.2	2.6	12.8 ①	1.6	12.1	②
1976–77	96.8 (1588) Gasoline	3.7	3.2	2.6	12.8 ①	1.6	12.1	②
1978	88.9 (1,457) Gasoline	3.7	3.2	2.6	12.8 ①	1.6	12.1	②
1977–78	89.7 (1471) Diesel	3.7	3.2	2.6	12.8 ①	1.6	12.1	②

① Dry refill; normal refill is 6.4 pts
② 1975–77 Rabbit, Scirocco—11.9 gals.
   1978 Rabbit, Scirocco—10.5 gals.

Three routine level checks—coolant (left), windshield washer reservoir (center), and battery (right)

ing. Use one of the many commercially available cleaners to flush out the system. These remove rust and scale which cut down on cooling efficiency. Refill with the correct water/antifreeze solution for anticipated temperatures. An antifreeze percentage chart is included in the "Appendix."

Steering Gear

The rack and pinion steering gear is filled with lubricant and sealed at the factory. If you notice any leaking, have it checked at the dealer.

Battery

The battery is located at left front of the engine compartment. Routinely check the battery electrolyte level and specific gravity. A few minutes occasionally spent monitoring battery condition is worth saving hours of frustration when your car won't start due to a dead battery. Only distilled water should be used to top up the battery, as tap water, in many areas, contains harmful minerals. Two tools which will facilitate battery maintenance are a hydrometer and a squeeze bulb filler. These are cheap and widely available at automotive parts stores, hardware stores, etc. The specific gravity of the electrolyte should be between 1.27 and 1.20. Keep the top of the battery clean, as a film of dirt can sometimes completely discharge a battery. A solution of baking soda and water may be used to clean the top surface, but be careful to flush this off with clear water and that none of the solution enters the filler holes. Clean the battery posts and clamps with a wire

brush to eliminate corrosion deposits. Special clamp and terminal cleaning brushes are available for just this purpose. Lightly coat the posts and clamps with petroleum jelly or chassis grease after cleaning them.

Tires and Wheels

Buy a tire pressure gauge and keep it in the glovebox of your car. Service station air gauges are generally either not working or inaccurate and should not be relied upon. The decal on the left door post gives the recommended air pressures for the standard tires. If you are driving on replacement tires of a different type, follow the inflation recommendations of the manufacturer and never exceed the maximum pressure stated on the sidewall. Always check tire pressure when the tires are cool because air pressure in-

Tread wear bars show up as horizontal bands across the tire when the tire is worn to less than $1/16$ in.

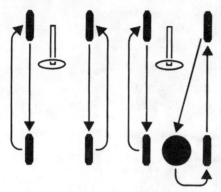

Tire rotation not including spare (left) or including spare (right)

Two kinds of inline fuel filters are used on gas engines. The carbureted models use this one. Fuel injected models use a larger canister type

creases with heat and readings will be 4–6 psi higher after the tire has been run. For continued expressway driving, increase the tire pressure by a few pounds in each tire. Never mix tires of different construction on your Rabbit or Scirocco. When replacing tires, ensure that the new tire(s) are the same size and type as those which will be remaining on the car. Intermixing bias ply tires with radial or bias belted can result in unpredictable and treacherous handling.

TIRE ROTATION

To equalize tire wear and thereby lengthen the mileage you obtain from your tires, rotate them every 5 or 6,000 miles. The pattern shown is for radial tires. Use an X rotation pattern if you've replaced the original tires with nonradials.

Fuel Filter

GASOLINE ENGINES

Early models (up to Chassis No. 175 3 394 505 Rabbit or 535 2 052 618 Scirocco) have a fuel filter located under the top cover of the fuel pump (see Chapter 4, Fuel Pump). To remove and/or clean it:

1. Disconnect the fuel line from the top cover of the pump.

2. Remove the single screw which retains the cover.

3. Lift off the cover and remove the strainer.

4. Clean the strainer in solvent and air dry.

5. Replace the strainer in the reverse order of removal.

Models following the above serial numbers have only a flow-through, in-line fuel filter located in the fuel line near the air cleaner.

This filter is easily replaced by removing the hose clamps from each end of the line and replacing the filter with a new one. Reinstall and tighten the clamps. Note the direction of flow, which is the direction of the white arrow.

NOTE: *1978 models use a larger fuel filter that cannot be used on earlier models.*

DIESEL ENGINES

The diesel engine uses a canister type fuel filter, which should be replaced according to the maintenance intervals in this chapter. The filter is located on the right-hand side of the engine compartment between the fender and the air cleaner.

To replace the filter:

1. Remove the 2 filter support mounting nuts. Remove the filter unit from the studs and turn it upside down on the studs.

2. Using an open end wrench on the end of the filter housing (or a small band wrench),

Remove the diesel fuel filter from the mounting studs

loosen (do not remove) the filter housing. Be careful; fuel will probably out.

3. Turn the filter right side up and unscrew the filter by hand. Discard the old filter.

4. Apply a thin film of diesel fuel to the new filter gasket and tighten the new filter by hand. Replace the filter support on the mounting studs.

5. Crank the engine until it starts and accelerate a few times until the engine runs smoothly. Check for leaks.

BLEEDING THE FUEL SYSTEM

Bleeding the fuel system is not required. After the filter or other fuel system parts

Invert the filter and loosen it

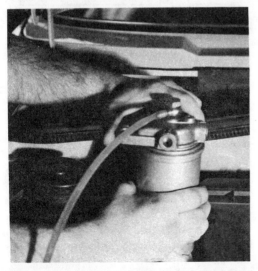

Turn the filter right side up and remove it by hand

have been replaced, simply crank the engine until it starts and accelerate a few times until the engine runs smoothly.

DRAINING WATER FROM THE DIESEL FUEL FILTER

Diesel fuel tends to collect water which will settle in the bottom of the filter housing. It is very important to drain the water out periodically.

Several types of filters have been installed.

Fuel Filter with Primer Pump and Vent Screw

1. Loosen the vent screw (A) and the drain plug and drain water out into a container until clean fuel appears. Close the vent screw, and the drain screw. Start the engine and accelerate until the engine runs smoothly.

Fuel filter with primer pump, vent screw (A)

Fuel Filter Without Primer Pump and With Vent Screw

Loosen the vent screw and drain plug and drain water out into a container until clean fuel appears. Close the drain plug and vent screw. Start the engine and accelerate a few times until the engine runs smoothly.

Fuel Filter Without Vent Screw

Disconnect the fuel return line at the injection pump. Loosen the filter drain plug and drain water out into a container until clean fuel appears. Reconnect the fuel return line at the injection pump. Start the engine and

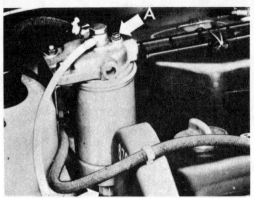

Fuel filter without primer pump, but with vent screw (A)

Fuel filter without vent screw. On all types of filters drain water by loosening the drain plug (arrow)

accelerate a few times until the engine runs smoothly.

LUBRICATION

Oil and Fuel Recommendations

GASOLINE ENGINES

Your Rabbit or Scirocco is designed to operate on regular lead-free fuel. The octane ratings are listed on the inside of the fuel filler door. Use of leaded gasoline will render the catalyst ineffective.

Oil must be selected with regard to the anticipated temperatures during the period before the next oil change. Using the chart, select the oil viscosity prior to the next oil change for the lowest expected temperature and you will be assured of easy cold starting and sufficient engine protection. The oil you pour into your engine should have the designation "SE" marked on the top of its container. Under the classification system adopted by the American Petroleum Institute (API) in May, 1970, "SE" is the highest designation for passenger car use. The "S" stands for passenger car and the second letter denotes a more specific application. "SA" oil, for instance, contains no additives and is suitable only for very light-duty usage. Oil designated "MS" (motor severe) may also be used, since this was the highest classification under the old API rating system.

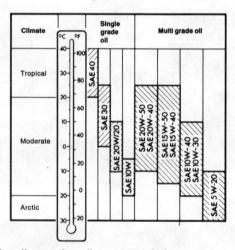

Gasoline engine oil recommendations

DIESEL ENGINES

The Rabbit diesel engine is designed to run on Diesel Fuel No. 2. Since diesel fuel is generally available along major truck routes, supply is not usually a problem, though it is wise to check in advance.

Several diesel station guides are available from fuel companies and are normally sold at diesel fuel stations.

Some U.S. States and Candian provinces require purchasers of diesel fuel to obtain a special permit to buy diesel fuel. Check with your local VW dealer or fuel supplier for regulations in your area.

Engine oils should be selected from the ac-

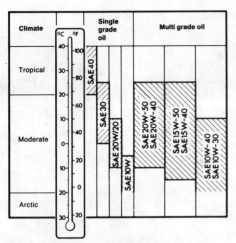

Diesel engine oil recommendations

companying chart. The SAE viscosity number should be chosen for the lowest anticipated temperature at which the engine will be required to start not for the temperature at the time the oil is changed.

Use only oils designated by the API (American Petroleum Institute) for service CC or MIL-L-46152. The letters CC should appear somewhere on the oil can. This indicates that the oil provides protection from rust, corrosion and high temperature deposits in diesel engines used in moderate to severe service.

Oil Changes

ENGINE

Change the oil according to the maintenance interval chart in this chapter. This interval is only for average driving. If your car is being used under dusty conditions, change the oil and filter sooner. The same thing goes for cars being driven in stop and go city traffic, where acid and sludge buildup is a problem.

Always drain the oil after the engine has been run long enough to bring it to the normal operating temperature. Hot oil will flow easier and more contaminants will be removed with the oil than if it were drained cold. A large capacity drain pan, which can be purchased at any automotive supply store, will be more than paid back by savings from do-it-yourself containers for the used oil. You will find that plastic bleach containers make excellent storage bottles. Two ecologically desirable solutions to the used oil disposal problem are to take it to a service station and ask to dump it into their sump tank or keep it

and use it as a preservative for exposed wood around your home.

To change the oil:

1. Run the engine until it reaches the normal operating temperature.

2. Slide a drain pan under the oil pan drain plug.

3. Loosen the drain plug with a socket or box wrench, and then remove it by hand. Push in on the plug as you turn it out, so that no oil escapes until the plug is completely removed.

4. Allow the oil to drain into the pan.

5. Install the drain plug, making sure that the brass gasket is still on the plug. Tighten the plug to 22 ft lbs.

6. Refill the engine with oil. Start the engine and check for leaks.

MANUAL TRANSAXLE

It is relatively easy to change your own gear oil. The oil level should be checked twice a year and changed every 30,000 miles or three years, whichever comes first. The only equipment required is a drain pan, a wrench to fit the filler and drain plugs, and an oil suction gun. Gear oil can be purchased in gallon cans at the larger automotive supply stores.

To change the oil:

1. Jack up the front of the car and support it safely on stands.

2. Slide drain pan under the transaxle.

3. Remove the filler plug and then the drain plug.

4. When the oil has been completely drained, install the drain plug. Tighten to 18 ft lbs.

Using the suction gun, refill the gearbox or rear axle up to the level of the filler plug. Use an SAE 80 or 90 gear oil.

6. Install and tighten the filler plug.

AUTOMATIC TRANSMISSION

The final drive section of the automatic transmission requires no attention other than an occasional level check. Top up with SAE 80 or 90 hypoid gear oil.

VW of America recommends that the automatic transmission fluid be replaced every 30,000 miles, or 20,000 miles if you use your car for frequent trailer towing, mountain driving, or other severe service.

To change the fluid:

1. Purchase 4 quarts of automatic transmission fluid (Type A or Dexron®) and a pan gasket.

2. Slide a drain pan under the transmis-

sion. Jack up the front of the car and support it safely on stands.

3. Remove the drain plug and allow all the fluid to drain.

4. Remove the pan retaining bolts and drop the pan.

5. Discard the old gasket and clean the pan with solvent.

6. Unscrew and clean the circular oil strainer.

7. Install the oil strainer, but don't tighten the bolt too much—specified torque is only 4 ft lbs.

8. Using a long-necked funnel, refill the transmission with about 4.2 pts of fluid. Check the level with the dipstick. Run the car for a few minutes and check again.

Oil Filter Changes

VW recommends changing the oil filter at every other oil change, but it is more beneficial to replace the filter every time the oil is changed.

To replace oil and filter:

1. Drain the crankcase into a pan of sufficient capacity. The plug is in the end of the pan.

The oil drain plug is in the end of the oil pan

2. The filter is located on the front of the engine block. Reach in and turn the filter off counterclockwise. If it's tight use a filter strap wrench.

3. Carefully lift the filter out of the engine compartment and dispose of it.

4. Clean the oil filter adapter on the engine with a clean rag.

5. Lightly oil the rubber seal on the new filter and spin it on to the engine. Tighten it until the seal is flush and then give it an additional ½ to ¾ turn.

The oil filter (diesel shown) is on the side of the engine block that faces the front of the car. Turn in the direction of the arrow to tighten it

6. Refill the engine, start the engine and check for leaks.

Chassis Greasing

The Rabbit and Scirocco require no chassis greasing and are not equipped with grease nipples. Check the axle and driveshaft and tierod rubber boots occasionally for leaking or cracking. At the same time, squirt a few drops of oil on the parking brake equalizer (point where cables V-off to the rear brakes). The front wheel bearings do not require greasing unless they are disassembled.

Body Lubrication

Periodic lubrication will prevent squeaky, hard-to-open doors and lids. About every three months, pry the plastic caps off the door hinges and squirt in enough oil to fill the chambers. Press the plug back into the hinge after filling. Lightly oil the door check pivots. Finally, spray graphite lock lubricant onto your key and insert it into the door a few times.

Wheel Bearings

See Chapter 9.

PUSHING, TOWING, AND JUMP STARTING

If your car is equipped with a manual transaxle, it may be push started in an extreme emergency. It should be recognized that there is the possibility of damaging bumpers and/or fenders of both cars. Make sure that the bumpers of both cars are evenly matched. Depress the clutch pedal, select Second or Third gear, and switch the ignition On. When the car reaches a speed of approximately 10 or 15 mph, release the clutch to start the engine DO NOT ATTEMPT TO PUSH START AN AUTOMATIC RABBIT OR SCIROCCO.

Both manual and automatic models may be towed short distances. Attach tow lines to the towing eye on the front suspension or the left or right bumper bracket at the rear. Automatic equipped cars must be towed in Neutral no farther than 30 miles and no faster than 30 mph, unless the front wheels are off the ground.

If you plan on towing a trailer, don't exceed 885 lbs (trailer without brakes). Towing a trailer with an automatic equipped car places an extra load on the transmission and a few items should be made note of here. Make doubly sure that the transmission fluid is at the correct level. Change the fluid more frequently if you're doing much trailer hauling. Start out in 1 or 2 and use the lower ranges when climbing hills. Aftermarket transmission coolers are available which greatly ease the load on your automatic and one should be considered if you often pull a trailer.

Jump starting is the favored method of starting a car with a dead battery. Make sure that the cables are properly connected, negative-to-negative and positive-to-positive, or you stand a change of damaging the electrical systems of both cars. Keep the engine running in the donor car. If the car still fails to start, call a garage—continual grinding on the starter will overheat the unit and make repair or replacement necessary.

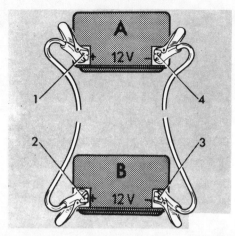

Jump starting a discharged battery (B) from a healthy battery (A). Make sure one cable is attached to the positive terminals (1,2) and the other cable to the negative terminals (3,4)

Jacking

The Rabbit and Scirocco are equipped with a single post, crank handle jack which fits the jacking points behind the front wheel and in front of the rear wheel. These are marked with triangular sections of the body stamping. Never use the tire changing jack for anything other than that. If you intend to use this book to perform your own maintenance, a good scissors or small hydraulic jack and two sturdy jackstands would be a wise purchase. Always chock the wheels when changing a tire or working beneath the car. It cannot be overemphasized, CLIMBING UNDER A CAR SUPPORTED BY JUST THE JACK IS EXTREMELY DANGEROUS. A jack can be safely placed under the front and rear jacking points, the engine crossmember, or the center of the rear axle beam. Take care that the jack pad is at least 4 in. square when jacking the rear axle, or you may damage it.

2

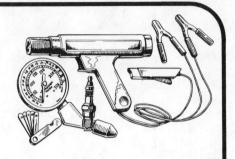

Tune-Up and Troubleshooting

TUNE-UP PROCEDURES

Diesel Rabbits do not require a tune-up as such. Your gasoline VW Rabbit should be tuned including points and plugs, at at least 12,000 mile intervals. The first one is provided under warranty along with a computer check, but from there on it's up to you to tune it yourself or pay to have it done. If you're experiencing some specific problem, turn to the "Troubleshooting" section at the rear of this chapter and follow the programmed format until you pinpoint the trouble. If you're just doing a tune-up to restore your Rabbit or Scirocco's pep and economy, proceed with the following steps.

The tune-up is a good time to take a look around the engine compartment for beginning problems and head them off before they get expensive. Look for oil and fuel leaks, deteriorating radiator or heater hoses, loose and/or frayed fan belt, etc. These little items have the tendency to develop into major headaches, so don't overlook anything.

Spark Plugs (Gasoline Engine Only)

Their primary job of igniting the air/fuel mixture aside, the spark plugs in your engine can also serve as very useful diagnostic tools.

Once removed, compare your spark plugs with the samples illustrated in section 4.6 of the "Troubleshooting" section at the end of this chapter. Typical plug conditions are shown along with their causes and remedies. Plugs which exhibit only normal wear and deposits can be cleaned, regapped, and installed. However, it is a good practice to replace them at every major tune-up.

The tool kit includes a spark plug socket and handle, but you will find it much more convenient to purchase a ½ in. drive, $^{13}/_{16}$ in. spark plug socket which can be turned with a ratchet handle. Using a small extension, all four plugs can be removed very quickly. Before removing the spark plug leads, number the towers on the distributor cap with tape. The firing order is 1-3-4-2, with the No. 1 cylinder at the right of the engine. This prevents mixups in the case of distributor cap replacement or spark plug wire replacement.

REMOVAL AND INSTALLATION

1. Grasp the spark plug boot and pull it straight out. Don't pull on the wire. If the boot(s) are cracked, replace them.
2. Place the spark plug socket firmly on the plug. Turn the spark plug out of the cylinder head in a counterclockwise direction.

NOTE: *The cylinder head is aluminum,*

Remove the spark plug wire by the boot; don't pull
on the cable

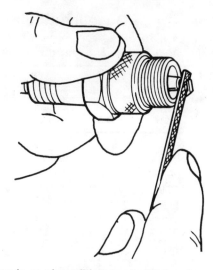

Plugs in good condition can be filed and re-used

*which is easily stripped. Remove plugs
only when the engine is cold.*

If removal is difficult, loosen the plug only
slightly and drip penetrating oil onto the
threads. Allow the oil time enough to work
and then unscrew the plug. This will prevent
damaging the threads in the cylinder head.
Be sure to keep the socket straight to avoid
breaking the ceramic insulator.

3. Continue on and remove spark plugs
Nos. 2, 3, and 4.

4. Inspect the plugs using the "Troubleshooting" section illustrations and then clean
or discard them according to condition.

New spark plugs come pre-gapped, but
double check the setting or reset them if you
desire a different gap. The recommended
spark plug gap is listed in the "Tune-Up
Specifications" chart. Use a spark plug wire
gauge for checking the gap. The wire should
pass through the electrode with just a slight
drag. Using the electrode bending tool on

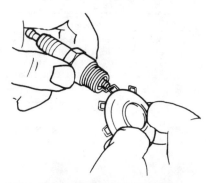

Check the plug gap with a wire gauge

the end of the gauge, bend the side electrode
to adjust the gap. Never attempt to adjust the
center electrode. Lightly oil the threads of
the replacement plug and install it hand-
tight. It is a good practice to use a torque
wrench to tighten the spark plugs on any car
and especially since the head is aluminum.
Install the ignition wire boots firmly on the
spark plugs.

Breaker Points and Condenser (Gasoline Engine only)

Snap off the two retaining clips on the distributor cap. Remove the cap and examine it
for cracks, deterioration, or carbon tracking.
Replace the cap, if necessary, by transferring
one wire at a time from the old cap to the
new one. Examine the rotor for corrosion or
wear and replace it if it's at all questionable.
Remove the dust shield. Check the points for
pitting and burning. Slight imperfections on

Remove the spark plug with a spark plug socket

Gasoline Engine Tune-Up Specifications

NOTE: *When analyzing compression test results, look for uniformity among cylinders, rather than specific pressure. The lowest reading cylinder should be within 20% of the highest.*

Year	Engine Displacement Cu in. (cc)	Spark Plugs Type	Gap (in.)	Distributor Point Dwell (deg)	Point Gap (in.)	Ignition Timing (deg) ●	Intake Valve Opens (deg)	Idle Speed (rpm)	Valve Clearance (in.) ① In	Ex
1975	89.7 (1,471)	W200 T30 N8Y	0.024–0.028	44–50	0.016	3 ATDC @ idle	4 BTDC	850–1000	0.008–0.012	0.016–0.020
1976	96.8 (1588)	W175 T30 N8Y	0.024–0.028	44–50	0.016	3 ATDC @ idle	4 BTDC	850–1000	0.008–0.012	0.016–0.020
1977	96.8 (1588)	W175 T30 N7Y	0.024–0.028	44–50	0.016	3 ATDC @ idle	4 BTDC	850–1000	0.008–0.012	0.016–0.020
1978	88.9 (1457)	W175 T30 N8Y	0.024–0.028	44–50	0.016	②	4 BTDC	850–1000	0.008–0.012	0.016–0.020

● Vacuum hose ON.
① Valve clearance need not be adjusted, it varies more than 0.002 in. from specification.
② 3 ATDC @ idle with CIS fuel injection
   7½ BTDC @ idle with 34 PICT-5 carburetor

CO Volume (%) at Idle:		US Models	Calif. Models
	Man trans	1.5 max	0.3 max
	Auto trans	1.0 max	0.3 max

Diesel Tune-Up Specifications

Model	Valve Clearance (cold) ① Intake (in.)	Exhaust (in.)	Intake Valve Opens (deg)	Injection Pump Setting (deg)	Injection Nozzle Pressure (psi) New	Used	Idle Speed (rpm)	Cranking Compression Pressure (psi)
1977–78 Diesel Rabbit	0.008–0.012	0.016–0.020	N.A.	Align marks	1849	1706	770–870	398 minimum

① Warm clearance given—Cold clearance: Intake   0.006–0.010
                                    Exhaust 0.014–0.018
Valve clearance need not be adjusted unless it varies more than 0.002 in. from specification.
N.A. Not Available

the contact surface may be filed off with a point file (fine emergy paper will also do), but it is usually wise to replace the breaker point set when tuning. Always replace the condenser when you replace the point set, unless you have access to a condenser tester.

To replace the breaker points:
1. Remove the rotor.
2. Unsnap the point connector from the terminal at the side of the distributor. Remove the retaining screw and lift out the point set.
3. Install the new point set, making sure that the pin on the bottom engages the hole in the breaker plate.
4. Install wire connector and the retaining screw (hand-tight).
5. Turn the fan belt or crankshaft pulley until the breaker arm rubbing block is on the high point of one of the cam lobes.

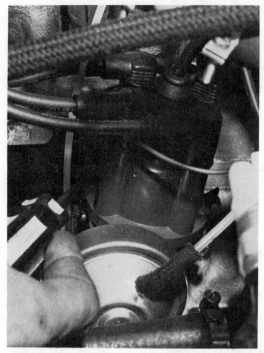

Unsnap the distributor cap retaining cups with a screwdriver

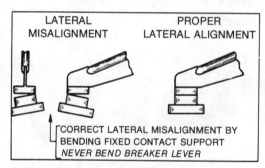

LATERAL MISALIGNMENT   PROPER LATERAL ALIGNMENT

CORRECT LATERAL MISALIGNMENT BY BENDING FIXED CONTACT SUPPORT
NEVER BEND BREAKER LEVER

Points must be correctly aligned

6. A 0.016 (0.40 mm) in. feeler gauge should just slip through the points. If the gap is incorrect, pivot a screwdriver in the point set notch and the two projections on the breaker plate to bring it within specifications.

7. When the gap is correct, tighten the retaining screw.

8. Lubricate the distributor cam with silicone grease.

9. Install the dust cover, rotor and distributor cap.

10. Check the dwell angle and the ignition timing as outlined in the following sections.

11. The condenser is mounted on the outside of the distributor. Undo the mounting screw and the terminal block to replace the condenser.

Dwell Angle (Gasoline Engine Only)

The dwell angle or cam angle is the number of degrees that the distributor cam rotates while the points are closed. There is an inverse relationship between dwell angle and point gap. Increasing the point gap will decrease the dwell angle and vice versa. Checking the dwell angle with a meter is a far more accurate method of measuring point opening than the feeler gauge method.

After setting the point gap to specification with a feeler gauge as described above, check the dwell angle with a meter. Attach the dwell meter according to the manufacturer's instruction sheet. A typical dwell meter hook-up is illustrated in the "Tune-Up" section at the end of the chapter. The negative lead is connected to the primary wire terminal No. 1 that runs from the coil to the distributor. Start the engine, let it idle and reach operating temperature, and observe the dwell on the meter. The reading should fall within the allowable range. If it does not, the gap will have to be reset or the breaker points will have to be replaced.

Ignition Timing (Gasoline Engine Only)

CAUTION: *When performing this or any other operation with the engine running, be very careful of the alternator belt and pulleys. Make sure that your timing light wires don't interfere with the belt.*

Ignition timing is an important part of the tune-up. It is always adjusted after the points are gapped (dwell angle changed), since altering the dwell affects the timing. Three basic types of timing lights are available, the neon, the DC, and the AC powered. Of the three, the DC light is the most frequently used by professional tuners. The bright flash put out by the DC light makes the timing marks stand out on even the brightest of days. Another advantage of the DC light is that you don't need to be near an electrical outlet. Neon timing lights are available for a few dollars, but their weak flash makes it necessary to use them in a fairly dark work area. One neon light lead is attached to the spark plug and the other to the plug wire. The DC light attaches to the spark plug and the wire with an adapter and two clips attach to the battery posts for power. The AC unit is simi-

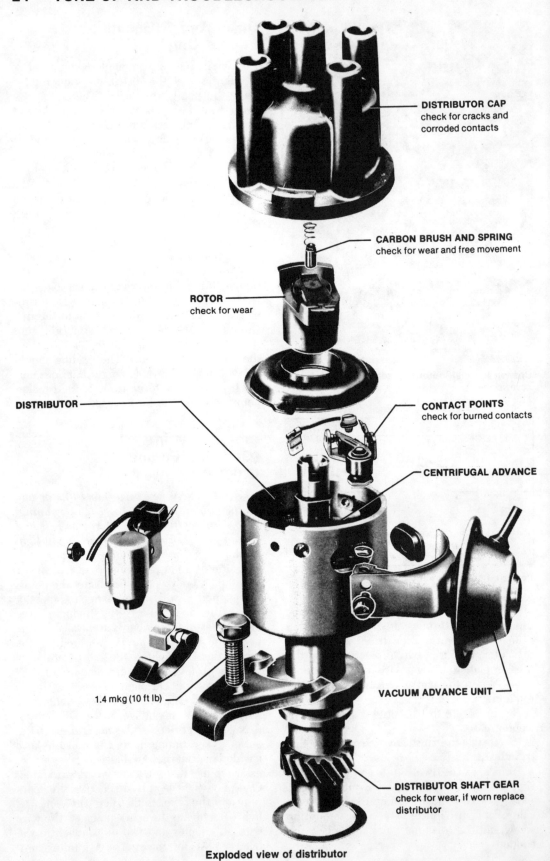

DISTRIBUTOR CAP
check for cracks and
corroded contacts

CARBON BRUSH AND SPRING
check for wear and free movement

ROTOR
check for wear

DISTRIBUTOR

CONTACT POINTS
check for burned contacts

CENTRIFUGAL ADVANCE

1.4 mkg (10 ft lb)

VACUUM ADVANCE UNIT

DISTRIBUTOR SHAFT GEAR
check for wear, if worn replace
distributor

Exploded view of distributor

lar, except that the power cable is plugged into a house outlet.

1. Attach the timing light as outlined above or according to the manufacturer's instructions. Hook-up a dwell/tachometer since you'll need an rpm indication for correct timing.

2. Locate the timing mark opening in the clutch or torque converter housing at the rear of the engine directly behind the distributor. The OT mark stands for TDC or 0° advance. The 3 mark designates 3° ATDC. Mark them with chalk so that they will be more visible. Don't disconnect the vacuum line.

3. Start the engine and allow it to reach the normal operating temperature. The engine should be running at normal idle speed.

4. Shine the timing light at the marks.

5. The light should now be flashing when the 3° line and the V-shaped pointer are aligned.

7. If not, loosen the distributor hold-down

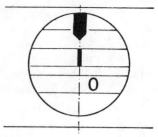

Timing mark (7½° BTDC—34 PICT-5 carburetor only)

bolt and rotate the distributor very slowly to align the marks.

8. Tighten the mounting nut when the ignition timing is correct.

9. Recheck the timing when the distributor is secured.

With ignition timing correctly adjusted, the spark plugs will fire at the exact instant in which the piston is nearing the top of the compression stroke, thus providing maximum power and economy.

Valve Lash (All Models)

Valve adjustment is one factor which determines how far the intake and exhaust valves open into the cylinder. If the valve clearance is too large, part of the lift of the camshaft will be used in removing the excessive clearance, therefore the valves will not open far enough. This has two ill effects; one, the valve gear will become noisy as the excess clearance is taken up and, two, the engine will perform poorly. This is because intake valves which don't open the full distance will admit a smaller air/fuel mixture into the cylinders. Exhaust valves which aren't opening the full amount create a greater backpressure in the cylinder which prevents the proper air/fuel mixture from entering the cylinder.

If the valve clearance is too small, the intake and exhaust valves will not fully seat on the cylinder head when they close. When a valve seats on the cylinder head it does two things; it seals the combustion chamber so that none of the gases in the cylinder can escape and it cools itself by transferring some of the heat absorbed from the combustion process through the cylinder head and into the cooling system. Therefore, if the valve clearance is too small, the engine will run poorly (due to gases escaping from the combustion chamber), and the valves will overheat and eventually warp (since they cannot properly

Locate the timing mark opening in the clutch or torque converter housing

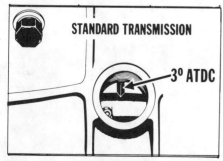

Timing marks (all except 34 PICT-5 carburetor)

transfer heat unless they fully seat on the cylinder head).

While all valve adjustments must be as accurate as possible, it is better to have the valve adjustment slightly loose than tight, as burned valves can result from too tight an adjustment.

ADJUSTMENT

VW recommends checking the valve clearance at 1,000 miles and then every 20,000 miles. The overhead cam acts directly on the valves through cam followers which fit over the springs and valves. Adjustment is made with an adjusting disc which fits into the cam follower. Different thickness discs result in changes in valve clearance.

NOTE: *Valve adjustment is rarely needed and, therefore, should not be considered a part of a normal tune-up.*

Valve clearance is checked with the engine at normal operating temperature.

1. Remove the air cleaner and hoses which attach to the camshaft cover.

2. Remove the eight bolts and lift off the camshaft cover.

Valve clearance is checked in the firing order, 1-3-4-2, and with the piston of the cylinder being checked at TDC of the compression stroke. Both valves will be closed at this position and the cam lobes pointing up. Turn

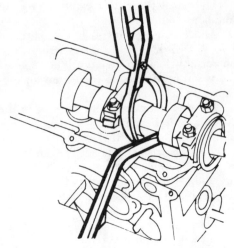

Removing or replacing clearance adjusting disc

the crankshaft pulley nut with a socket wrench to position the camshaft for checking.

3. With the No. 1 piston at TDC of the compression stroke, determine the clearance with a feeler gauge. Intake clearance should be 0.008–0.012 in. (0.20–0.30 mm); exhaust clearance 0.016–0.020 in. (0.40–0.50 mm).

4. Continue on to check the other three cylinders in the firing order, turning the crankshaft to bring that piston to the top of the compression stroke. Record the valve clearances as you go along.

Remove the camshaft cover (diesel engine shown)

Check the valve clearance with a feeler gauge. The camshaft lobe should be pointing up

If adjustment is necessary, the disc(s) will have to be removed and replaced with thicker or thinner ones which will yield the correct clearance. Discs are available in 0.002 in. (0.05 mm) increments from 0.12 in. (3.00 mm) to 0.17 in (4.25 mm). The disc size is etched into the underside. The etched side always faces the cam follower. VW recommends that two special tools be used to remove and install the adjustment discs. One is a pry bar (VW tool 10–208) to compress the valve springs and the other a pair of special pliers (VW tool 546) to remove the disc. The tools cost about $30 and are available from VW dealers (if they'll order them) or from Zelenda Tool and Machine Company, Forest Hills, NY 11374. A flat metal plate can be used to compress the spring if you are careful not to gouge the camshaft lobes. The cam follower has two slots which permit the disc to be lifted out. Again, you can improvise with a thin-bladed screwdriver. An assistant to pry the spring down while you remove the disc would be the ideal way to perform the operation.

NOTE: *When adjusting clearances on a diesel, the pistons must not be at TDC. Turn the crankshaft ¼ turn past TDC, so that the valves do not contact the pistons when the tappets are depressed.*

5. Replace the adjustment discs as necessary to bring the clearance within the 0.002 in. (0.05 mm) tolerance.

6. Recheck all valve clearances after adjustment.

7. Install the camshaft cover with a new gasket and replace the air cleaner.

Carburetor

The 1975–76 Rabbit and Scirocco use a Zenith 32/32-2B2 two-barrel carburetor with a vacuum-operated secondary throat. Beginning October 1, 1977 (1978 models) Rabbits except California may use a Solex 34 Pict-5 carburetor.

Idle speed adjustment screw (carburetors)

Idle mixture adjustment screw (carburetors)

ZENITH 32/32-2B2 CARBURETOR

Idle Speed Adjustment

1. Start the engine and run it until the normal operating temperature is reached.

2. Hook-up a tachometer to the engine and observe the idle speed.

3. If the idle speed differs from 925 rpm ±25 rpm, turn the curb idle screw to correct it. Make sure that you are turning the correct screw as shown in the illustration. Do not mistake the idle mixture screw for the curb idle screw.

Idle Mixture Adjustment

This adjustment should only be performed if you have access to an accurate CO meter, otherwise leave it to your dealer or a service garage.

1. Run the engine until it reaches normal operating temperature.

2. Check that ignition timing and idle speed are as specified.

On the Solex 34 PICT-5 Carburetor, adjust the idle speed at (A) and the CO at (B)

3. Adjust the CO level with the idle mixture screw to 2%.

SOLEX 34 PICT-5 CARBURETOR

The choke must be fully open and the engine at normal operating temperature.

1. Remove the hose from the charcoal filter at the air intake elbow. Plug the hose.

2. Remove the air injection hose at the air cleaner. Plug the hose.

3. Make sure no electrical equipment is ON. In particular the cooling fan must be OFF.

4. Connect a tachometer. Adjust the idle speed to specifications at the idle speed adjusting screw (A). The CO content can be adjusted at screw (B) if a CO meter is available.

5. Disconnect the tachometer and reconnect 11 hoses.

CIS FUEL INJECTION

Idle Speed and Mixture Ajustment

This adjustment can be made only with a

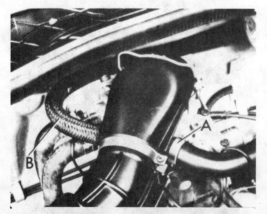

Disconnect the charcoal filter hose (B) at the elbow before adjusting idle speed on 34 PICT-5

Idle speed adjustment screw (arrow)—CIS fuel injection

CO adjustment tool (P377)—CIS fuel injection

CO meter and CO adjusting tool (VW-P377). Adjust at normal operating temperature. Check ignition timing and idle speed with vacuum lines connected.

Remove the charcoal filter hose from the air cleaner (except 1978 and later models) and turn the high beams and A/C on. Remove the plug from the CO adjusting hole and insert the special tool. Turn the screw clockwise to raise the CO percentage and counterclockwise to decrease it.

NOTE: *Do not push down on the tool or accelerate the engine with the tool in place.*

Remove the tool after each adjustment and accelerate the engine briefly before reading CO percentage.

DIESEL INJECTION SYSTEM

Idle Speed Adjustment

The idle speed should be adjusted with the engine warm, at normal operating temperature. Because the diesel engine has no conventional ignition such as the gasoline engine, you will also need an adaptor (VW 1324) to connect the dwell-tach or use the tachometer in the dash, if equipped. The adaptor is an impulse sensor with a magnetic base that is attached to the valve cover. The adaptor is powered by two leads attached to the battery and the tach lead is attached to the top of the adaptor. Without the adaptor or in-dash tach, you cannot accurately set idle

speed. Check with the manufacturer of the dwell tach to be sure the tach will work on diesel engines.

Adjust the idle speed to 850–950 rpm with the idle adjusting screw (arrow). When you are finished, lock the screw with a dab of paint or with non hardening thread sealer.

A special adaptor (VW 1324) is necessary to use an external tachometer on diesel engines

Adjust the diesel engine idle speed at the screw (arrow) on the injection pump. Be sure to lock the screw in place with sealer or paint after adjustment

Engine Tune-Up

NOTE: *Many tune-up procedures on the following pages apply only to the gasoline engine.*

Engine tune-up is a procedure performed to restore engine performance, deteriorated due to normal wear and loss of adjustment. The three major areas considered in a routine tune-up are compression, ignition, and carburetion, although valve adjustment may be included.

A tune-up is performed in three steps: *analysis*, in which it is determined whether normal wear is responsible for performance loss, and which parts require replacement or service; *parts replacement or service;* and *adjustment*, in which engine adjustments are returned to original specifications. Since the advent of emission control equipment, precision adjustment has become increasingly critical, in order to maintain pollutant emission levels.

Analysis

The procedures below are used to indicate where adjustments, parts service or replacement are necessary within the realm of a normal tune-up. If, following these tests, all systems appear to be functioning properly, proceed to the Troubleshooting Section for further diagnosis.

NOTE: *Do not attempt this on the diesel engine unless you have a screw in gauge of at least 600 psi capacity. Disconnect the wire from stop control on injection pump. A special tool (US 2775) is also needed to remove the injector.*

—Remove all spark plugs, noting the cylinder in which they were installed. Remove the air cleaner, and position the throttle and choke in the full open position. Disconnect the coil high tension lead from the coil and the distributor cap. Insert a compression gauge into the spark plug port of each cylinder, in succession, and crank the engine with the starter to obtain the highest possible reading. Record the readings, and compare the highest to the lowest on the compression pressure limit chart. If the difference exeeds the limits on the chart, or if all readings are excessively low, proceed to a wet compression check (see Troubleshooting Section).

—Evaluate the spark plugs according to the spark plug chart in the Troubleshooting Section, and proceed as indicated in the chart.

—Remove the distributor cap, and inspect it inside and out for cracks and/or carbon tracks, and inside for excessive wear or burning of the rotor contacts. If any of these faults are evident, the cap must be replaced.

—Check the breaker points for burning, pitting or wear, and the contact heel resting on the distributor cam for excessive wear. If defects are noted, replace the entire breaker point set.

—Remove and inspect the rotor. If the

Maxi. Press. Lbs. Sq. In.	Min. Press. Lbs. Sq. In.	Max. Press. Lbs. Sq. In.	Min. Press. Lbs. Sq. In.
134	101	188	141
136	102	190	142
138	104	192	144
140	105	194	145
142	107	196	147
146	110	198	148
148	111	200	150
150	113	202	151
152	114	204	153
154	115	206	154
156	117	208	156
158	118	210	157
160	120	212	158
162	121	214	160
164	123	216	162
166	124	218	163
168	126	220	165
170	127	222	166
172	129	224	168
174	131	226	169
176	132	228	171
178	133	230	172
180	135	232	174
182	136	234	175
184	138	236	177
186	140	238	178

Compression pressure limits © Buick Div. G.M. Corp.)

Spark Plug Torque

Thread size	Cast-Iron heads	Aluminum heads
10 mm.	14	11
14 mm.	30	27
18 mm.	34*	32
7/8 in.—18	37	35

* 17 ft. lbs. for tapered plugs using no gaskets.

clean the inside with a dry rag, and remove corrosion from the rotor contact points with fine emery cloth. Remove the spark plug wires one by one, and clean the wire ends and the inside of the towers. If the boots are loose, they should be replaced.

If the cap is to be replaced, transfer the wires one by one, cleaning the wire ends and replacing the boots if necessary.

—If the original points are to remain in service, clean them lightly with emery cloth, lubricate the contact heel with grease specifically designed for this purpose. Rotate the crankshaft until the heel rests on a high point of the distributor cam, and adjust the point gap to specifications.

When replacing the points, remove the original points and condenser, and wipe out the inside of the distributor housing with a clean, dry rag. Lightly lubricate the contact heel and pivot point, and install the points and condenser. Rotate the crankshaft until the heel rests on a high point of the distributor cam, and adjust the point gap to specifications.

NOTE: *Always replace the condenser when changing the points.*

—If the rotor is to be reused, clean the contacts with solvent. Do not alter the spring tension of the rotor center contact. Install the rotor and the distributor cap.

—Replace the coil high tension lead and/or the spark plug leads as necessary.

—Clean the carburetor using a spray solvent (e.g., Gumout Spray). Remove the varnish from the throttle bores, and clean the linkage. Disconnect and plug the fuel line, and run the engine until it runs out of fuel. Partially fill the float chamber with solvent, and reconnect the fuel line. In extreme cases, the jets can be pressure flushed by inserting a rubber plug into the float vent, running the spray nozzle through it, and spraying the solvent until it squirts out of the venturi fuel dump.

—Clean and tighten all wiring connections in the primary electrical circuit.

contacts are burned or worn, or if the rotor is excessively loose on the distributor shaft (where applicable), the rotor must be replaced.

—Inspect the spark plug leads and the coil high tension lead for cracks or brittleness. If any of the wires appear defective, the entire set should be replaced.

—Check the air filter to ensure that it is functioning properly.

Parts Replacement and Service

The determination of whether to replace or service parts is at the mechanic's discretion; however, it is suggested that any parts in questionable condition be replaced rather than reused.

—Clean and regap, or replace, the spark plugs as needed. Lightly coat the threads with engine oil and install the plugs.

CAUTION: *Do not over-torque taperseat spark plugs, or plugs being installed in aluminum cylinder heads.*

—If the distributor cap is to be reused,

Additional Services

The following services *should* be performed in conjunction with a routine tune-up to ensure efficient performance.

—Inspect the battery and fill to the proper level with distilled water. Remove the cable clamps, clean clamps and posts thoroughly, coat the posts lightly with petroleum jelly, reinstall and tighten.

—Inspect all belts, replace and/or adjust as necessary.

—Test the PCV valve (if so equipped), and clean or replace as indicated. Clean all crankcase ventilation hoses, or replace if cracked or hardened.

—Adjust the valves (if necessary) to manufacturer's specifications.

Adjustments

—Connect a dwell-tachometer between the distributor primary lead and ground. The diesel requires an adaptor (VW 1324) to connect a tachometer. Remove the distributor cap and rotor. With the ignition off, crank the engine with a remote starter switch and measure the point dwell angle. Adjust the dwell angle to specifications.

NOTE: *Increasing the gap decreases the dwell angle and vice-versa.*

Install the rotor and distributor cap.

—Connect a timing light according to the manufacturer's specifications. Identify the proper timing marks with chalk or paint.

NOTE: *Luminescent (day-glo) paint is excellent for this purpose.*

Start the engine, and run it until it reaches operating temperature. Disconnect and plug any distributor vacuum lines, and adjust idle to the speed required to adjust timing, according to specifications. Loosen the distributor clamp and adjust timing to specifications by rotating the distributor in the engine.

NOTE: *To advance timing, rotate distributor opposite normal direction of rotor rotation, and vice-versa.*

—Adjust the idle speed, mixture, and idle quality, as specified in the car sections. Final idle adjustments should be made with the air cleaner installed.

CAUTION: *Due to strict emission control requirements on 1969 and later models, special test equipment (CO meter, SUN Tester) may be necessary to properly adjust idle mixture to specifications.*

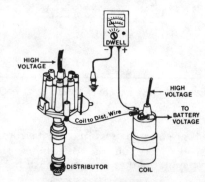

Typical dwell meter hook-up (gasoline engine)

Troubleshooting

NOTE: *This section applies to gasoline engines only. See the following sections for diesel engine troubleshooting.*

The following section is designed to aid in the rapid diagnosis of engine problems. The systematic format is used to diagnose problems ranging from engine starting difficulties to the need for engine overhaul. It is assumed that the user is equipped with basic hand tools and test equipment (tach-dwell meter, timing light, voltmeter, and ohmmeter).

Troubleshooting is divided into two sections. The first, *General Diagnosis*, is used to locate the problem area. In the second, *Specific Diagnosis*, the problem is systematically evaluated.

General Diagnosis

Problem: Symptom	*Begin at Specific Diagnosis, Number* _____
Engine Won't Start:	
Starter doesn't turn	1.1, 2.1
Starter turns, engine doesn't	2.1
Starter turns engine very slowly	1.1, 2.4
Starter turns engine normally	3.1, 4.1
Starter turns engine very quickly	6.1
Engine fires intermittently	4.1
Engine fires consistently	5.1, 6.1
Engine Runs Poorly:	
Hard starting	3.1, 4.1, 5.1, 8.1
Rough idle	4.1, 5.1, 8.1
Stalling	3.1, 4.1, 5.1, 8.1
Engine dies at high speeds	4.1, 5.1
Hesitation (on acceleration from standing stop)	5.1, 8.1
Poor pickup	4.1, 5.1, 8.1
Lack of power	3.1, 4.1, 5.1, 8.1
Backfire through the carburetor	4.1, 8.1, 9.1
Backfire through the exhaust	4.1, 8.1, 9.1
Blue exhaust gases	6.1, 7.1
Black exhaust gases	5.1
Running on (after the ignition is shut off)	3.1, 8.1
Susceptible to moisture	4.1
Engine misfires under load	4.1, 7.1, 8.4, 9.1
Engine misfires at speed	4.1, 8.4
Engine misfires at idle	3.1, 4.1, 5.1, 7.1, 8.4

Engine Noise Diagnosis

Problem: Symptom	Probable Cause
Engine Noises:①	
Metallic grind while starting	Starter drive not engaging completely
Constant grind or rumble	*Starter drive not releasing, worn main bearings
Constant knock	Worn connecting rod bearings
Knock under load	Fuel octane too low, worn connecting rod bearings
Double knock	Loose piston pin
Metallic tap	*Collapsed or sticky valve lifter, excessive valve clearance, excessive end play in a rotating shaft
Scrape	*Fan belt contacting a stationary surface
Tick while starting	S.U. electric fuel pump (normal), starter brushes
Constant tick	*Generator brushes, shreaded fan belt
Squeal	*Improperly tensioned fan belt
Hiss or roar	*Steam escaping through a leak in the cooling system or the radiator overflow vent
Whistle	*Vacuum leak
Wheeze	Loose or cracked spark plug

①—It is extremely difficult to evaluate vehicle noises. While the above are general definitions of engine noises, those starred (*) should be considered as possibly originating elsewhere in the car. To aid diagnosis, the following list considers other potential sources of these sounds.

Metallic grind:
Throwout bearing; transmission gears, bearings, or synchronizers; differential bearings, gears; something metallic in contact with brake drum or disc.

Metallic tap:
U-joints; fan-to-radiator (or shroud) contact.

Scrape:
Brake shoe or pad dragging; tire to body contact; suspension contacting undercarriage or exhaust; something non-metallic contacting brake shoe or drum.

Tick:
Transmission gears; differential gears; lack of radio suppression; resonant vibration of body panels; windshield wiper motor or transmission; heater motor and blower.

Squeal:
Brake shoe or pad not fully releasing; tires (excessive wear, uneven wear, improper inflation); front or rear wheel alignment (most commonly due to improper toe-in).

Hiss or whistle:
Wind leaks (body or window); heater motor and blower fan.

Roar:
Wheel bearings; wind leaks (body and window).

Index

Topic		Group
Battery	*	1
Cranking system	*	2
Primary electrical system	*	3
Secondary electrical system	*	4
Fuel system	*	5
Engine compression	*	6
Engine vaccuum	**	7
Secondary electrical system	**	8
Valve train	**	9
Exhaust system	**	10
Cooling system	**	11
Engine lubrication	**	12

* The engine need not be running
**The engine must be running

Sample Section

Test and Procedure	Results and Indications	Proceed to
4.1—Check for spark: Hold each spark plug wire approximately ¼″ from ground with gloves or a heavy, dry rag. Crank the engine and observe the spark.	→ If no spark is evident:	→4.2
	→ If spark is good in some cases:	→4.3
	→ If spark is good in all cases:	→4.6

Specific Diagnosis

This section is arranged so that following each test, instructions are given to proceed to another, until a problem is diagnosed.

1.1—Inspect the battery visually for case condition (corrosion, cracks) and water level.	If case is cracked, replace battery:	1.4
	If the case is intact, remove corrosion with a solution of baking soda and water (**CAUTION:** *do not get the solution into the battery*), and fill with water:	1.2
1.2—Check the battery cable connections: Insert a screwdriver between the battery post and the cable clamp. Turn the headlights on high beam, and observe them as the screwdriver is gently twisted to ensure good metal to metal contact.	If the lights brighten, remove and clean the clamp and post; coat the post with petroleum jelly, install and tighten the clamp:	1.4
	If no improvement is noted:	1.3

Testing battery cable connections using a screwdriver

1.3—Test the state of charge of the battery using an individual cell tester or hydrometer.	If indicated, charge the battery. **NOTE:** *If no obvious reason exists for the low state of charge (i.e., battery age, prolonged storage), the charging system should be tested:*	1.4

Spec. Grav. Reading	Charged Condition
1.260–1.280	Fully Charged
1.230–1.250	Three Quarter Charged
1.200–1.220	One Half Charged
1.170–1.190	One Quarter Charged
1.140–1.160	Just About Flat
1.110–1.130	All The Way Down

State of battery charge

Electrolyte temperature (° F)	Specific gravity correction
+120	+016
+100	+012 ⎱ ADD
	+008 ⎰ to reading
+80	+004
	no correction
+60	−004
	−008
+40	−012
	−016
+20	−020
	−024 ⎱ SUBTRACT
0	−028 ⎰ from reading
	−032
−20	−036
	−040

The effect of temperature on the specific gravity of battery electrolyte

1.4—Visually inspect battery cables for cracking, bad connection to ground, or bad connection to starter.	If necessary, tighten connections or replace the cables:	2.1

Tests in Group 2 are performed with coil high tension lead disconnected to prevent accidental starting.

2.1—Test the starter motor and solenoid: Connect a jumper from the battery post of the solenoid (or relay) to the starter post of the solenoid (or relay).	If starter turns the engine normally:	2.2
	If the starter buzzes, or turns the engine very slowly:	2.4
	If no response, replace the solenoid (or relay).	3.1
	If the starter turns, but the engine doesn't, ensure that the flywheel ring gear is intact. If the gear is undamaged, replace the starter drive.	3.1

Test and Procedure	Results and Indications	Proceed to
2.2—Determine whether ignition override switches are functioning properly (clutch start switch, neutral safety switch), by connecting a jumper across the switch(es), and turning the ignition switch to "start".	If starter operates, adjust or replace switch:	**3.1**
	If the starter doesn't operate:	**2.3**
2.3—Check the ignition switch "start" position: Connect a 12V test lamp between the starter post of the solenoid (or relay) and ground. Turn the ignition switch to the "start" position, and jiggle the key.	If the lamp doesn't light when the switch is turned, check the ignition switch for loose connections, cracked insulation, or broken wires. Repair or replace as necessary:	**3.1**
	If the lamp flickers when the key is jiggled, replace the ignition switch.	**3.3**

Checking the ignition switch "start" position

2.4—Remove and bench test the starter, according to specifications in the car section.	If the starter does not meet specifications, repair or replace as needed:	**3.1**
	If the starter is operating properly:	**2.5**
2.5—Determine whether the engine can turn freely: Remove the spark plugs, and check for water in the cylinders. Check for water on the dipstick, or oil in the radiator. Attempt to turn the engine using an 18″ flex drive and socket on the crankshaft pulley nut or bolt.	If the engine will turn freely only with the spark plugs out, and hydrostatic lock (water in the cylinders) is ruled out, check valve timing:	**9.2**
	If engine will not turn freely, and it is known that the clutch and transmission are free, the engine must be disassembled for further evaluation:	**Next Chapter**
3.1—Check the ignition switch "on" position: Connect a jumper wire between the distributor side of the coil and ground, and a 12V test lamp between the switch side of the coil and ground. Remove the high tension lead from the coil. Turn the ignition switch on and jiggle the key.	If the lamp lights:	**3.2**
	If the lamp flickers when the key is jiggled, replace the ignition switch:	**3.3**
	If the lamp doesn't light, check for loose or open connections. If none are found, remove the ignition switch and check for continuity. If the switch is faulty, replace it:	**3.3**

Checking the ignition switch "on" position

Test and Procedure	Results and Indications	Proceed to
3.2—Check the ballast resistor or resistance wire for an open circuit, using an ohmmeter. Some 1976 and all later models have resistor wire in place of a ballast resistor. It is a clear wire with violet stripe.	If resistance is zero, replace the resistor or resistance wiring.	**3.3**
3.3—Visually inspect the breaker points for burning, pitting or excessive wear. Gray coloring of the point contact surfaces is normal. Rotate the crankshaft until the contact heel rests on a high point of the distributor cam and adjust the point gap to specifications.	If the breaker points are intact, clean the contact surfaces with fine emery cloth, and adjust the point gap to specifications. If pitted or worn, replace the points and condenser, and adjust the gap to specification. **NOTE:** *Always lubricate the distributor cam according to manufacture's recommendations when servicing the breaker points.*	**3.4**
3.4—Connect a dwell-meter between the distributor primary lead and ground. Crank the engine and observe the point dwell angle.	If necessary, adjust the dwell angle. **NOTE:** *Increasing the point gap decreases the dwell angle and vice-versa.* If the dwell meter shows little or no reading;	**3.6** **3.5**

Dwell meter hook-up

Dwell angle

Test and Procedure	Results and Indications	Proceed to
3.5—Check the condenser for short: connect an ohmmeter across the condenser body and the pigtail lead.	If any reading other than infinite is noted, replace the condenser:	**3.6**

Checking the condenser for short

Test and Procedure	Results and Indications	Proceed to
3.6—Test the coil primary resistance: Connect an ohmmeter across the coil primary terminals, and read the resistance on the low scale. Note whether an external ballast resistor or resistance wire is utilized.	Coils utilizing ballast resistors or resistance wires should have approximately 1.0 ohms resistance. Coils with internal resistors should have approximately 4.0 ohms resistance. If values far from the above are noted, replace the coil.	**4.1**

Testing the coil primary resistance

Test and Procedure	Results and Indications	Proceed to
4.1—Check for spark: Hold each spark plug wire approximately ¼″ from ground with gloves or a heavy, dry rag. Crank the engine, and observe the spark.	If no spark is evident:	**4.2**
	If spark is good in some cylinders:	**4.3**
	If spark is good in all cylinders:	**4.6**
4.2—Check for spark at the coil high tension lead: Remove the coil high tension lead from the distributor and position it approximately ¼″ from ground. Crank the engine and observe spark. **CAUTION:** *This test should not be performed on cars equipped with transistorized ignition.*	If the spark is good and consistent:	**4.3**
	If the spark is good but intermittent, test the primary electrical system starting at 3.3:	**3.3**
	If the spark is weak or non-existent, replace the coil high tension lead, clean and tighten all connections and retest. If no improvement is noted:	**4.4**
4.3—Visually inspect the distributor cap and rotor for burned or corroded contacts, cracks, carbon tracks, or moisture. Also check the fit of the rotor on the distributor shaft (where applicable).	If moisture is present, dry thoroughly, and re-test per 4.1:	**4.1**
	If burned or excessively corroded contacts, cracks, or carbon tracks are noted, replace the defective part(s) and retest per 4.1:	**4.1**
	If the rotor and cap appear intact, or are only slightly corroded, clean the contacts thoroughly (including the cap towers and spark plug wire ends) and retest per 4.1: If the spark is good in all cases:	**4.6**
	If the spark is poor in all cases:	**4.5**
4.4—Check the coil secondary resistance: Connect an ohmmeter across the distributor side of the coil and the coil tower. Read the resistance on the high scale of the ohmmeter.	The resistance of a satisfactory coil should be between 4,000 and 10,000 ohms. If resistance is considerably higher (i.e. 40,000 ohms) replace the coil and retest per 4.1. **NOTE:** *this does not apply to high performance coils.*	**4.1**

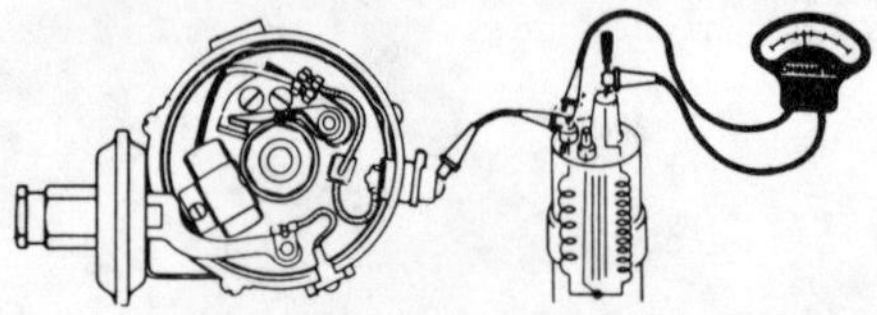

Testing the coil secondary resistance

Test and Procedure	Results and Indications	Proceed to
4.5—Visually inspect the spark plug wires for cracking or brittleness. Ensure that no two wires are positioned so as to cause induction firing (adjacent and parallel). Remove each wire, one by one, and check resistance with an ohmmeter.	Replace any cracked or brittle wires. If any of the wires are defective, replace the entire set. Replace any wires with excessive resistance (over 8000Ω per foot for suppression wire), and separate any wires that might cause induction firing.	**4.6**
4.6—Remove the spark plugs, noting the cylinders from which they were removed, and evaluate according to the chart below.	See following.	**See following.**

	Condition	Cause	Remedy	Proceed to
	Electrodes eroded, light brown deposits.	Normal wear. Normal wear is indicated by approximately .001″ wear per 1000 miles.	Clean and regap the spark plug if wear is not excessive: Replace the spark plug if excessively worn:	**4.7**
	Carbon fouling (black, dry, fluffy deposits).	If present on one or two plugs:		
		Faulty high tension lead(s).	Test the high tension leads:	**4.5**
		Burnt or sticking valve(s).	Check the valve train: (Clean and regap the plugs in either case.)	**9.1**
		If present on most or all plugs: Overly rich fuel mixture, due to restricted air filter, improper carburetor adjustment, improper choke or heat riser adjustment or operation.	Check the fuel system:	**5.1**
	Oil fouling (wet black deposits)	Worn engine components. **NOTE:** *Oil fouling may occur in new or recently rebuilt engines until broken in.*	Check engine vacuum and compression: Replace with new spark plug	**6.1**
	Lead fouling (gray, black, tan, or yellow deposits, which appear glazed or cinder-like).	Combustion by-products.	Clean and regap the plugs: (Use plugs of a different heat range if the problem recurs.)	**4.7**
	Gap bridging (deposits lodged between the electrodes).	Incomplete combustion, or transfer of deposits from the combustion chamber.	Replace the spark plugs:	**4.7**
	Overheating (burnt electrodes, and extremely white insulator with small black spots).	Ignition timing advanced too far.	Adjust timing to specifications:	**8.2**
		Overly lean fuel mixture.	Check the fuel system:	**5.1**
		Spark plugs not seated properly.	Clean spark plug seat and install a new gasket washer: (Replace the spark plugs in all cases.)	**4.7**

	Condition	Cause	Remedy	Proceed to
	Fused spot deposits on the insulator.	Combustion chamber blow-by.	Clean and regap the spark plugs:	4.7
	Pre-ignition (melted or severely burned electrodes, blistered or cracked insulators, or metallic deposits on the insulator).	Incorrect spark plug heat range.	Replace with plugs of the proper heat range:	4.7
		Ignition timing advanced too far.	Adjust timing to specifications:	8.2
		Spark plugs not being cooled efficiently.	Clean the spark plug seat, and check the cooling system:	11.1
		Fuel mixture too lean.	Check the fuel system:	5.1
		Poor compression.	Check compression:	6.1
		Fuel grade too low.	Use higher octane fuel:	4.7

Test and Procedure	Results and Indications	Proceed to
4.7—Determine the static ignition timing. Using the crankshaft pulley timing marks as a guide, locate top dead center on the compression stroke of the number one cylinder.	The rotor should be pointing toward the no. 1 tower in the distributor cap, and the armature spoke for that cylinder should be lined up with the stator.	4.8
4.8—Check coil polarity: Connect a voltmeter negative lead to the coil high tension lead, and the positive lead to ground (**NOTE:** *reverse the hook-up for positive ground cars*). Crank the engine momentarily. Checking coil polarity	If the voltmeter reads up-scale, the polarity is correct:	5.1
	If the voltmeter reads down-scale, reverse the coil polarity (switch the primary leads):	5.1
5.1—Determine that the air filter is functioning efficiently: Hold paper elements up to a strong light, and attempt to see light through the filter.	Clean permanent air filters in gasoline (or manufacturer's recommendation), and allow to dry. Replace paper elements through which light cannot be seen:	5.2
5.2—Determine whether a flooding condition exists: Flooding is identified by a strong gasoline odor, and excessive gasoline present in the throttle bore(s) of the carburetor.	If flooding is not evident:	5.3
	If flooding is evident, permit the gasoline to dry for a few moments and restart. If flooding doesn't recur:	5.6
	If flooding is persistent:	5.5
5.3—Check that fuel is reaching the carburetor: Detach the fuel line at the carburetor inlet. Hold the end of the line in a cup (not styrofoam), and crank the engine.	If fuel flows smoothly:	5.6
	If fuel doesn't flow (**NOTE:** *Make sure that there is fuel in the tank*), or flows erratically:	5.4

Test and Procedure	Results and Indications	Proceed to
5.4—Test the fuel pump: Disconnect all fuel lines from the fuel pump. Hold a finger over the input fitting, crank the engine (with electric pump, turn the ignition or pump on); and feel for suction.	If suction is evident, blow out the fuel line to the tank with low pressure compressed air until bubbling is heard from the fuel filler neck. Also blow out the carburetor fuel line (both ends disconnected):	5.6
	If no suction is evident, replace or repair the fuel pump: **NOTE:** *Repeated oil fouling of the spark plugs, or a no-start condition, could be the result of a ruptured vacuum booster pump diaphragm, through which oil or gasoline is being drawn into the intake manifold (where applicable).*	5.6
5.5—Check the needle and seat: Tap the carburetor in the area of the needle and seat.	If flooding stops, a gasoline additive (e.g., Gumout) will often cure the problem:	5.6
	If flooding continues, check the fuel pump for excessive pressure at the carburetor (according to specifications). If the pressure is normal, the needle and seat must be removed and checked, and/or the float level adjusted:	5.6
5.6—Test the accelerator pump by looking into the throttle bores while operating the throttle.	If the accelerator pump appears to be operating normally:	5.7
	If the accelerator pump is not operating, the pump must be reconditioned. Where possible, service the pump with the carburetor(s) installed on the engine. If necessary, remove the carburetor. Prior to removal:	5.7
5.7—Determine whether the carburetor main fuel system is functioning: Spray a commercial starting fluid into the carburetor while attempting to start the engine.	If the engine starts, runs for a few seconds, and dies:	5.8
	If the engine doesn't start:	6.1
5.8—Uncommon fuel system malfunctions: See below:	If the problem is solved:	6.1
	If the problem remains, remove and recondition the carburetor.	

Condition	Indication	Test	Usual Weather Conditions	Remedy
Vapor lock	Car will not restart shortly after running.	Cool the components of the fuel system until the engine starts.	Hot to very hot	Ensure that the exhaust manifold heat control valve is operating. Check with the vehicle manufacturer for the recommended solution to vapor lock on the model in question.
Carburetor icing	Car will not idle, stalls at low speeds.	Visually inspect the throttle plate area of the throttle bores for frost.	High humidity, 32–40°F.	Ensure that the exhaust manifold heat control valve is operating, and that the intake manifold heat riser is not blocked.

Condition	Indication	Test	Usual Weather Conditions	Remedy
Water in the fuel	Engine sputters and stalls; may not start.	Pump a small amount of fuel into a glass jar. Allow to stand, and inspect for droplets or a layer of water.	High humidity, extreme temperature changes.	For droplets, use one or two cans of commercial gas dryer (Dry Gas) For a layer of water, the tank must be drained, and the fuel lines blown out with compressed air.

Test and Procedure	Results and Indications	Proceed to
6.1—Test engine compression: Remove all spark plugs. Insert a compression gauge into a spark plug port, crank the engine to obtain the maximum reading, and record.	If compression is within limits on all cylinders:	7.1
	If gauge reading is extremely low on all cylinders:	6.2
	If gauge reading is low on one or two cylinders: (If gauge readings are identical and low on two or more adjacent cylinders, the head gasket must be replaced.)	6.2

Testing compression

Compression pressure limits

Maxi. Press. Lbs. Sq. In.	Min. Press. Lbs. Sq. In.	Maxi. Press. Lbs. Sq. In.	Min. Press. Lbs. Sq. In.	Max. Press. Lbs. Sq. In.	Min. Press. Lbs. Sq. In.	Max. Press. Lbs. Sq. In.	Min. Press. Lbs. Sq. In.
134	101	162	121	188	141	214	160
136	102	164	123	190	142	216	162
138	104	166	124	192	144	218	163
140	105	168	126	194	145	220	165
142	107	170	127	196	147	222	166
146	110	172	129	198	148	224	168
148	111	174	131	200	150	226	169
150	113	176	132	202	151	228	171
152	114	178	133	204	153	230	172
154	115	180	135	206	154	232	174
156	117	182	136	208	156	234	175
158	118	184	138	210	157	236	177
160	120	186	140	212	158	238	178

Test and Procedure	Results and Indications	Proceed to
6.2—Test engine compression (wet): Squirt approximately 30 cc. of engine oil into each cylinder, and retest per 6.1.	If the readings improve, worn or cracked rings or broken pistons are indicated:	Next Chapter
	If the readings do not improve, burned or excessively carboned valves or a jumped timing chain are indicated: NOTE: *A jumped timing chain is often indicated by difficult cranking.*	7.1
7.1—Perform a vacuum check of the engine: Attach a vacuum gauge to the intake manifold beyond the throttle plate. Start the engine, and observe the action of the needle over the range of engine speeds.	See below.	See below

	Reading	Indications	Proceed to
	Steady, from 17–22 in. Hg.	Normal:	8.1

	Reading	Indications	Proceed to
	Low and steady.	Late ignition or valve timing, or low compression:	6.1
	Very low.	Vacuum leak:	7.2
	Needle fluctuates as engine speed increases.	Ignition miss, blown cylinder head gasket, leaking valve or weak valve spring:	6.1, 8.3
	Gradual drop in reading at idle.	Excessive back pressure in the exhaust system:	10.1
	Intermittent fluctuation at idle.	Ignition miss, sticking valve:	8.3, 9.1
	Drifting needle.	Improper idle mixture adjustment, carburetors not synchronized (where applicable), or minor intake leak. Synchronize the carburetors, adjust the idle, and retest. If the condition persists:	7.2
	High and steady.	Early ignition timing:	8.2

Test and Procedure	Results and Indications	Proceed to
7.2—Attach a vacuum gauge per 7.1, and test for an intake manifold leak. Squirt a small amount of oil around the intake manifold gaskets, carburetor gaskets, plugs and fittings. Observe the action of the vacuum gauge.	If the reading improves, replace the indicated gasket, or seal the indicated fitting or plug:	8.1
	If the reading remains low:	7.3
7.3—Test all vacuum hoses and accessories for leaks as described in 7.2. Also check the carburetor body (dashpots, automatic choke mechanism, throttle shafts) for leaks in the same manner.	If the reading improves, service or replace the offending part(s):	8.1
	If the reading remains low:	6.1
8.1—Check the point dwell angle: Connect a dwell meter between the distributor primary wire and ground. Start the engine, and observe the dwell angle from idle to 3000 rpm.	If necessary, adjust the dwell angle. **NOTE:** *Increasing the point gap reduces the dwell angle and vice-versa.* If the dwell angle moves outside specifications as engine speed increases, the distributor should be removed	

Test and Procedure	Results and Indications	Proceed to
	and checked for cam accuracy, shaft endplay and concentricity, bushing wear, and adequate point arm tension (**NOTE:** *Most of these items may be checked with the distributor installed in the engine, using an oscilloscope*):	8.2
8.2—Connect a timing light (per manufacturer's recommendation) and check the dynamic ignition timing. Disconnect and plug the vacuum hose(s) to the distributor if specified, start the engine, and observe the timing marks at the specified engine speed.	If the timing is not correct, adjust to specifications by rotating the distributor in the engine: (Advance timing by rotating distributor opposite normal direction of rotor rotation, retard timing by rotating distributor in same direction as rotor rotation.)	8.3
8.3—Check the operation of the distributor advance mechanism(s): To test the mechanical advance, disconnect all but the mechanical advance, and observe the timing marks with a timing light as the engine speed is increased from idle. If the mark moves smoothly, without hesitation, it may be assumed that the mechanical advance is functioning properly. To test vacuum advance and/or retard systems, alternately crimp and release the vacuum line, and observe the timing mark for movement. If movement is noted, the system is operating.	If the systems are functioning: If the systems are not functioning, remove the distributor, and test on a distributor tester:	8.4 8.4
8.4—Locate an ignition miss: With the engine running, remove each spark plug wire, one by one, until one is found that doesn't cause the engine to roughen and slow down.	When the missing cylinder is identified:	4.1
9.1—Evaluate the valve train: Remove the valve cover, and ensure that the valves are adjusted to specifications. A mechanic's stethoscope may be used to aid in the diagnosis of the valve train. By pushing the probe on or near push rods or rockers, valve noise often can be isolated. A timing light also may be used to diagnose valve problems. Connect the light according to manufacturer's recommendations, and start the engine. Vary the firing moment of the light by increasing the engine speed (and therefore the ignition advance), and moving the trigger from cylinder to cylinder. Observe the movement of each valve.	See below.	See below

Observation	Probable Cause	Remedy	Proceed to
Metallic tap heard through the stethoscope.	Sticking hydraulic lifter or excessive valve clearance.	Adjust valve. If tap persists, remove and replace the lifter:	**10.1**
Metallic tap through the stethoscope, able to push the rocker arm (lifter side) down by hand.	Collapsed valve lifter.	Remove and replace the lifter:	**10.1**
Erratic, irregular motion of the valve stem.*	Sticking valve, burned valve.	Recondition the valve and/or valve guide:	**Next Chapter**
Eccentric motion of the pushrod at the rocker arm.*	Bent pushrod.	Replace the pushrod:	**10.1**
Valve retainer bounces as the valve closes.*	Weak valve spring or damper.	Remove and test the spring and damper. Replace if necessary:	**10.1**

*—When observed with a timing light.

Test and Procedure	Results and Indications	Proceed to
9.2—Check the valve timing: Locate top dead center of the No. 1 piston, and install a degree wheel or tape on the crankshaft pulley or damper with zero corresponding to an index mark on the engine. Rotate the crankshaft in its direction of rotation, and observe the opening of the No. 1 cylinder intake valve. The opening should correspond with the correct mark on the degree wheel according to specifications.	If the timing is not correct, the timing cover must be removed for further investigation:	
10.1—Determine whether the exhaust manifold heat control valve is operating: Operate the valve by hand to determine whether it is free to move. If the valve is free, run the engine to operating temperature and observe the action of the valve, to ensure that it is opening.	If the valve sticks, spray it with a suitable solvent, open and close the valve to free it, and retest. If the valve functions properly: If the valve does not free, or does not operate, replace the valve:	**10.2** **10.2**
10.2—Ensure that there are no exhaust restrictions: Visually inspect the exhaust system for kinks, dents, or crushing. Also note that gasses are flowing freely from the tailpipe at all engine speeds, indicating no restriction in the muffler or resonator.	Replace any damaged portion of the system:	**11.1**

Test and Procedure	Results and Indications	Proceed to
11.1—Visually inspect the fan belt for glazing, cracks, and fraying, and replace if necessary. Tighten the belt so that the longest span has approximately ½″ play at its midpoint under thumb pressure.	Replace or tighten the fan belt as necessary:	**11.2**
11.2—Check the fluid level of the cooling system.	If full or slightly low, fill as necessary: If extremely low:	**11.5** **11.3**
11.3—Visually inspect the external portions of the cooling system (radiator, radiator hoses, thermostat elbow, water pump seals, heater hoses, etc.) for leaks. If none are found, pressurize the cooling system to 14–15 psi.	If cooling system holds the pressure: If cooling system loses pressure rapidly, reinspect external parts of the system for leaks under pressure. If none are found, check dipstick for coolant in crankcase. If no coolant is present, but pressure loss continues: If coolant is evident in crankcase, remove cylinder head(s), and check gasket(s). If gaskets are intact, block and cylinder head(s) should be checked for cracks or holes. If the gasket(s) is blown, replace, and purge the crankcase of coolant: **NOTE:** *Occasionally, due to atmospheric and driving conditions, condensation of water can occur in the crankcase. This causes the oil to appear milky white. To remedy, run the engine until hot, and change the oil and oil - filter.*	**11.5** **11.4** **12.6**
11.4— Check for combustion leaks into the cooling system: Pressurize the cooling system as above. Start the engine, and observe the pressure gauge. If the needle fluctuates, remove each spark plug wire, one by one, noting which cylinder(s) reduce or eliminate the fluctuation. Radiator pressure tester	Cylinders which reduce or eliminate the fluctuation, when the spark plug wire is removed, are leaking into the cooling system. Replace the head gasket on the affected cylinder bank(s).	
11.5—Check the radiator pressure cap: Attach a radiator pressure tester to the radiator cap (wet the seal prior to installation). Quickly pump up the pressure, noting the point at which the cap releases.	If the cap releases within ± 1 psi of the specified rating, it is operating properly: If the cap releases at more than ± 1 psi of the specified rating, it should be replaced:	**11.6** **11.6**

Testing the radiator pressure cap

Test and Procedure	Results and Indications	Proceed to
11.6—Test the thermostat: Start the engine cold, remove the radiator cap, and insert a thermometer into the radiator. Allow the engine to idle. After a short while, there will be a sudden, rapid increase in coolant temperature. The temperature at which this sharp rise stops is the thermostat opening temperature.	If the thermostat opens at or about the specified temperature:	**11.7**
	If the temperature doesn't increase: (If the temperature increases slowly and gradually, replace the thermostat.)	**11.7**
11.7—Check the water pump: Remove the thermostat elbow and the thermostat, disconnect the coil high tension lead (to prevent starting), and crank the engine momentarily.	If coolant flows, replace the thermostat and retest per 11.6:	**11.6**
	If coolant doesn't flow, reverse flush the cooling system to alleviate any blockage that might exist. If system is not blocked, and coolant will not flow, recondition the water pump.	—
12.1—Check the oil pressure gauge or warning light: If the gauge shows low pressure, or the light is on, for no obvious reason, remove the oil pressure sender. Install an accurate oil pressure gauge and run the engine momentarily.	If oil pressure builds normally, run engine for a few moments to determine that it is functioning normally, and replace the sender.	—
	If the pressure remains low:	**12.2**
	If the pressure surges:	**12.3**
	If the oil pressure is zero:	**12.3**
12.2—Visually inspect the oil: If the oil is watery or very thin, milky, or foamy, replace the oil and oil filter.	If the oil is normal:	**12.3**
	If after replacing oil the pressure remains low:	**12.3**
	If after replacing oil the pressure becomes normal:	—
12.3—Check to ensure that the oil pump is not cavitating (sucking air instead of oil): See that the crankcase is neither over nor underfull, and that the pickup in the sump is in the proper position and free from sludge.	Fill or drain the crankcase to the proper capacity, and clean the pickup screen in solvent if necessary. If no improvement is noted:	**12.5**
12.4—Inspect the oil pump drive and the oil pump:	If the pump drive or the oil pump appear to be defective, service as necessary and retest per 12.1:	**12.1**
	If the pump drive and pump appear to be operating normally, the engine should be disassembled to determine where blockage exists:	**Next Chapter**
12.5—Purge the engine of ethylene glycol coolant: Completely drain the crankcase and the oil filter. Obtain a commercial butyl cellosolve base solvent, designated for this purpose, and follow the instructions precisely. Following this, install a new oil filter and refill the crankcase with the proper weight oil. The next oil and filter change should follow shortly thereafter (1000 miles).		

Troubleshooting

Note: *This section applies to diesel engines only.*

Troubleshooting Diesel Engines

Problem	Possible Causes
Starter will not crank engine	Battery terminals loose or broken
	Battery discharged
	Starter switch damaged, or wires loose or broken
	Starter clutch or solenoid malfunction
	Starter drive locked
	Hydraulic lock, water or oil in combustion chamber
	Blow plug light still "ON" (dashboard)
Failure to start or hard starting	Correct starting procedures not being followed
	Cold start aid inoperative
	Battery low, slow cranking speed
	Starter equipment malfunctioning
	Engine oil too heavy
	Blocked exhaust system
	Air filter dirty
	Low engine compression due to defective valves or piston rings
	Insufficient fuel in tank
	Water or ice in fuel tank
	Excessive fuel device inoperative
	Fuel injection parts scored, poor delivery
	Advance mechanism in advance position. It should be in retarded position when engine is to be started.

Problem	Possible Causes
Failure to start or hard starting	Fuel injection pump not timed properly
	Air in the fuel system
	Fuel oil filter plugged or restricted
	Fuel lift pump not operating
	Leak in high pressure delivery lines
Engine runs, but misses NOTE: *The first signs of injector trouble usually appear as:* –A knock in one or more cylinders, –Overheated engine, –Loss of power, –Smoky black exhaust, –Increased fuel consumption. The faulty injector can be located by slightly loosening the pipe joint at each injector in turn with the engine at fast idle (1000–1200 rpm). If the engine speed remains constant (does not change), after loosening the joint, the injector is faulty. Do not loosen the fuel line with the engine running, and do not remove the injector. The system is under tremendous pressure (up to 1850 psi) and is enough to cause diesel fuel to penetrate skin.	Restricted fuel lines Water in fuel or poor quality fuel Air leaks in fuel suction line Injectors improperly adjusted or plugged Low compression, intake or exhaust valves leaking Leaking supercharger air connection Restricted drain line
Excessive vibration	Engine bearings worn Engine supports broken or loose Difference in compression pressures between cylinders Injector setting pressures unequal Unequal fuel delivery, line resistance Air in fuel system
Low Engine Torque NOTE: *The first signs of injector trouble usually appear as:* –A knock in one or more cylinders, –Overheated engine, –Loss of power, –Smoky black exhaust, –Increased fuel consumption. The faulty injector can be located by slightly loosening the pipe joint at each injector in turn with the engine at fast idle (1000–1200 rpm). If the engine speed remains constant (does not change), after loosening the joint, the injector is faulty. Do not loosen the fuel line with the engine running, and do not remove the injector. The system is under tremendous pressure (up to 1850 psi) and is enough to cause diesel fuel to penetrate skin.	Excessive exhaust back pressure Engine valve timing not correct Fuel filters dirty High pressure fuel line leaks Poor atomization of fuel Dirty or cracked injectors Fuel injection pump to engine timing wrong Throttle stop set too low Inferior quality fuel Advance device not working Brakes binding
Engine Knocks NOTE: *The first signs of injector trouble usually appear as:* –A knock in one or more cylinders, –Overheated engine, –Loss of power, –Smoky black exhaust, –Increased fuel consumption. The faulty injector can be located by slightly loosening the pipe joint at each injector in turn with	Low coolant level Engine overloaded Crankshaft vibration damper malfunction Excessive crankshaft end clearance Flywheel loose or unbalanced Broken or worn piston rings Incorrect bearing clearances

Problem	Possible Causes
the engine at fast idle (1000–1200 rpm). If the engine speed remains constant (does not change), after loosening the joint, the injector is faulty. Do not loosen the fuel line with the engine running, and do not remove the injector. The system is under tremendous pressure (up to 1850 psi) and is enough to cause diesel fuel to penetrate skin.	Damaged or worn main or connecting rod bearings Broken tooth in engine gear train Worn or scored cylinder liners or pistons Broken valve springs Fuel injection pump timing too early Poor atomization of fuel Octane value of fuel low
Excessive Smoke *BLACK SMOKE* consists of a large number of particles of carbon; this carbon forms when the fuel is heated in oxygen-lean regions in the combustion chamber. *BLUE SMOKE* consists of a large number of particles of fuel oil; these particles are recondensed droplets of unburned fuel or incompletely burned fuel. These small particles cause blue light to be scattered. When an engine is running fast but under light load, regions of the combustion chamber may be at too low a temperature to permit ignition and blue smoke would appear. When viewed in transmitted light, the blue smoke appears brown. *WHITE SMOKE* consists of a large number of particles of fuel oil. To produce white smoke, the fuel must have time to condense into larger droplets than for blue smoke. A cold engine running at light load and low speed could produce white smoke.	Restricted air intake High exhaust back pressure Intake manifold or cylinder head gasket leakage Cracked cylinder head or block Broken or worn piston rings Engine in need of overhaul Incorrect valve timing Worn or scored cylinder liners or pistons Engine overload Low compression Inferior quality fuel Restricted fuel lines Plugged injector spray holes Incorrect injector timing Injectors improperly adjusted Fuel injection pump to engine timing retarded Injector pump improperly adjusted Broken fuel delivery valve or valve sticking
Engine gradually loses power; then stops NOTE: *The first signs of injector trouble usually appear as:* –A knock in one or more cylinders, –Overheated engine, –Loss of power, –Smoky black exhaust, –Increased fuel consumption. The faulty injector can be located by slightly loosening the pipe joint at each injector in turn with the engine at fast idle (1000–1200 rpm). If the engine speed remains constant (does not change), after loosening the joint, the injector is faulty. Do not loosen the fuel line with the engine running, and do not remove the injector. The system is under tremendous pressure (up to 1850 psi) and is enough to cause diesel fuel to penetrate skin.	Low compression Engine valve clearance too small Air leak at suction side of fuel lines Choked fuel filter Damaged control linkage Fuel tank vent clogged Leak off line blocked Nozzle and delivery valve stuck open
Engine cannot reach maximum speed	Poor condition of engine Throttle stop improperly adjusted Maximum speed setting too low Broken or wrong type governor springs Dirty air filter

Problem	Possible Causes
Excessive fuel consumption NOTE: *The first signs of injector trouble usually appear as:* –A knock in one or more cylinders, –Overheated engine, –Loss of power, –Smoky black exhaust, –Increased fuel consumption. The faulty injector can be located by slightly loosening the pipe joint at each injector in turn with the engine at fast idle (1000–1200 rpm). If the engine speed remains constant (does not change), after loosening the joint, the injector is faulty. Do not loosen the fuel line with the engine running, and do not remove the injector. The system is under tremendous pressure (up to 1850 psi) and is enough to cause diesel fuel to penetrate skin.	Restricted air intake High exhaust back pressure Engine overloaded Engine in need of overhaul Inferior quality fuel Restricted fuel lines or filter Fuel leaks external or internal Plugged injector spray holes Injectors not adjusted properly Cracked injector body or cap
Excessive oil consumption	Broken or worn piston rings Worn or scored cylinder liners or pistons External or internal oil leaks Faulty cylinder oil control Wrong grade oil for conditions Engine in need of overhaul Loose crankcase breather vent
Low oil pressure	Incorrect bearing clearances Engine overloaded Insufficient coolant Worn water pump Coolant thermostat not working Loose fan belts Clogged coolant passages Clogged oil cooler Radiator core openings restricted Air in cooling system Leaking coolant hoses, connections or gaskets Insufficient radiator capacity Oil suction line restricted or cracked Oil pickup screen blocked Crankcase oil level too low Wrong grade of oil for conditions Engine in need of overhaul
Overheating (high coolant temperature) NOTE: *The first signs of injector trouble usually appear as:* –A knock in one or more cylinders, –Overheated engine, –Loss of power, –Smoky black exhaust, –Increased fuel consumption. The faulty injector can be located by slightly loos-	Low coolant level Air leaks in suction line Low coolant level Engine overloaded Injectors not properly adjusted Injector pipe partially clogged

Problem	*Possible Causes*
ening the pipe joint at each injector in turn with the engine at fast idle (1000–1200 rpm). If the engine speed remains constant (does not change), after loosening the joint, the injector is faulty. Do not loosen the fuel line with the engine running, and do not remove the injector. The system is under tremendous pressure (up to 1850 psi) and is enough to cause diesel fuel to penetrate skin.	Faulty injectors
	Injector timing too early
	Worn or scored cylinder liners or pistons
	Broken valve springs
	Crankshaft vibration damper faulty
	Excessive crankshaft end clearance
	Flywheel loose or unbalanced
	Broken or worn piston rings
	Incorrect bearing clearances
	Engine in need of overhaul
	Broken tooth in engine gear train

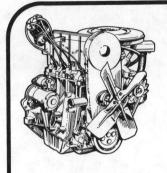

3

Engine and
Engine Rebuilding

ENGINE ELECTRICAL

Distributor

The distributor is a conventional, single breaker point unit. It incorporates both centrifugal and vacuum ignition timing mechanisms. Centrifugal advance is controlled by two weights located beneath the breaker plate. As engine speed increases, centrifugal force moves the weights out from the distributor shaft and advances the ignition by changing the position of the cam in relation to the shaft. This advanced positioning of the cam will then open the breaker points sooner and ignite the air/fuel mixture quickly enough in relation to piston speed. Centrifugal advance is necessary because as engine speed increases, the time period available to ignite the mixture decreases. At idle speed, the ignition setting is 3° ATDC. This is adequate for the spark plug to ignite the mixture at 925 rpm, but not at, say, 2,500 rpm. The weights, governed by springs, move out at a predetermined rate to advance the timing to match engine speed.

Centrifugal advance is not completely sufficient to provide the proper advance under all conditions, and so we also have vacuum advance/retard. Under light load conditions, such as very gradual acceleration and low

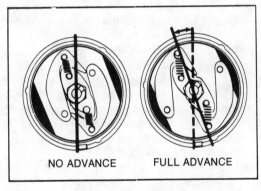

NO ADVANCE   FULL ADVANCE

Centrifugal advance weight operation

speed cruising, the throttle opening is not sufficient to draw enough air/fuel mixture into the cylinder. Vacuum advance is used to provide the extra spark advance needed to ignite the smaller mixture. The round can on the side of the distributor is the vacuum advance/retard unit. The rubber hose supplies vacuum from the intake manifold to draw on the diaphragm in the unit which is connected by a link to the breaker plate in the distributor. Under part-throttle operation, the vacuum advance moves the breaker plate as necessary to provide the correct advance for efficient operation. At idle, the vacuum retard unit retards the timing to reduce exhaust emission.

The distributor is gear driven by an intermediate shaft which also drives the fuel pump. The distributor shaft also turns the oil pump. The distributor is located toward the rear of the engine on the left-side and is easily accessible.

REMOVAL AND INSTALLATION

NOTE: *Aside from replacing the cap, rotor, breaker points, and the condenser, refer all distributor repair to a VW dealer or ignition specialty shop. They are equipped with a distributor test machine which permits diagnosis of any problems.*

1. Disconnect the coil high-tension wire from the distributor. This is the large wire which goes into the center of the cap.

2. Detach the smaller primary wire which also connects from the coil to the distributor.

3. Unsnap the clips and remove the distributor cap. Position it out of the way.

4. Using the fan belt or the crankshaft pulley nut, turn the engine until the rotor aligns with the index mark on the outer edge of the distributor. This is the No. 1 position. Matchmark the bottom of the distributor housing and its mounting flange on the engine. This is extra insurance that we'll get the distributor back in correctly.

5. Loosen and remove the hex bolt and lift off the retaining flange. Lift the distributor straight out of the engine.

If the engine has not been disturbed while the distributor was out i.e., the crankshaft was not turned, then reinstall the distributor in the reverse order of removal. Carefully align the match marks.

If the engine has been rotated while the distributor was out, then proceed as follows:

1. Turn the crankshaft so that the No. 1 piston is on its compression stroke and the OT timing marks are aligned with the V-shaped pointer.

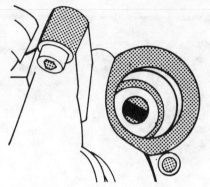
Oil pump driveshaft must be parallel to the crankshaft

2. Turn the distributor so that the rotor points approximately 15° before the No. 1 cylinder position on the distributor.

3. Insert the distributor into the engine block. If the oil pump drive doesn't engage, remove the distributor and, using a long screwdriver, turn the pump shaft so that it is parallel to the centerline of the crankshaft.

4. Install the distributor, aligning the matchmarks. Tighten the flange retaining nut.

5. Install the cap. Adjust the ignition timing as outlined in Chapter 2.

Alternator

ALTERNATOR PRECAUTIONS

The Rabbit and Scirocco are equipped with alternating current (AC) generators (alternators). Either a Bosch or Motorola unit may be used. Unlike the direct current (DC) generators used in many older cars, there are several precautions which must be strictly observed in order to avoid damaging the unit. They are:

1. Reversing the battery connections will result in damage to the diodes.

Firing Order

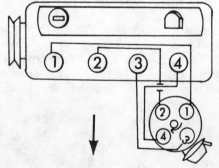

Rotor/distributor alignment for No. 1 cylinder

Firing order—1-3-4-2

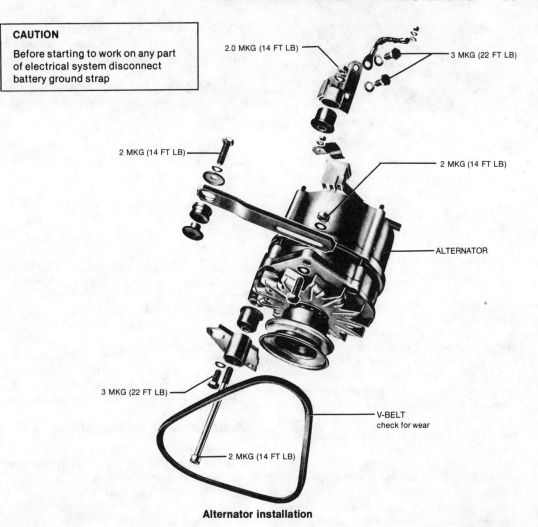

CAUTION

Before starting to work on any part of electrical system disconnect battery ground strap

2.0 MKG (14 FT LB)

3 MKG (22 FT LB)

2 MKG (14 FT LB)

2 MKG (14 FT LB)

ALTERNATOR

3 MKG (22 FT LB)

V-BELT
check for wear

2 MKG (14 FT LB)

Alternator installation

2. Booster batteries should be connected from negative to negative, and positive to positive.

3. Never use a fast charger as a booster to start cars with AC circuits.

4. When servicing the battery with a fast charger, always disconnect the car battery cables.

5. Never attempt to polarize an AC generator.

6. Avoid long soldering times when replacing diodes or transistors. Prolonged heat is damaging to AC generators.

7. Do not use test lamps of more than 12 volts (V) for checking diode continuity.

8. Do not short across or ground any of the terminals on the AC generator.

9. The polarity of the battery, generator, and regulator must be matched and considered before making any electrical connections within the system.

10. Never operate the AC generator on an open circuit. Make sure that all connections within the circuit are clean and tight.

11. Disconnect the battery terminals when performing any service on the electrical system. This will eliminate the possibility of accidental reversal of polarity.

12. Disconnect the battery ground cable if arc welding is to be done on any part of the car.

REMOVAL AND INSTALLATION

The alternator and voltage regulator are combined in one housing. No voltage adjustment can be made with this unit. As with the distributor, repairs to the alternator should be made by an authorized VW dealer. The regulator can be replaced without removing the alternator, just unbolt it from the rear.

1. Disconnect the battery cables.

2. Remove the multiconnector retaining bracket and unplug the connector from the rear of the alternator.

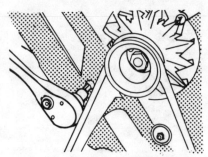

Removing the lower alternator bolt through the timing cover

3. Loosen and remove the top mounting nut and bolt.

4. Using a hex socket inserted through the timing belt cover (not necessary to remove the cover), loosen the lower mounting bolt.

5. Slide the alternator over and remove the alternator belt.

6. Remove the lower nut and bolt. Don't lose the spacers or rubber isolators.

7. Remove the alternator.

NOTE: *Remember when installing the alternator that it is not necessary to polarize an AC generating system.*

8. Install the alternator with the lower bolt. Don't tighten it at this point.

9. Install the alternator belt over the pulleys.

10. Loosely install the top mounting bolt and pivot the alternator over until the belt is correctly tensioned as explained in the next procedure.

11. Finally tighten the top and bottom bolts to 14 ft lbs.

12. Connect the alternator and battery wires.

BELT REPLACEMENT AND TENSIONING

1. Loosen the top alternator mounting bolt.

2. Using a hex socket inserted through the timing belt cover (it's not necessary to remove the cover), loosen the lower mounting bolt.

3. Using a pry bar, such as a large screwdriver or ratchet handle, slide the alternator over and remove the belt.

4. Slip the new belt over the pulleys.

5. Pry the alternator over until the belt deflection midway between the crankshaft pulley and the alternator pulley is $\frac{3}{8}$–$\frac{9}{16}$ in. (10–15 mm).

6. Securely tighten the mounting bolts.

Starter

Beginning approximately July, 1975, a new type starter is used, which is not interchangeable with the old design. A starter support bracket is no longer used. The old type is used on automatic transmission cars and manual transmission cars up to Chassis No. 175 3 439 592 (Rabbit) or 535 2 058 507 (Scirocco). Manual transmission cars after these chassis numbers use the new design starters. Service procedures are not affected.

REMOVAL AND INSTALLATION

1. Disconnect the battery ground cable.

2. Jack up the right front of the car and support with a sturdy stand.

3. Mark with tape and then disconnect the two small wires from the starter solenoid. One wire connects to the ignition coil and the second to the ignition switch through the wiring harness.

4. Disconnect the large cable, which is the positive battery cable, from the solenoid.

5. Remove the two starter retaining nuts.

6. Unscrew the socket head bolt. Pull the starter straight out and to the front.

7. Installation of the starter is carried out in reverse order of removal. On automatic

NEW TYPE   OLD TYPE

New and old type starters are not interchangeable

Starter installation—manual transmission. Be sure the bolts (2) have enough clearance in the elongated holes of the bracket (1) so there is no strain

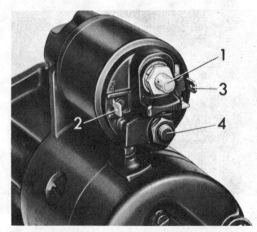

Starter installation—(1) from battery (+) terminal, (2) from terminal 15A to ignition coil, (3) from starter switch and (4) field winding connection

Routing starter wires on new type starters

Install the cover and clamp (2) on automatic transmission starters

transmission models install the cover and clamp (which holds the cover). On later manual transmission models, route the battery and starter wires so that the positive (+) terminal leads point to the rear of the car.

OVERHAUL

Use the following procedure to replace brushes or starter drive.

1. Remove the solenoid.
2. Remove the end bearing cap.
3. Loosen both of the long housing screws.
4. Remove the lockwasher and spacer washers.
5. Remove the long housing screws and remove the end cover.
6. Pull the two field coil brushes out of the brush housing.
7. Remove the brush housing assembly.
8. Loosen the nut on the solenoid housing, remove the sealing disc, and remove the solenoid operating lever.
9. Loosen the large screws on the side of the starter body and remove the field coil along with the brushes.

NOTE: If the brushes require replacement, the field coil and brushes and/or the brush housing and its brushes must be replaced as a unit. Have the armature commutator turned at a machine shop if it is out-of-round, scored, or grooved.

10. If the starter drive is being replaced, push the stop ring down and remove the circlip on the end of the shaft. Remove the stop ring and remove the drive.
11. Assembly of the starter is the reverse order of disassembly. Use a gear puller to install the stop ring in its groove. Use a new circlip on the shaft.

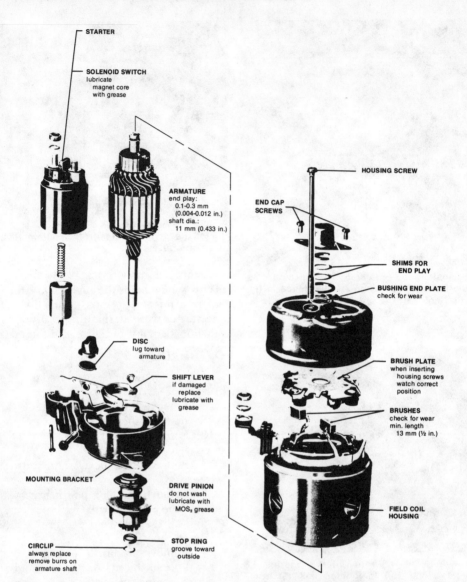

STARTER

SOLENOID SWITCH
lubricate
magnet core
with grease

ARMATURE
end play:
0.1-0.3 mm
(0.004-0.012 in.)
shaft dia.:
11 mm (0.433 in.)

HOUSING SCREW

END CAP
SCREWS

SHIMS FOR
END PLAY

BUSHING END PLATE
check for wear

DISC
lug toward
armature

SHIFT LEVER
if damaged
replace
lubricate with
grease

BRUSH PLATE
when inserting
housing screws
watch correct
position

BRUSHES
check for wear
min. length
13 mm (½ in.)

MOUNTING BRACKET

DRIVE PINION
do not wash
lubricate with
MOS₂ grease

FIELD COIL
HOUSING

CIRCLIP
always replace
remove burrs on
armature shaft

STOP RING
groove toward
outside

Exploded view of typical starter (new style shown)

SOLENOID REPLACEMENT

1. Remove the starter.

2. Remove the nut which secures the connector strip on the end of the solenoid.

3. Take out the two retaining screws on the mounting bracket and withdraw the solenoid after it has been unhooked from the operating lever.

4. Installation is the reverse of removal. In order to facilitate engagement of the lever, the pinion should be pulled out as far as possible when inserting the solenoid.

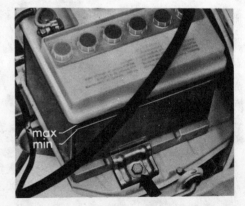

max
min

The battery is retained by a clamp (arrow)

Battery

REMOVAL AND INSTALLATION

CAUTION: *Battery electrolyte (acid) is highly corrosive and can damage both you and the paintwork. Be careful when lifting the battery in and out of the engine compartment.*

1. Disconnect the positive and negative battery cables.
2. Put on heavy work gloves.
3. Loosen the retaining clamp bolt and remove the clamp.
4. Disconnect the small electrical lead for the computer sensor.
5. Lift the battery carefully out of the tray.
6. Clean all corrosion deposits from the battery tray and the retaining plate. Spray them with rust preventative paint.

7. Install the battery in reverse order of removal. Polish the inside of the cables and give them a coat of petroleum jelly before installation.

ENGINE MECHANICAL

Design

GASOLINE ENGINE

The engine is an inline four-cylinder with single overhead camshaft. The engine is inclined 30° to the rear. The center of gravity is in front of the axle, thereby providing lighter steering and better handling. The crankshaft runs in five bearings with thrust being taken on the center bearing. The cylinder block is

Battery and Starter Specifications
(All models use 12 volt, negative ground system)

Year	Model	Battery Amp Hour Capacity	Lock Test Amps	Volts	Torque (ft/lbs)	No Load Test Amps	Volts	RPM	Brush Spring Tension (oz)	Minimum Brush Length (in.)
1974–78	All	45/54*	280–370	7.5	2.42	33–55	11.5	6000–8000	35.5	0.5

* w/AC

General Engine Specifications

Year	Engine Displacement Cu in. (cc)	Carburetor Type	Horsepower @ rpm (SAE)	Torque @ rpm (ft lbs) (SAE)	Bore x Stroke (in.)	Compression Ratio	Oil Pressure @ rpm (psi)
1975	89.7 (1,471)	2 bbl Zenith	70 @ 6000	81 @ 3500	3.01 x 3.15	8.2 : 1	40 @ 2500
1976	96.8 (1,588)	2-bbl	71 @ 5600	82 @ 3300	3.13 x 3.15	8.2 : 1	40 @ 2500
1977	96.8 (1,588)	CSI fuel injection	78 @ 5500	90 @ 3300	3.13 x 3.15	8.0 : 1	40 @ 2500
1978	88.9 (1.457)	CSI fuel injection	71 @ 5800	73 @ 3500	3.13 x 2.89	8.0 : 1	40 @ 2500
1977–78 Diesel	89.7 (1,471)	Fuel injection	48 @ 5800	58 @ 5000	3.01 x 3.15	23.5 : 1	27 @ 2000

Valve Specifications

Year	Seat Angle (deg)	Spring Test Pressure (lbs @ in.)	Stem to Guide Clearance (in.)		Stem Diameter (in.)	
			Intake	Exhaust	Intake	Exhaust
1975–78	45	96–106① @0.92 in.	0.001–0.002	0.001–0.002	0.314	0.314

① Outer spring, inner spring test pressure is 46–51 lbs @ 0.72 in.
NOTE: *Exhaust valves must be ground by hand.*

Crankshaft and Connecting Rod Specifications
All measurements are given in inches.

Year	Crankshaft				Connecting Rod		
	Main Brg Journal Dia	Main Brg Oil Clearance	Shaft End-Play	Thrust on No.	Journal Diameter	Oil Clearance	Side Clearance (max)
1975–78	2.126	0.001–0.003①	0.001–.003②	3	1.811	0.001–0.003	0.015

NOTE: *Main and connecting rod bearings are available in three undersizes.*
① Wear limit 0.003–0.007
② Wear limit—0.015

Piston and Ring Specifications
(All measurements in inches)

Year	Piston Clearance	Ring Gap			Ring Size Clearance		
		Top Compression	Bottom Compression	Oil Control	Top Compression	Bottom Compression	Oil Control
1975–78	0.0011①	0.012–0.018	0.012–0.018	0.010–0.016	0.001–0.002	0.001–0.002	0.001–0.002
1977–78 Diesel	0.0011	0.012–0.020	0.012–0.020	0.010–0.016	0.002–0.004	0.002–0.003	0.001–0.002

NOTE: *Three piston sizes are available to accommodate overbores up to 0.040 in.*
① Wear limit—0.027 in.

Torque Specifications
(All readings in ft lbs)

Year	Cylinder Head Bolts	Rod* Bearing Bolts	Main Bearing Bolts	Crankshaft Pulley Bolt	Flywheel to Crankshaft Bolts	Manifold	
						In	Ex
1975–78	54①	33	47	58	54②	18	18
1977–78 Diesel	61③	33	47	58	54	—	18

① Cold; 61 ft lbs warm—1978 54 ft lbs plus ¼ turn
② Pressure plate to crankshaft bolts
* Always use new bolts
③ Cold—69 ft lbs warm

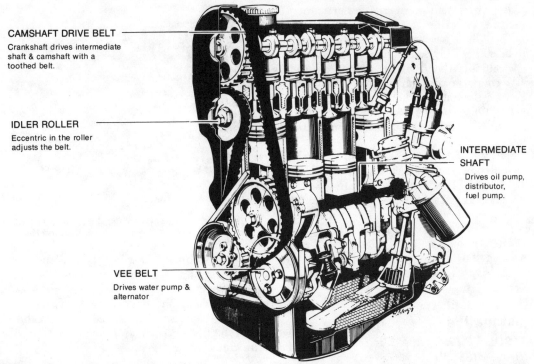

CAMSHAFT DRIVE BELT
Crankshaft drives intermediate
shaft & camshaft with a
toothed belt.

IDLER ROLLER
Eccentric in the roller
adjusts the belt.

**INTERMEDIATE
SHAFT**
Drives oil pump,
distributor,
fuel pump.

VEE BELT
Drives water pump &
alternator

Cutaway view of Rabbit gasoline engine. The diesel engine is very similar, using as many parts from the gasoline engine as possible.

cast iron. A steel reinforced belt drives the intermediate shaft and camshaft. The intermediate shaft drives the oil pump, distributor, and fuel pump.

The cylinder head is lightweight aluminum alloy. The intake and exhaust manifolds are mounted on the same side of the cylinder head. The valves are opened and closed by the camshaft lobes operating on cupped cam followers which fit over the valves and springs. This design results in lighter valve train weight and fewer moving parts. The Rabbit and Scirocco engine combines low maintenance and high power output along with low emissions and excellent fuel mileage.

DIESEL ENGINE

VW introduced the diesel engine option on 1977 Rabbit models.

The key difference between the gasoline and diesel engine is that the diesel has no carburetor and no electrical ignition system. There are no plugs, points or coil to replace. Combustion occurs when a fine mist of diesel fuel is sprayed into hot compressed air (1650° F.) under high pressure (850 psi). The air is heated by the compression as the piston moves up on the compression stroke. The

diesel engine has a compression ratio of 23.5:1 compared to the gasoline engine's compression ratio of 8.2:1.

VW's diesel block, flywheel, bearings and crankshaft are identical to those in the Rabbit gasoline engine. The connecting rod wrist pins were strengthened and new pistons and cylinder head, made of aluminum for lightness, were designed.

The cylinder head has an overhead camshaft to actuate the valves and the cam is driven by a flexible toothed belt which also operates the fuel injection pump.

The Rabbit diesel has a spherical precombustion chamber in which combustion begins. The burning fuel/air mixture is given a swirl pattern by the chamber's shape. The swirl promotes more complete combustion as the combustion process continues in the main combustion chamber. Using the swirl chamber has other advantages: it reduces the peak load which the force of combustion would normally exert on pistons, rods, bearings and crankshaft, enabling VW to use many standard components; and it also permits the VW diesel to be revved to the relatively high speed of 5000 rpm.

Starting a cold engine on a chilly day is different and takes slightly more time. Warm weather starts and warm engine starts are immediate, as with a gasoline version. Each of the cylinders has an electric glow plug to preheat them for cold starts. Depending on how cold it is, the driver must wait from 15 to 60 seconds before starting. A light on the dashboard indicates when preheating is completed. Once the engine is warmed up, there is no need to preheat for subsequent restarting.

The VW diesel is also equipped with a manual cold-start device that looks like a choke knob. It advances the timing for the fuel injection so that the fuel is injected into the hot compressed air earlier to make the engine start more easily. The engine accelerates better and the puff of blue smoke typical of a cold-starting diesel is reduced. Once the car is driven away, the knob is pushed in.

Engine Removal and Installation

GASOLINE ENGINE WITH MANUAL TRANSMISSION

The engine and transmission are removed as an assembly. You don't have to remove the hood, but it might make the job easier.

NOTE: *On A/C cars do not loosen any hoses. Remove compressor with hoses attached.*

1. Disconnect the battery ground cable.
2. Drain the coolant by unbolting the lower water pump flange or by removing the hoses.
3. Remove the radiator with the air ducts and fan. Remove the condenser.
4. Detach all the electrical wires connecting the engine to the body.

Engine disconnects: (1) front mount, (2) clutch cable, and (3) speedometer cable

Engine disconnects: (1) exhaust pipe bracket, (2) exhaust pipe, and (3) rear transmission mount

5. Disconnect the plug the fuel line at the fuel pump. Detach the coolant hoses at the left end of the engine. Disconnect the accelerator cable and remove the air cleaner.
6. Disconnect the speedometer cable from the transmission (seal the hole). Detach the clutch cable.
7. Remove the engine support to the right of the starter.
8. Remove the headlight caps inside the engine compartment.
9. Unbolt the driveshafts from the transmission and wire them up.
10. Unbolt the exhaust pipe from the manifold and unbolt the exhaust pipe brace.
11. Unbolt the transmission rear mount from the body (alongside the tunnel).
12. Detach the ground strap from the transmission and body.
13. Remove the shift linkage.
14. Attach a chain sling to the alternator bracket and the lifting eye at the left end of the engine. Lift the engine and transmission slightly.
15. Detach the engine carrier from the body and remove the left transmission carrier.
16. Lift the engine/transmission assembly carefully out of the car.
17. To separate the engine and transmission, remove the TDC sensor and turn the flywheel to align the lug on the flywheel (to the left of TDC) with the pointer in the opening. Remove the cover plate over the driveshaft flange and remove the engine to transmission bolts and the transmission housing cover plate.

To install the engine:
18. To attach the transmission to the engine, the recess in the flywheel edge must

Align the engine/transmission mounts at front mount (A), left mount (B), and rear mount (C)

be at 3 O'Clock (facing the left end of the engine). Torque the engine to transmission bolts to 40 ft lbs. Lift the engine/transmission assembly into place and loosely attach the left transmission carrier to the transmission. Align the assembly, then bolt the engine and transmission carrier to the body. Torque the 10 mm bolts to 29 ft lbs. Torque the driveshaft flange bolts to 32 ft lbs. Refill the cooling system.

NOTE: *When installing the engine/transmission, the mounts must be properly aligned, in the following order.*

1. *Loosen the front mount bolts.*
2. *Loosen the left transmission mount.*
3. *Loosen the rear transmission mount.*
4. *Loosen the right transmission mount.*
5. *Center the engine/transmission in the transmission mounts. Tighten the bolts.*

6. *Center the rubber core of the front mount in the housing and tighten the bolts.*
7. *Check adjustment of shift linkage.*

Move the engine/transmission front to rear to center the left and right transmission mounts in the brackets

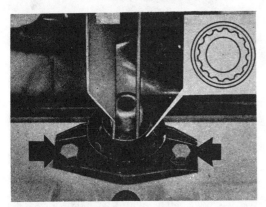

Align the front mount so the rubber core is centered in the housing

Move the engine/transmission assembly side to side so that the rear mount is straight

GASOLINE ENGINE WITH AUTOMATIC TRANSMISSION

The engine and transmission are removed as an assembly. You don't have to remove the hood, but it might make the job easier. The transmission should be in park.

NOTE: *On A/C cars, do not loosen any A/C lines. Remove the compressor with hoses attached.*

1. Disconnect both battery cables.

2. Drain the coolant by unbolting the lower water pump flange or by removing the hoses.

3. Remove the radiator with the air ducts and fan. Remove the condenser.

4. Remove the air cleaner.

5. Detach the speedometer cable from the transmission.

6. Detach all electrical wires connecting the engine to the body. Detach the coolant hoses.

7. Remove the screws holding the accelerator cable bracket to the carburetor float bowl, shift into P, detach the end of the gearshift selector cable from the transmission, detach the accelerator cable from the carburetor and from the pedal at the transmission, and remove the two bracket bolts behind this linkage on the transmission.

8. Unbolt the exhaust pipe from the manifold.

9. Remove the rear transmission mount.

10. Remove the converter cover plate and remove the three torque converter to drive plate bolts.

11. Attach a chain sling to the alternator bracket and the lifting eye at the left end of the engine. It may be necessary to remove the alternator. Lift the engine and transmission slightly.

12. Detach the engine front mounting support; remove the left transmission carrier and the right engine carrier.

13. Lift the engine/transmission assembly carefully out of the car.

14. The transmission can now be detached from the engine.

To install the engine:

15. The engine to transmission bolts should be torqued to 40 ft lbs. Lift the engine/transmission assembly into place and install the left transmission carrier, tightening first the body, then the transmission bolts. Lower the assembly to attach the engine carrier to the body, tightening the bolts to 40 ft lbs. Install the engine mounting support. Torque converter bolts should be torqued to 21 ft lbs and drive shaft bolts to 32 ft lbs. Refill the cooling system. Check the adjustment of transmission and carburetor linkages.

DIESEL ENGINES

The diesel engine is removed with the transmission attached.

1. Disconnect the battery.

2. Disconnect the radiator hoses and drain the coolant. It can be saved for reuse, if it's not too old.

3. Remove the radiator complete with fan.

4. Remove the alternator.

5. Disconnect the fuel filter and set it aside near the windshield washer reservoir.

6. Detach the supply and return lines from the injection pump.

7. Disconnect the accelerator cable from the lever on the injection pump and remove the injection pump complete with bracket.

Disconnect the fuel supply line (6) and return line (7) from the injection pump. Disconnect the accelerator cable (8) from pump lever and remove the bracket (9)

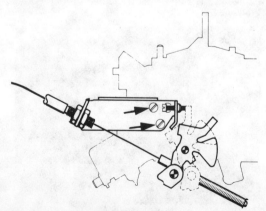

Remove the accelerator cable bracket screws (arrows) without disturbing the settings

Remove the relay lever (13), connecting rod (14) and selector rod (15)

8. Disconnect the cold start cable from the pump.

9. Disconnect and label all electrical wires and leads.

10. Remove the front transmission mount.

11. Disconnect the clutch cable.

12. Remove the relay rod and connecting rod from the transmission and turn the relay lever shaft to the rear.

13. Disconnect the selector rod.

14. Remove the rear support.

15. Disconnect the exhaust pipe at the manifold and remove the rear transmission mount.

16. Attach a lifting sling to the engine and take the weight from the engine mounts. Remove the left and right transmission mounts.

17. Carefully guide the engine out of the car while turning it slightly.

18. To separate the engine from the transmission, unscrew the plug from the TDC sensor opening and turn the flywheel to align the mark on the flywheel with the pointer. The engine/transmission can only be separated in this position.

19. Remove the cover plate over the driveshaft flange and remove the engine-to-transmission bolts.

20. Press the engine off the transmission.

21. Installation is the reverse of removal. Turn the flywheel so that the recess in the flywheel is level with the driveshaft flange. Lower the engine into the car and attach the left transmission mount to the transmission first. In this order, align the rear transmission mount, center the engine/transmission and center the front transmission mount. Adjust the acclerator and cold start cables and bleed the injection system. See installation

note under "Gasoline Engine with Manual Transmission" removal and installation.

Timing Belt Cover
REMOVAL AND INSTALLATION

1. Loosen the alternator mounting bolts.

2. Pivot the alternator over and slip the drive belt off the pulleys.

3. Unscrew the cover retaining nuts and remove the cover. Don't lose any of the washers or spacers.

4. Reposition the spacers on the studs and then install the washers and nuts.

5. Install the alternator belt and adjust the tension.

Timing Belt

NOTE: *The Rabbit and Scirocco timing belt is designed to last for more than 60,000 miles and does not normally require tension adjustments. If the belt is removed or replaced, the basic valve timing must be checked and the belt retensioned.*

REMOVAL, INSTALLATION, AND TENSIONING
Gasoline Engines

1. Remove the timing belt cover.

2. While holding the large hex on the tension pulley, loosen the pulley locknut.

3. Release the tensioner from the timing belt.

4. Slide the belt off the three toothed pulleys and remove it.

5. Using the larger bolt on the crankshaft pulley, turn the engine until the No. 1 cylinder is at TDC of the compression stroke. At this point, both valves will be closed and the OT mark will be aligned with the pointer on the bellhousing.

6. Check that the timing mark on the rear face of the camshaft pulley is aligned with the camshaft cover as shown. If it's not, turn the pulley so that it does.

7. Check that the V-notch in the crankshaft pulley aligns with the dot mark on the intermediate shaft as shown. If they don't, turn the crankshaft until they do.

CAUTION: *If the timing marks are not correctly aligned with the No. 1 piston at TDC of the compression stroke and the belt is installed, valve timing will be incorrect. Poor performance and possible engine*

Releasing the tensioner. Turn in direction (a) to tension the belt and (b) to release tension. Check tension at midpoint (c).

Remove the belt by sliding it off the pulleys

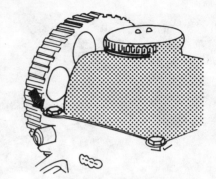

Camshaft sprocket alignment

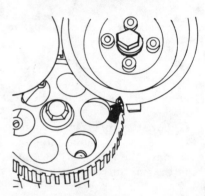

Crankshaft and intermediate shaft sprocket alignment

damage can result from the improper valve timing.

8. Install the belt on the pulleys.

9. Adjust tensioner by turning the large tensioner hex to the right. Tension is correct when you can just twist the belt 90° with two fingers at the midpoint between the camshaft pulley and the intermediate shaft pulley. Tighten the locknut to 32 ft lbs.

10. Install the timing belt cover and check the ignition timing as described in Chapter 2.

Diesel Engine

The drive belt on the Rabbit diesel also drives the injection pump. It is necessary that this procedure be followed exactly to ensure proper valve timing and injection pump timing. You will also need special tool VW 210 to properly tension the belt.

1. Remove the alternator belt.

2. Remove the timing belt cover and rocker cover.

3. Set the engine at TDC on No. 1 cylinder. In this position both valves of No. 1 cylinder will be closed and the OT mark on the flywheel will be aligned with the pointer on the bell housing.

4. Use a pin or suitable bolt to hold the injection pump sprocket and camshaft sprocket in position. The pin or bolt must be exactly the size of the hole. There can be no "slop" in the gears.

5. Loosen the tensioner.

6. Remove the belt and belt shield from the drive gears.

To install the belt:

7. Check that the TDC mark is aligned with the flywheel mark.

8. Loosen the camshaft sprocket bolt ½

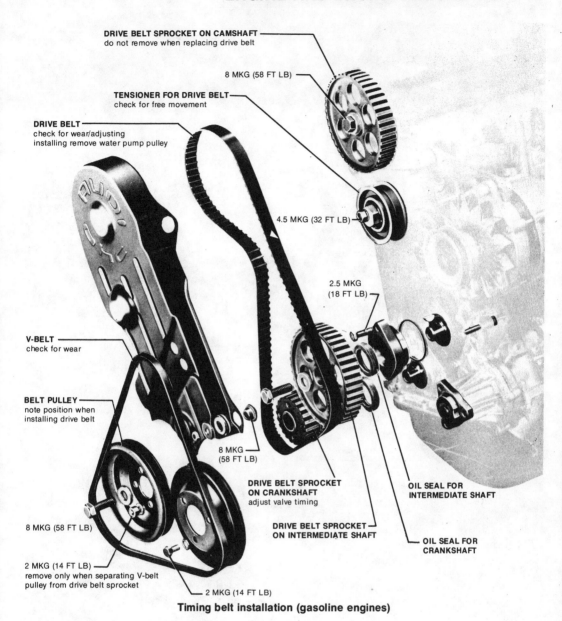

DRIVE BELT SPROCKET ON CAMSHAFT
do not remove when replacing drive belt

8 MKG (58 FT LB)

TENSIONER FOR DRIVE BELT
check for free movement

DRIVE BELT
check for wear/adjusting
installing remove water pump pulley

4.5 MKG (32 FT LB)

2.5 MKG
(18 FT LB)

V-BELT
check for wear

BELT PULLEY
note position when
installing drive belt

8 MKG
(58 FT LB)

DRIVE BELT SPROCKET
ON CRANKSHAFT
adjust valve timing

OIL SEAL FOR
INTERMEDIATE SHAFT

DRIVE BELT SPROCKET
ON INTERMEDIATE SHAFT

OIL SEAL FOR
CRANKSHAFT

8 MKG (58 FT LB)

2 MKG (14 FT LB)
remove only when separating V-belt
pulley from drive belt sprocket

2 MKG (14 FT LB)

Timing belt installation (gasoline engines)

turn and tap the gear loose from the camshaft with a rubber mallet.

9. Install the drive belt and remove the pin from the camshaft and injection pump gears.

10. Tension the belt by turning the tensioner to the right.

11. Check the belt tension between the camshaft and injection pump sprockets. On VW 210 special tool, the scale should read 12–13.

12. Tighten the camshaft sprocket bolt.

13. Turn the crankshaft 2 complete turns in the direction of normal rotation and check the belt tension again.

Timing Gears
REMOVAL AND INSTALLATION
All Engines

The camshaft, intermediate shaft, and crankshaft pulleys are located by keys on their respective shafts and each is retained by a bolt. To remove any or all of the pulleys, first remove the timing belt cover and belt and then use the following procedure.

NOTE: *When removing the crankshaft pulley, don't remove the four socket head bolts which retain the outer belt pulley to the timing belt pulley.*

1. Remove the center bolt.

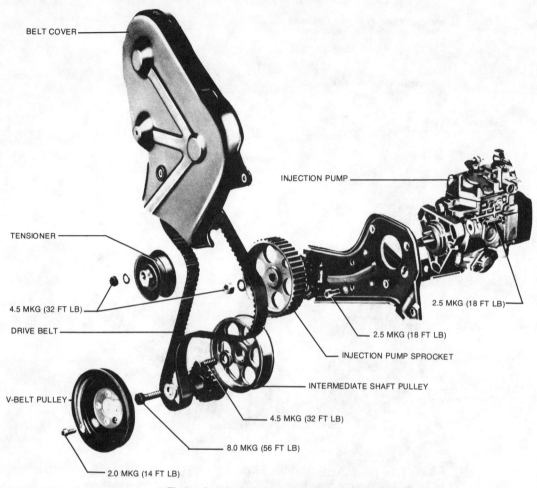

BELT COVER

INJECTION PUMP

TENSIONER

4.5 MKG (32 FT LB)

DRIVE BELT

V-BELT PULLEY

2.5 MKG (18 FT LB)

2.5 MKG (18 FT LB)

INJECTION PUMP SPROCKET

INTERMEDIATE SHAFT PULLEY

4.5 MKG (32 FT LB)

8.0 MKG (56 FT LB)

2.0 MKG (14 FT LB)

Timing belt installation (diesel engines)

2. Gently pry the pulley off the shaft.

3. If the pulley is stubborn in coming off, use a gear puller. Don't hammer on the pulley.

4. Remove the pulley and key.

5. Install the pulley in the reverse order of removal.

6. Tighten the center bolt to 58 ft lbs.

7. Install the timing belt, check valve timing, tension belt, and install the cover.

Camshaft

REMOVAL AND INSTALLATION

1. Remove the timing belt.

2. Remove the camshaft sprocket.

3. Remove the air cleaner.

4. Remove the camshaft cover.

5. Unscrew and remove the Nos. 1, 3, and 5 bearing caps (No. 1 is at front of engine).

6. Unscrew the Nos. 2 and 4 bearing caps, diagonally and in increments.

Remove the nuts holding the camshaft bearing caps

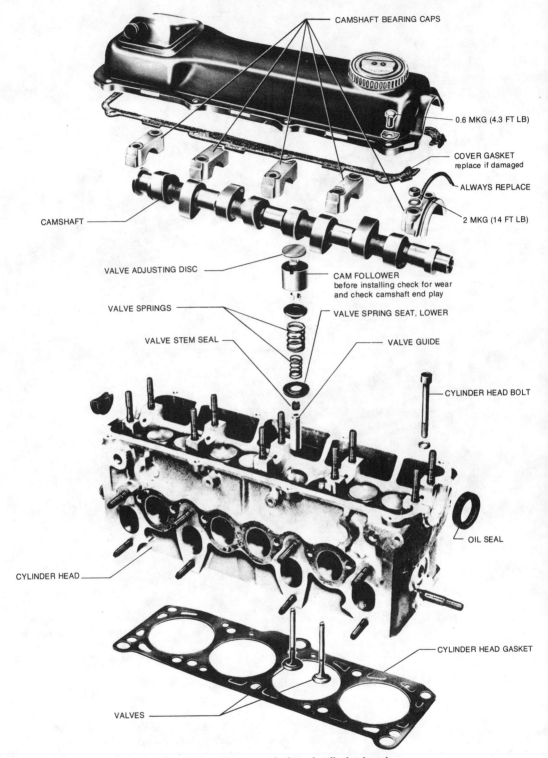

CAMSHAFT BEARING CAPS

0.6 MKG (4.3 FT LB)

COVER GASKET
replace if damaged

ALWAYS REPLACE

2 MKG (14 FT LB)

CAMSHAFT

VALVE ADJUSTING DISC

CAM FOLLOWER
before installing check for wear
and check camshaft end play

VALVE SPRINGS

VALVE SPRING SEAT, LOWER

VALVE STEM SEAL

VALVE GUIDE

CYLINDER HEAD BOLT

OIL SEAL

CYLINDER HEAD

CYLINDER HEAD GASKET

VALVES

Gasoline engine camshaft and cylinder head

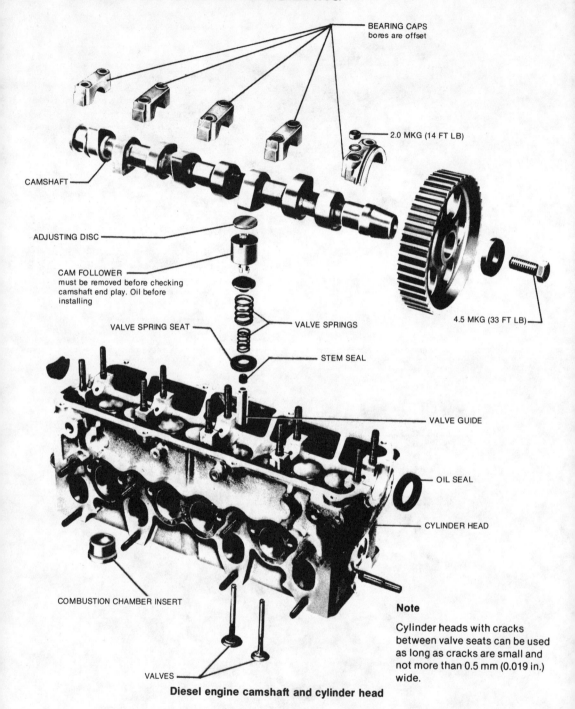

BEARING CAPS
bores are offset

2.0 MKG (14 FT LB)

CAMSHAFT

ADJUSTING DISC

CAM FOLLOWER
must be removed before checking
camshaft end play. Oil before
installing

4.5 MKG (33 FT LB)

VALVE SPRING SEAT

VALVE SPRINGS

STEM SEAL

VALVE GUIDE

OIL SEAL

CYLINDER HEAD

COMBUSTION CHAMBER INSERT

VALVES

Note

Cylinder heads with cracks
between valve seats can be used
as long as cracks are small and
not more than 0.5 mm (0.019 in.)
wide.

Diesel engine camshaft and cylinder head

7. Lift the camshaft out of the cylinder head.

8. Lubricate the camshaft journals and lobes with assembly lube or gear oil before installing it in the cylinder head.

9. Replace the camshaft oil seal with a new one whenever the cam is removed.

10. Install the Nos. 1, 3, and 5 bearing caps and tighten the nuts to 14 ft lbs. The caps should be installed so that they read right side up from the driver's seat.

11. Install the Nos. 2 and 4 bearing caps and diagonally tighten the nuts to 14 ft lbs.

NOTE: *If checking end-play, install a dial indicator so that the feeler touches the camshaft snout. End-play should be no more than 0.006 in. (0.15 mm).*

12. Replace the seal in the No. 1 bearing

The camshaft bearing caps are numbered for identification (Arrows)

cap. If necessary, replace the end plug in the cylinder head.

13. Install the camshaft cover.

14. Install the camshaft pulley and the timing belt as previously described.

15. Check the valve clearance as outlined in Chapter 2.

Cylinder Head

REMOVAL AND INSTALLATION

Carbureted Engines

The engine should be cold before the cylinder head can be removed. The head is retained by 10 socket head bolts. It can be removed without removing the intake and exhaust manifolds.

NOTE: *Beginning approximately July 1977, 12 point socket head bolts were used in place of 6 point older version. These*

NEW
POLYGON

OLD
HEXAGON

New and old style head bolts

should be used in complete sets only and need not be retorqued after the mileage interval.

1. Disconnect the battery ground cable.

2. Drain the cooling system.

3. Remove the air cleaner. Disconnect the fuel line.

4. Disconnect the radiator, heater, and choke hoses.

5. Disconnect all electrical wires. Remove the spark plug wires.

6. Separate the exhaust manifold from the exhaust pipe.

7. Disconnect the EGR line from the exhaust manifold. Remove the EGR valve and filter from the intake manifold.

8. Remove the carburetor.

9. On California cars, disconnect the air pump fittings.

10. Remove the timing belt cover and belt.

11. Loosen the cylinder head bolts in the sequence of 10 to 1 as shown in the illustration.

12. Remove the bolts and lift the cylinder head straight off.

13. Install the new cylinder head gasket with the word "TOP" going up.

14. Install bolts Nos. 7 and 8 first, these holes are smaller and will properly locate the gasket and cylinder head.

15. Install the remaining bolts. Tighten them in three stages in the 1 through 10 sequence shown. Cylinder head tightening torque is 54 ft lbs.

NOTE: *After approximately 300 miles, retighten these cylinder head bolts.*

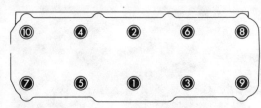

Tighten the head bolts in this sequence

16. Install the remaining components in the reverse order of removal.

Fuel Injected Engines

The cylinder head is retained by Allen bolts. When installing the head gasket, the TOP or OBEN goes up. Install No. 7 and 8 bolts first; these are shorter and will locate the head and gasket.

1. Drain the cooling system.
2. Disconnect the air duct from the throttle valve assembly.
3. Disconnect the throttle cable.
4. Remove the injectors and disconnect the line from the cold start valve.
5. Disconnect the radiator and heater hoses.
6. Disconnect all fluid lines and hoses.
7. Remove the auxiliary air regulator from the intake manifold.
8. Disconnect all electrical leads.
9. Separate the exhaust manifold from the exhaust pipe.
10. Remove the intake manifold.
11. Remove the timing belt cover and belt.
12. Installation is the reverse of removal. After 1000 miles, loosen and retighten all bolts.

Diesel Engines

The head is retained by Allen bolts. The engine should be cold when the head is removed. The word TOP or OBEN on the new gasket should face up.

1. Disconnect the battery ground cable.
2. Drain the cooling system.
3. Remove the air cleaner.
4. Disconnect the fuel lines. Disconnect and tag all electrical wires and leads.
5. Separate the exhaust manifold from the pipe. Disconnect the radiator and heater hoses.
6. Remove the timing cover and belt (See timing belt replacement).
7. Loosen the cylinder head bolts in the reverse order of the tightening sequence.
8. Remove the head. Do not lay the head on the gasket surface with the injectors in-

stalled. Support it at the ends on strips of wood.

9. Install the cylinder head with a new gasket. Be sure the new gasket has the same number of notches and the same identifying number as the old one, unless the pistons were also replaced. In this case, see Piston Replacement.

Install bolts 8 and 10 first and torque the bolts to the specification in the proper sequence. After 1000 miles, loosen all bolts ⅓ turn and retorque the bolts.

OVERHAUL

The "Engine Rebuilding" section contains general information on cylinder head refinishing. This job is best left to a dealer or a competent machinist, as they will have the correct tools. Valve guides are a shrink fit. Always install new valve seals. Valve seats are not replaceable.

Intake Manifold

REMOVAL AND INSTALLATION

Carbureted Engines

1. Remove the air cleaner. Drain the cooling system.
2. Disconnect the accelerator cable.
3. Disconnect the EGR valve connections.
4. Detach all electrical leads.
5. Disconnect the coolant hoses.
6. Disconnect the fuel line from the carburetor.
7. Remove the vacuum hoses from the carburetor.
8. Loosen and remove the six retaining bolts and lift off the manifold.
9. Install a new gasket. Fit the manifold and tighten the bolts from the inside out. Tightening torque is 18 ft lbs.
10. Install the remaining components in the reverse order of removal. Refill the cooling system.

Fuel Injected Engines

1. Disconnect the air duct from the throttle valve body. Drain the cooling system.
2. Disconnect the accelerator cable.
3. Remove the injectors and disconnect the cold start valve.
4. Disconnect all coolant hoses.
5. Disconnect all vacuum and emission control hoses.
6. Remove the auxiliary air regulator.
7. Disconnect all electrical leads.

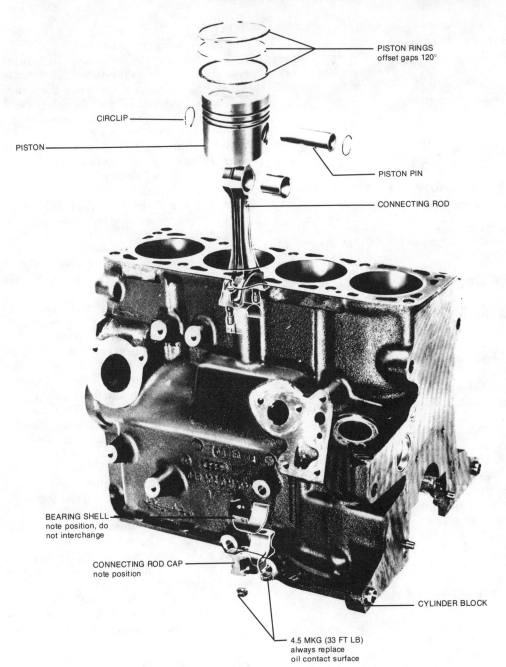

PISTON RINGS
offset gaps 120°

CIRCLIP

PISTON

PISTON PIN

CONNECTING ROD

BEARING SHELL
note position, do
not interchange

CONNECTING ROD CAP
note position

CYLINDER BLOCK

4.5 MKG (33 FT LB)
always replace
oil contact surface

Cylinder block, pistons, connecting rods and bearings

8. Disconnect the EGR line.

9. Remove the manifold.

10. Installation is the reverse of removal.

Exhaust Manifold

REMOVAL AND INSTALLATION

1. Disconnect the EGR tube from the exhaust manifold (if equipped).

2. On California cars, remove the air pump components which are in the way.

3. Remove the air cleaner hose from the exhaust manifold.

4. Disconnect the intake manifold support.

5. Separate the exhaust pipe from the manifold.

6. Remove the eight retaining nuts and remove the manifold.

7. Clean the cylinder head and manifold mating surfaces.

8. Using a new gasket, install the exhaust manifold.

9. Tighten the nuts to 18 ft lbs. Work from the insde out.

10. Install the remaining components in the reverse order of removal. Use a new manifold flange gasket if the old one is deteriorated.

Pistons and Connecting Rods

REMOVAL AND INSTALLATION

Gasoline Engines

NOTE: *A complete step-by-step engine rebuilding section is included at the end of this chapter.*

1. Follow the instructions under "Cylinder Head" removal and "Timing Belt" removal.

2. Remove the oil pan as described later in this chapter.

3. This procedure would be much more easily performed with the engine out of the car.

4. Pistons should be removed in the order: 1-3-4-2. Turn the crankshaft until the piston to be removed is at the bottom of its stroke.

5. Place a cloth on the head of the piston to be removed and, using a ridge reamer, remove the deposits from the upper end of the cylinder bore.

NOTE: *Never remove more than 1/32 in. from the ring travel area when removing the ridges.*

6. Mark all connecting rod bearing caps so that they may be returned to their original locations in the engine. Mark all pistons so they can be returned to their original cylinders.

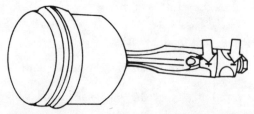

Matchmark the connecting rod and cap before disassembly

7. Remove the connecting rod caps.

8. Push the connecting rod and piston out through the top of the cylinder with a hammer handle.

CAUTION: *Don't score the cylinder walls or the crankshaft journal.*

9. Using an internal micrometer, measure the bores across the thrust faces of the cylinder and parallel to the axis of the crankshaft at a minimum of four equally spaced locations. The bore must not be out-of-round by more than 0.005 in. and it must not taper more than 0.010 in. Taper is the difference in wear between two bore measurements in any cylinder. See the "Engine Rebuilding" section for complete details.

10. If the cylinder bore is in satisfactory conditon, place each ring in the bore in turn and square it in the bore with the head of the piston. Measure the ring gap. If the ring gap is greater than the limit, get a new ring. If the ring gap is less thanthe limit, file the end of the ring to obtain the correct gap.

11. Check the ring side clearance by installing rings on the piston, and inserting a feeler gauge of the correct dimension between the ring and the lower land. The gauge should slide freely around the ring circumference without binding. Any wear will form a step on the lower land. Remove any pistons having high steps. Before checking the ring side clearance, be sure that the ring grooves are clean and free of carbon, sludge, or grit.

12. Piston rings should be installed so that their ends are at three equal spacings. Avoid installing the rings with their ends in line with the piston pin bosses and the thrust direction.

13. Install the pistons in their original bores, if you are reusing the same pistons. Install short lengths of rubber hose over the connecting rod bolts to prevent damage to the cylinder walls or rod journal.

NOTE: *1978 models have different pistons than 1977 and earlier models. New pistons cannot be used in earlier models.*

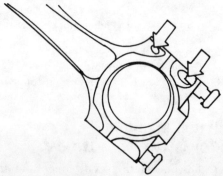

When assembling the connecting rod and cap, align the forged marks

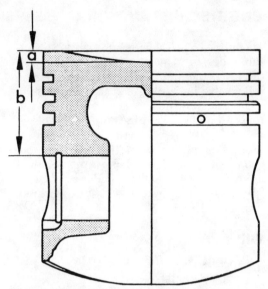

New pistons have been installed in the 1978 gasoline engines. A = 0.002 in.—B = 1.338 in.

14. Install a ring compressor over the rings on the piston. Lower the piston and rod assembly into the bore until the ring compressor contacts the block. Using a wooden hammer handle, push the piston into the bore while guiding the rod onto the journal.

NOTE: *The arrow on the piston should face toward the front of the engine.*

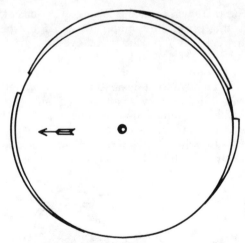

The arrow on the piston must face to the right (the front of the engine)

Diesel Engine

The same basic procedures apply to the diesel engine as well as the gasoline engine. The one important difference is that whenever

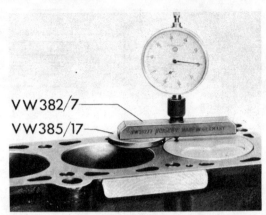

Piston projection measurement on diesel engine

new pistons or short block are installed, the piston projection must be checked.

A spacer (VW 385/17) and bar with micrometer (VW 382/7) are necessary, and should be set up as shown to measure the maximum amount of piston projection above the deck height.

Select a cylinder head gasket from the following chart.

Piston Projection (mm)	Gasket Identification No. of Notches	Part Number
0.43–0.63	2	068 103 383
0.63–0.82	3	068 103 383C
0.82–0.92	4	068 103 383G
0.92–1.02	5	068 103 383H

NOTE: *1978 models (beginning with engine CK 024 944) have pistons with a new piston height and a thicker cylinder head gasket. These pistons are marked with a ".9" next to installation direction arrow. New pistons can be used in earlier cars, but only in sets of 4.*

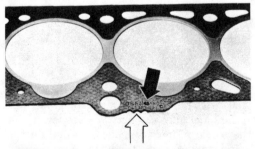

Diesel engine cylinder head gaskets are identified by a number (black arrow) and notches (white arrow)

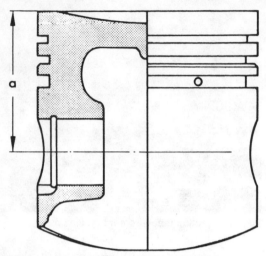

Beginning with Sept, 1977 production, the piston height (A) on diesel engines was increased from 1.759 in. to 1.768 in.

New diesel pistons (since Sept, 1977) are identified by a number "9" next to the arrow denoting installation direction

Engine Rebuilding Notes

Use the "Engine Rebuilding" section at the end of the chapter for cylinder head, block, and crankshaft refinishing. The main bearing shells with the lubricating grooves always go in the block, not the caps, for proper oiling. There is a piston size code stamped on the cylinder block above the water pump. Bring this number to the dealer when ordering a replacement piston(s).

ENGINE LUBRICATION

The lubrication system is a conventional wet-sump design. The gear type oil pump is driven by the intermediate shaft. A pressure relief valve limits pressure and prevents extreme pressure from developing in the system. All oil is filtered by a full-flow replaceable filter. A by-pass valve assures lubrication in the event that the filter becomes plugged. The oil pressure switch is located at the end of the cylinder head galley [the end of the system] to assure accurate pressure readings.

Oil Pan

REMOVAL AND INSTALLATION

1. Drain the oil pan.
2. Loosen and remove the socket head, oil pan retaining bolts.
3. Lower the pan from the car.
4. Install the pan using a new gasket and sealer.
5. Tighten the retaining bolts to 7 ft lbs in a crosswise pattern.
6. Refill the engine with oil. Start the engine and check for leaks.

Rear Main Oil Seal

REPLACEMENT

The rear main oil seal is located in a housing on the rear of the cylinder block. To replace the seal, it is necessary to remove the engine and perform the work on an engine stand or work bench.

1. Remove the transmission and flywheel.
2. Using a screwdriver, very carefully pry the old seal out of the support ring.
3. Remove the seal.
4. Lightly oil the replacement seal and then press it into place using a canister top or

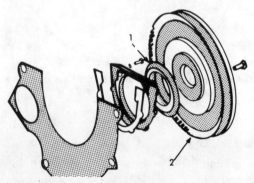

Rear main oil seal (1) and flywheel (2)

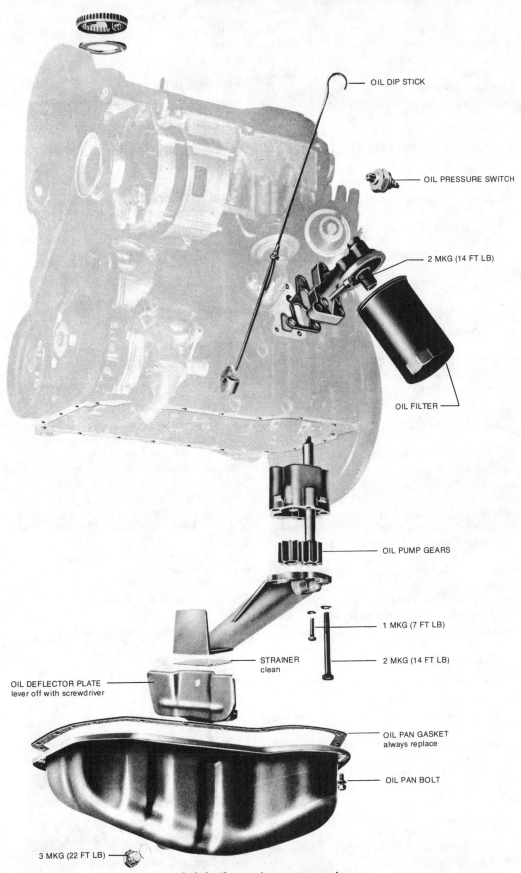

OIL DIP STICK

OIL PRESSURE SWITCH

2 MKG (14 FT LB)

OIL FILTER

OIL PUMP GEARS

1 MKG (7 FT LB)

2 MKG (14 FT LB)

STRAINER
clean

OIL DEFLECTOR PLATE
lever off with screwdriver

OIL PAN GASKET
always replace

OIL PAN BOLT

3 MKG (22 FT LB)

Lubrication system components

other circular piece of flat metal. Be careful not to damage the seal or score the crankshaft.

5. Install the flywheel and transmission. Flywheel-to-engine bolts are tightened to 36 ft lbs.

Oil Pump
REMOVAL AND INSTALLATION

1. Remove the oil pan.
2. Remove the two mounting bolts.
3. Pull oil pump down and out of the engine.
4. Unscrew the two bolts and separate the pump halves.
5. Remove the driveshaft and gear from the upper body.
6. Clean the bottom half in solvent. Pry up the metal edges to remove the filter screen for cleaning.
7. Examine the gears and driveshaft for wear or damage. Replace them if necessary.
8. Reassemble the pump halves.
9. Prime the pump with oil and install in the reverse order of removal.

ENGINE COOLING

The cooling system consists of a belt-driven, external water pump, thermostat, radiator, and thermo-switch controlled electric cooling fan. When the engine is cold the thermostat is closed and blocks the water from the radiator so that the coolant is only circulated through the engine. When the engine warms up, the thermostat opens and the radiator is included in the coolant circuit. The thermo-switch is positioned in the bottom of the radiator and turns the electrical fan on at 199° F, off at 186° F. This reduces power loss and engine noise.

Radiator and Fan
REMOVAL AND INSTALLATION

1. Drain the cooling system.
2. Remove the inner shroud mounting bolts.
3. Disconnect the lower radiator hose.
4. Disconnect the thermo-switch lead.
5. Remove the lower radiator shroud.
6. Remove the lower radiator mounting units.
7. Disconnect the upper radiator hose.
8. Detach the upper radiator shroud.
9. Disconnect the heater and intake manifold hoses.

10. Remove the side mounting bolts and lift the radiator and fan out as an assembly.
11. Installation is the reverse of removal.

Thermostat
REMOVAL AND INSTALLATION

The thermostat is located in the bottom radiator hose neck on the water pump.

1. Drain the cooling system.
2. Remove the two retaining bolts from the lower water pump neck.
NOTE: *It's not necessary to disconnect the hose.*
3. Move neck, with hoses attached, out of the way.
4. Remove the thermostat.
5. Install a new seal on the water pump neck.
6. Install the thermostat with the spring end up.
7. Replace the water pump neck and tighten the two retaining bolts.

Water Pump
REMOVAL AND INSTALLATION

1. Drain the cooling system.
2. Remove the alternator and drive belt as outlined earlier in this chapter.
3. Remove the timing belt cover.
4. Disconnect the lower radiator hose, engine hose, and heater hose from the water pump.
5. Remove the four pump retaining bolts. Notice where the different length bolts are located.
6. Turn the pump slightly and lift it out of the engine block.
7. Installation is the reverse of removal. Use a new seal on the mating surface of the engine.

Water pump mounting bolts

Engine Rebuilding

This section describes, in detail, the procedures involved in rebuilding a typical engine. The procedures specifically refer to an inline engine, however, they are basically identical to those used in rebuilding engines of nearly all design and configurations. Procedures for servicing atypical engines (i.e., horizontally opposed) are described in the appropriate section, although in most cases, cylinder head reconditioning procedures described in this chapter will apply.

The section is divided into two sections. The first, Cylinder Head Reconditioning, assumes that the cylinder head is removed from the engine, all manifolds are removed, and the cylinder head is on a workbench. The camshaft should be removed from overhead cam cylinder heads. The second section, Cyl-

Torque (ft. lbs.)*

	U.S./Bolt Grade (SAE)							Metric/Bolt Grade				
Bolt Diameter (inches)	⬡ 1 and 2	⬡ 5	⬡ 6	⬡ 8	Wrench Size (inches) Bolt	Wrench Size (inches) Nut		Bolt Diameter (mm)	5D 5D	8G 8G	10K 10K	12K 12K	Wrench Size (mm) Bolt and Nut
1/4	5	7	10	10.5	3/8	7/16		6	5	6	8	10	10
5/16	9	14	19	22	1/2	9/16		8	10	16	22	27	14
3/8	15	25	34	37	9/16	5/8		10	19	31	40	49	17
7/16	24	40	55	60	5/8	3/4		12	34	54	70	86	19
1/2	37	60	85	92	3/4	13/16		14	55	89	117	137	22
9/16	53	88	120	132	7/8	7/8		16	83	132	175	208	24
5/8	74	120	167	180	15/16	1		18	111	182	236	283	27
3/4	120	200	280	296	1 1/8	1 1/8		22	182	284	394	464	32
7/8	190	302	440	473	1 5/16	1 5/16		24	261	419	570	689	36
1	282	466	660	714	1 1/2	1 1/2							

*—Torque values are for lightly oiled bolts. CAUTION: Bolts threaded into aluminum require much less torque.

inder Block Reconditioning, covers the block, pistons, connecting rods and crankshaft. It is assumed that the engine is mounted on a work stand, and the cylinder head and all accessories are removed.

Procedures are identified as follows:

Unmarked—Basic procedures that must be performed in order to successfully complete the rebuilding process.

Starred (*)—Procedures that should be performed to ensure maximum performance and engine life.

Double starred (**)—Procedures that may be performed to increase engine performance and reliability. These procedures are usually reserved for extremely heavy-duty or competition usage.

In many cases, a choice of methods is also provided. Methods are identified in the same manner as procedures. The choice of method for a procedure is at the discretion of the user.

The tools required for the basic rebuilding procedure should, with minor exceptions, be those included in a mechanic's tool kit. An accurate torque wrench, and a dial indicator (reading in thousandths) mounted on a universal base should be available. Bolts and nuts with no torque specification should be tightened according to size (see chart). Special tools, where required, all are readily available from the major tool suppliers (i.e., Craftsman, Snap-On, K-D). The services of a competent automotive machine shop must also be readily available.

When assembling the engine, any parts that will be in frictional contact must be pre-lubricated, to provide protection on initial start-up. Vortex Pre-Lube, STP, or any product specifically formulated for this purpose may be used. NOTE: *Do not use engine oil.* Where semi-permanent (locked but removable) installation of bolts or nuts is desired, threads should be cleaned and coated with Loctite. Studs may be permanently installed using Loctite Stud and Bearing Mount.

Aluminum has become increasingly popular for use in engines, due to its low weight and excellent heat transfer characteristics. The following precautions must be observed when handling aluminum engine parts:

—Never hot-tank aluminum parts.

—Remove all aluminum parts (identification tags, etc.) from engine parts before hot-tanking (otherwise they will be removed during the process).

—Always coat threads lightly with engine oil or anti-seize compounds before installation, to prevent seizure.

—Never over-torque bolts or spark plugs in aluminum threads. Should stripping occur, threads can be restored according to the following procedure, using Heli-Coil thread inserts:

Tap drill the hole with the stripped threads to the specified size (see chart). Using the specified tap (NOTE: *Heli-Coil tap sizes refer to the size thread being replaced, rather than the actual tap size*), tap the hole for the Heli-

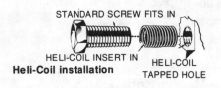

Heli-Coil installation

STANDARD SCREW FITS IN
HELI-COIL INSERT IN
HELI-COIL TAPPED HOLE

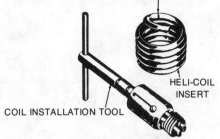

Heli-Coil and installation tool

NOTCH
HELI-COIL INSERT
COIL INSTALLATION TOOL

Heli-Coil Specifications

	Heli-Coil Insert		Drill	Tap	Insert. Tool	Extracting Tool
Thread Size	Part No.	Insert Length (In.)	Size	Part No.	Part No.	Part No.
1/2 -20	1185-4	3/8	17/64(.266)	4 CPB	528-4N	1227-6
5/16-18	1185-5	15/32	Q(.332)	5 CPB	528-5N	1227-6
3/8 -16	1185-6	9/16	X(.397)	6 CPB	528-6N	1227-6
7/16-14	1185-7	21/32	29/64(.453)	7 CPB	528-7N	1227-16
1/2 -13	1185-8	3/4	33/64(.516)	8 CPB	528-8N	1227-16

Coil. place the insert on the proper installation tool (see chart). Apply pressure on the insert while winding it clockwise into the hole, until the top of the insert is one turn below the surface. Remove the installation tool, and break the installation tang from the bottom of the insert by moving it up and down. If the Heli-Coil must be removed, tap the removal tool firmly into the hole, so that it engages the top thread, and turn the tool counter-clockwise to extract that insert.

Snapped bolts or studs may be removed, using a stud extractor (unthreaded) or Vise-Grip pliers (threaded). Penetrating oil (e.g., Liquid Wrench) will often aid in breaking frozen threads. In cases where the stud or bolt is flush with, or below the surface, proceed as follows:

Drill a hole in the broken stud or bolt, approximately $1/2$ its diameter. Select a screw extractor (e.g., Easy-Out) of the proper size, and tap it into the stud or bolt. Turn the extractor counter-clockwise to remove the stud or bolt.

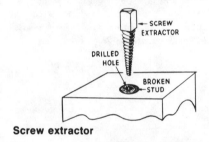

Screw extractor

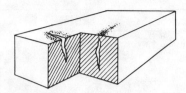

Magnaflux indication of cracks

Magnaflux and Zyglo are inspection techniques used to locate material flaws, such as stress cracks. Magnafluxing coats the part with fine magnetic particles, and subjects the part to a magnetic field. Cracks cause breaks in the magnetic field, which are outlined by the particles. Since Magnaflux is a magnetic process, it is applicable only to ferrous materials. The Zyglo process coats the material with a fluorescent dye penetrant, and then subjects it to blacklight inspection, under which cracks glow brightly. Parts made of any material may be tested using Zyglo. While Magnaflux and Zyglo are excellent for general inspection, and locating hidden defects, specific checks of suspected cracks may be made at lower cost and more readily using spot check dye. The dye is sprayed onto the suspected area, wiped off, and the area is then sprayed with a developer. Cracks then will show up brightly. Spot check dyes will only indicate surface cracks; therefore, structural cracks below the surface may escape detection. When questionable, the part should be tested using Magnaflux or Zyglo.

NOTE: *This engine rebuilding section is a guide to accepted engine rebuilding procedures. Every effort is made to illustrate the engine(s) used by this manufacturer; but, occasionally, typical examples of standard engine rebuilding practice are illustrated.*

Cylinder Head Reconditioning

Procedure	Method
Identify the valves: 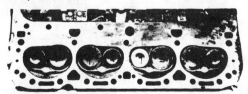 **Valve identification**	Invert the cylinder head, and number the valve faces front to rear, using a permanent felt-tip marker.

Procedure	Method
Remove the valves and springs:	Using an appropriate valve spring compressor (depending on the configuration of the cylinder head), compress the valve springs. Lift out the keepers with needlenose pliers, release the compressor, and remove the valve, spring, and spring retainer.
Check the valve stem-to-guide clearance: Checking the valve stem-to-guide clearance	Clean the valve stem with lacquer thinner or a similar solvent to remove all gum and varnish. Clean the valve guides using solvent and an expanding wire-type valve guide cleaner. Mount a dial indicator so that the stem is at 90° to the valve stem, as close to the valve guide as possible. Move the valve off its seat, and measure the valve guide-to-stem clearance by moving the stem back and forth to actuate the dial indicator. Measure the valve stems using a micrometer, and compare to specifications, to determine whether stem or guide wear is responsible for excessive clearance.
De-carbon the cylinder head and valves: Removing carbon from the cylinder head	Chip carbon away from the valve heads, combustion chambers, and ports, using a chisel made of hardwood. Remove the remaining deposits with a stiff wire brush. **NOTE: *Ensure that the deposits are actually removed, rather than burnished.***
Hot-tank the cylinder head:	Have the cylinder head hot-tanked to remove grease, corrosion, and scale from the water passages. **NOTE: *In the case of overhead cam cylinder heads, consult the operator to determine whether the camshaft bearings will be damaged by the caustic solution.***
Degrease the remaining cylinder head parts:	Using solvent (i.e., Gunk), clean the rockers, rocker shaft(s) (where applicable), rocker balls and nuts, springs, spring retainers, and keepers. Do not remove the protective coating from the springs.
Check the cylinder head for warpage: 1 & 3 CHECK DIAGONALLY 2 CHECK ACROSS CENTER  Checking the cylinder head for warpage	Place a straight-edge across the gasket surface of the cylinder head. Using feeler gauges, determine the clearance at the center of the straight-edge. Measure across both diagonals, along the longitudinal centerline, and across the cylinder head at several points. If warpage exceeds .003″ in a 6″ span, or .006″ over the total length, the cylinder head must be resurfaced. **NOTE: *If warpage exceeds the manufacturers maximum tolerance for material removal, the cylinder head must be replaced.*** When milling the cylinder heads of V-type engines, the intake manifold mounting position is altered, and must be corrected by milling the manifold flange a proportionate amount.

Procedure	Method

** Porting and gasket matching:

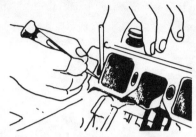

Marking the cylinder head for gasket matching

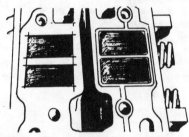

Port configuration before and after gasket matching

** Coat the manifold flanges of the cylinder head with Prussian blue dye. Glue intake and exhaust gaskets to the cylinder head in their installed position using rubber cement and scribe the outline of the ports on the manifold flanges. Remove the gaskets. Using a small cutter in a hand-held power tool (i.e., Dremel Moto-Tool), gradually taper the walls of the port out to the scribed outline of the gasket. Further enlargement of the ports should include the removal of sharp edges and radiusing of sharp corners. Do not alter the valve guides. **NOTE:** *The most efficient port configuration is determined only by extensive testing. Therefore, it is best to consult someone experienced with the head in question to determine the optimum alterations.*

** Polish the ports:

Relieved and polished ports

** Using a grinding stone with the above mentioned tool, polish the walls of the intake and exhaust ports, and combustion chamber. Use progressively finer stones until all surface imperfections are removed. **NOTE:** *Through testing, it has been determined that a smooth surface is more effective than a mirror polished surface in intake ports, and vice-versa in exhaust ports.*

* Knurling the valve guides:

Cut-away view of a knurled valve guide

* Valve guides which are not excessively worn or distorted may, in some cases, be knurled rather than replaced. Knurling is a process in which metal is displaced and raised, thereby reducing clearance. Knurling also provides excellent oil control. The possibility of knurling rather than replacing valve guides should be discussed with a machinist.

Checking/replacing the valve guides: NOTE: *Valve guides should only be replaced if damaged or if an oversize valve stem is not available.*

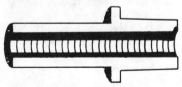

** Check the valve guides by inserting a new valve in the guide and rocking it back and forth against a dial indicator. The dial indicator reading shows wear (max. 0.039 in. intake or 0.051 in. exhaust).

Worn guides can be pressed out from the combustion chamber side. Coat new guides with oil and press them in from the camshaft side as far as they will go. Once the guide is seated, do not use more than 1 ton pressure.

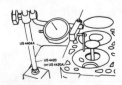

Checking valve guide for wear

Procedure	Method

Ream the valve guides:

Reaming valve guides with a hand reamer

Using the proper cutting lubricant, ream the valve guides to the individual valves.

Replacing valve seat inserts:

Replacement of valve seat inserts which are worn beyond resurfacing or broken, if feasible, must be done by a machine shop.

Resurfacing (grinding) the valve face:

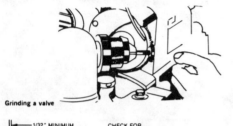

Grinding a valve

Critical valve dimensions

Using a valve grinder, resurface the valves according to specifications. **CAUTION:** *Valve face angle is not always identical to valve seat angle.* A minimum margin of $1/32''$ should remain after grinding the valve. The valve stem tip should also be squared and resurfaced, by placing the stem in the V-block of the grinder, and turning it while pressing lightly against the grinding wheel.

Resurfacing the valve seats using reamers:

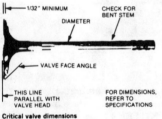

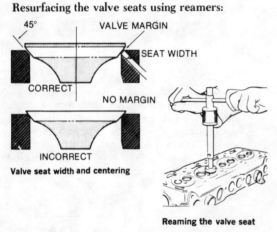

Valve seat width and centering

Reaming the valve seat

Select a reamer of the correct seat angle, slightly larger than the diameter of the valve seat, and assemble it with a pilot of the correct size. Install the pilot into the valve guide, and using steady pressure, turn the reamer clockwise. **CAUTION:** *Do not turn the reamer counter-clockwise.* Remove only as much material as necessary to clean the seat. Check the concentricity of the seat (see below). If the dye method is not used, coat the valve face with Prussian blue dye, install and rotate it on the valve seat. Using the dye marked area as a centering guide, center and narrow the valve seat to specifications with correction cutters. **NOTE:** *When no specifications are available, minimum seat width for exhaust valves should be $5/64''$, intake valves $1/16''$.* After making correction cuts, check the position of the valve seat on the valve face using Prussian blue dye.

---

* Resurfacing the valve seats using a grinder:

Select a pilot of the correct size, and a coarse stone of the correct seat angle. Lubricate the pilot if necessary, and install the tool in the valve guide. Move the stone on and off the seat at approximately two cycles per second, until all flaws are removed from the seat. Install a fine stone, and finish the seat. Center and narrow the seat using correction stones, as described above.

Procedure	*Method*
Checking the valve seat concentricity:	Coat the valve face with Prussian blue dye, install the valve, and rotate it on the valve seat. If the entire seat becomes coated, and the valve is known to be concentric, the seat is concentric.

Checking the valve seat concentricity using a dial gauge

* Install the dial gauge pilot into the guide, and rest the arm on the valve seat. Zero the gauge, and rotate the arm around the seat. Run-out should not exceed .002".

* **Lapping the valves: NOTE:** *Valve lapping is done to ensure efficient sealing of resurfaced valves and seats. Valve lapping alone is not recommended for use as a resurfacing procedure.*

* Invert the cylinder head, lightly lubricate the valve stems, and install the valves in the head as numbered. Coat valve seats with fine grinding compound, and attach the lapping tool suction cup to a valve head (**NOTE:** *Moisten the suction cup*). Rotate the tool between the palms, changing position and lifting the tool often to prevent grooving. Lap the valve until a smooth, polished seat is evident. Remove the valve and tool, and rinse away all traces of grinding compound.

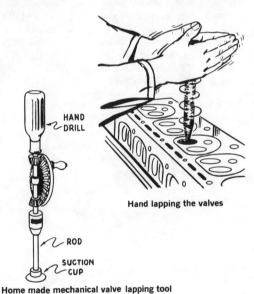

HAND DRILL

Hand lapping the valves

ROD

SUCTION CUP

Home made mechanical valve lapping tool

** Fasten a suction cup to a piece of drill rod, and mount the rod in a hand drill. Proceed as above, using the hand drill as a lapping tool. **CAUTION:** *Due to the higher speeds involved when using the hand drill, care must be exercised to avoid grooving the seat.* Lift the tool and change direction of rotation often.

Check the valve springs:

Place the spring on a flat surface next to a square. Measure the height of the spring, and rotate it against the edge of the square to measure distortion. If spring height varies (by comparison) by more than $1/16"$ or if distortion exceeds $1/16"$, replace the spring.

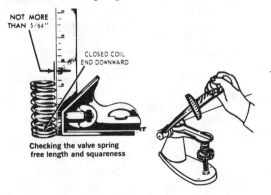

NOT MORE THAN 5/64"

CLOSED COIL END DOWNWARD

Checking the valve spring free length and squareness

Checking the valve spring tension

** In addition to evaluating the spring as above, test the spring pressure at the installed and compressed (installed height minus valve lift) height using a valve spring tester. Springs used on small displacement engines (up to 3 liters) should be ± 1 lb of all other springs in either position. A tolerance of ± 5 lbs is permissible on larger engines.

Procedure	Method
* Install valve stem seals:  **Installing valve stem seals**	* Due to the pressure differential that exists at the ends of the intake valve guides (atmospheric pressure above, manifold vacuum below), oil is drawn through the valve guides into the intake port. This has been alleviated somewhat since the addition of positive crankcase ventilation, which lowers the pressure above the guides. Several types of valve stem seals are available to reduce blow-by. Certain seals simply slip over the stem and guide boss, while others require that the boss be machined. Recently, Teflon guide seals have become popular. Consult a parts supplier or machinist concerning availability and suggested usages. **NOTE:** *When installing seals, ensure that a small amount of oil is able to pass the seal to lubricate the valve guides; otherwise, excessive wear may result.*
Install the valves:	Lubricate the valve stems, and install the valves in the cylinder head as numbered. Lubricate and position the seals (if used, see above) and the valve springs. Install the spring retainers, compress the springs, and insert the keys using needlenose pliers or a tool designed for this purpose. **NOTE:** *Retain the keys with wheel bearing grease during installation.*
Checking valve spring installed height: 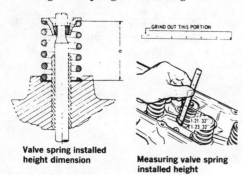 **Valve spring installed height dimension** **Measuring valve spring installed height**	Measure the distance between the spring pad and the lower edge of the spring retainer, and compare to specifications. If the installed height is incorrect, add shim washers between the spring pad and the spring. **CAUTION:** *Use only washers designed for this purpose.*
** CC'ing the combustion chambers:  **CC'ing the combustion chamber**	** Invert the cylinder head and place a bead of sealer around a combustion chamber. Install an apparatus designed for this purpose (burette mounted on a clear plate; see illustration) over the combustion chamber, and fill with the specified fluid to an even mark on the burette. Record the burette reading, and fill the combustion chamber with fluid. (**NOTE:** *A hole drilled in the plate will permit air to escape.*) Subtract the burette reading, with the combustion chamber filled, from the previous reading, to determine combustion chamber volume in cc's. Duplicate this procedure in all combustion chambers on the cylinder head, and compare the readings. The volume of all combustion chambers should be made equal to that of the largest. Combustion chamber volume may be increased in two ways. When only a small change is required (usually), a small cutter or coarse stone

Procedure	Method
	may be used to remove material from the combustion chamber. **NOTE:** *Check volume frequently.* Remove material over a wide area, so as not to change the configuration of the combustion chamber. When a larger change is required, the valve seat may be sunk (lowered into the head). **NOTE:** *When altering valve seat, remember to compensate for the change in spring installed height.*
Inspect the camshaft bushings and the camshaft (overhead cam engines):	See next section.

Cylinder Block Reconditioning

Procedure	Method
Checking the main bearing clearance: 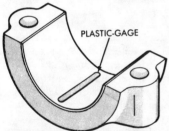PLASTIC-GAGE Installing Plastigage on lower bearing shell 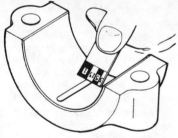Measuring Plastigage to determine bearing clearance	Invert engine, and remove cap from the bearing to be checked. Using a clean, dry rag, thoroughly clean all oil from crankshaft journal and bearing insert. **NOTE:** *Plastigage is soluble in oil; therefore, oil on the journal or bearing could result in erroneous readings.* Place a piece of Plastigage along the full length of journal, reinstall cap, and torque to specifications. Remove bearing cap, and determine bearing clearance by comparing width of Plastigage to the scale on Plastigage envelope. Journal taper is determined by comparing width of the Plastigage strip near its ends. Rotate crankshaft 90° and retest, to determine journal eccentricity. **NOTE:** *Do not rotate crankshaft with Plastigage installed.* If bearing insert and journal appear intact, and are within tolerances, no further main bearing service is required. If bearing or journal appear defective, cause of failure should be determined before replacement.
	* Remove crankshaft from block (see below). Measure the main bearing journals at each end twice (90° apart) using a micrometer, to determine diameter, journal taper and eccentricity. If journals are within tolerances, reinstall bearing caps at their specified torque. Using a telescope gauge and micrometer, measure bearing I.D. parallel to piston axis and at 30° on each side of piston axis. Subtract journal O.D. from bearing I.D. to determine oil clearance. If crankshaft journals appear defective, or do not meet tolerances, there is no need to measure bearings; for the crankshaft will require grinding and/or undersize bearings will be required. If bearing appears defective, cause for failure should be determined prior to replacement.

Causes of bearing failure

Procedure	Method
Checking the connecting rod bearing clearance:	Connecting rod bearing clearance is checked in the same manner as main bearing clearance, using Plastigage. Before removing the crankshaft, connecting rod side clearance also should be measured and recorded.
	* Checking connecting rod bearing clearance, using a micrometer, is identical to checking main bearing clearance. If no other service is required, the piston and rod assemblies need not be removed.
Removing the crankshaft:  Connecting rod matching marks	Using a punch, mark the corresponding main bearing caps and saddles according to position (i.e., one punch on the front main cap and saddle, two on the second, three on the third, etc.). Using number stamps, identify the corresponding connecting rods and caps, according to cylinder (if no numbers are present). Remove the main and connecting rod caps, and place sleeves of plastic tubing over the connecting rod bolts, to protect the journals as the crankshaft is removed. Lift the crankshaft out of the block.
Remove the ridge from the top of the cylinder: 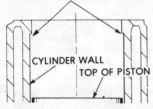 Cylinder bore ridge	In order to facilitate removal of the piston and connecting rod, the ridge at the top of the cylinder (unknown area; see illustration) must be removed. Place the piston at the bottom of the bore, and cover it with a rag. Cut the ridge away using a ridge reamer, exercising extreme care to avoid cutting too deeply. Remove the rag, and remove cuttings that remain on the piston. **CAUTION:** *If the ridge is not removed, and new rings are installed, damage to rings will result.*
Removing the piston and connecting rod: 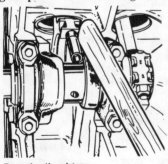 Removing the piston	Invert the engine, and push the pistons and connecting rods out of the cylinders. If necessary, tap the connecting rod boss with a wooden hammer handle, to force the piston out. **CAUTION:** *Do not attempt to force the piston past the cylinder ridge* (see above).
Service the crankshaft:	Ensure that all oil holes and passages in the crankshaft are open and free of sludge. If necessary, have the crankshaft ground to the largest possible undersize.
	** Have the crankshaft Magnafluxed, to locate stress cracks. Consult a machinist concerning additional service procedures, such as surface hardening (e.g., nitriding, Tuftriding) to improve wear characteristics, cross drilling and chamfering the oil holes to improve lubrication, and balancing.

Procedure	Method
Removing freeze plugs:	Drill a small hole in the center of the freeze plugs. Thread a large sheet metal screw into the hole and remove the plug with a slide hammer.
Remove the oil gallery plugs:	Threaded plugs should be removed using an appropriate (usually square) wrench. To remove soft, pressed in plugs, drill a hole in the plug, and thread in a sheet metal screw. Pull the plug out by the screw using a slide hammer.
Hot-tank the block:	Have the block hot-tanked to remove grease, corrosion, and scale from the water jackets. **NOTE: *Consult the operator to determine whether the camshaft bearings will be damaged during the hot-tank process.***
Check the block for cracks:	Visually inspect the block for cracks or chips. The most common locations are as follows:
	Adjacent to freeze plugs.
	Between the cylinders and water jackets.
	Adjacent to the main bearing saddles.
	At the extreme bottom of the cylinders.
	Check only suspected cracks using spot check dye (see introduction). If a crack is located, consult a machinist concerning possible repairs.
	** Magnaflux the block to locate hidden cracks. If cracks are located, consult a machinist about feasibility of repair.
Install the oil gallery plugs and freeze plugs:	Coat freeze plugs with sealer and tap into position using a piece of pipe, slightly smaller than the plug, as a driver. To ensure retention, stake the edges of the plugs. Coat threaded oil gallery plugs with sealer and install. Drive replacement soft plugs into block using a large drift as a driver.
	* Rather than reinstalling lead plugs, drill and tap the holes, and install threaded plugs.
Check the bore diameter and surface:	Visually inspect the cylinder bores for roughness, scoring, or scuffing. If evident, the cylinder bore must be bored or honed oversize to eliminate imperfections, and the smallest possible oversize piston used. The new pistons should be given to the machinist with the block, so that the cylinders can be bored or honed exactly to the piston size (plus clearance). If no flaws are evident, measure the bore diameter using a telescope gauge and micrometer, or dial gauge, parallel and perpendicular to the engine centerline, at the top (below the ridge) and bottom of the bore. Subtract the bottom measurements from the top to determine taper, and the parallel to the centerline measurements from the perpendicular measurements to determine eccentricity. If the measurements are not within specifications, the cylinder must be bored or honed, and an oversize piston installed. If the measurements are within specifications the cylinder may be used as is, with only finish honing (see below). **NOTE: *Prior to submitting the block for boring, perform the following operation(s).***

1, 2, 3 Piston skirt seizure resulted in this pattern. Engine must be rebored

4. Piston skirt and oil ring seizure caused this damag Engine must be rebored

Procedure	*Method*

5, 6 Score marks caused by a split piston skirt. Damage is not serious enough to warrant reboring

7. Ring seized longitudinally, causing a score mark 1 3/16" wide, on the land side of the piston groove. The honing pattern is destroyed and the cylinder must be rebored

8. Result of oil ring seizure. Engine must be rebored

9. Oil ring seizure here was not serious enough to warrant reboring. The honing marks are still visible

Cylinder wall damage

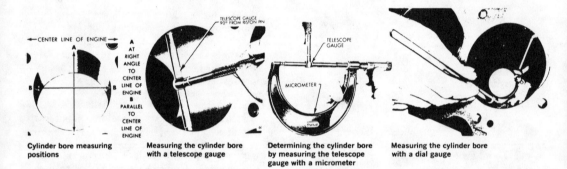

Cylinder bore measuring positions

Measuring the cylinder bore with a telescope gauge

Determining the cylinder bore by measuring the telescope gauge with a micrometer

Measuring the cylinder bore with a dial gauge

Procedure	Method
Check the block deck for warpage:	Using a straightedge and feeler gauges, check the block deck for warpage in the same manner that the cylinder head is checked (see Cylinder Head Reconditioning). If warpage exceeds specifications, have the deck resurfaced. **NOTE:** *In certain cases a specification for total material removal (cylinder head and block deck) is provided. This specification must not be exceeded.*
* Check the deck height:	The deck height is the distance from the crankshaft centerline to the block deck. To measure, invert the engine, and install the crankshaft, retaining it with the center main cap. Measure the distance from the crankshaft journal to the block deck, parallel to the cylinder centerline. Measure the diameter of the end (front and rear) main journals, parallel to the centerline of the cylinders, divide the diameter in half, and subtract it from the previous measurement. The results of the front and rear measurements should be identical. If the difference exceeds .005", the deck height should be corrected. **NOTE:** *Block deck height and warpage should be corrected concurrently.*

Procedure	Method

Check the cylinder block bearing alignment:

Checking main bearing saddle alignment

Remove the upper bearing inserts. Place a straightedge in the bearing saddles along the centerline of the crankshaft. If clearance exists between the straightedge and the center saddle, the block must be align-bored.

Clean and inspect the pistons and connecting rods:

RING EXPANDER

Removing the piston rings

Ring Groove Cleaner

Cleaning the piston ring grooves

Connecting rod length checking dimension

Using a ring expander, remove the rings from the piston. Remove the retaining rings (if so equipped) and remove piston pin. **NOTE: *If the piston pin must be pressed out, determine the proper method and use the proper tools; otherwise the piston will distort.*** Clean the ring grooves using an appropriate tool, exercising care to avoid cutting too deeply. Thoroughly clean all carbon and varnish from the piston with solvent. **CAUTION:** *Do not use a wire brush or caustic solvent on pistons.* Inspect the pistons for scuffing, scoring, cracks, pitting, or excessive ring groove wear. If wear is evident, the piston must be replaced. Check the connecting rod length by measuring the rod from the inside of the large end to the inside of the small end using calipers (see illustration). All connecting rods should be equal length. Replace any rod that differs from the others in the engine.

* Have the connecting rod alignment checked in an alignment fixture by a machinist. Replace any twisted or bent rods.

* Magnaflux the connecting rods to locate stress cracks. If cracks are found, replace the connecting rod.

Fit the pistons to the cylinders:

90°

Measuring the piston for fitting

Using a telescope gauge and micrometer, or a dial gauge, measure the cylinder bore diameter perpendicular to the piston pin, 2½″ below the deck. Measure the piston perpendicular to its pin on the skirt. The difference between the two measurements is the piston clearance. If the clearance is within specifications or slightly below (after boring or honing), finish honing is all that is required. If the clearance is excessive, try to obtain a slightly larger piston to bring clearance within specifications. Where this is not possible, obtain the first oversize piston, and hone (or if necessary, bore) the cylinder to size.

Procedure	Method
Assemble the pistons and connecting rods:  Installing piston pin lock rings	Inspect piston pin, connecting rod small end bushing, and piston bore for galling, scoring, or excessive wear. If evident, replace defective part(s). Measure the I.D. of the piston boss and connecting rod small end, and the O.D. of the piston pin. If within specifications, assemble piston pin and rod. **CAUTION:** *If piston pin must be pressed in, determine the proper method and use the proper tools; otherwise the piston will distort.* Install the lock rings; ensure that they seat properly. If the parts are not within specifications, determine the service method for the type of engine. In some cases, piston and pin are serviced as an assembly when either is defective. Others specify reaming the piston and connecting rods for an oversize pin. If the connecting rod bushing is worn, it may in many cases be replaced. Reaming the piston and replacing the rod bushing are machine shop operations.
Clean and inspect the camshaft:  Checking the camshaft for straightness Camshaft lobe measurement	Degrease the camshaft, using solvent, and clean out all oil holes. Visually inspect cam lobes and bearing journals for excessive wear. If a lobe is questionable, check all lobes as indicated below. If a journal or lobe is worn, the camshaft must be reground or replaced. **NOTE:** *If a journal is worn, there is a good chance that the bushings are worn.* If lobes and journals appear intact, place the front and rear journals in V-blocks, and rest a dial indicator on the center journal. Rotate the camshaft to check straightness. If deviation exceeds .001″, replace the camshaft.
	* Check the camshaft lobes with a micrometer, by measuring the lobes from the nose to base and again at 90° (see illustration). The lift is determined by subtracting the second measurement from the first. If all exhaust lobes and all intake lobes are not identical, the camshaft must be reground or replaced.
Replace the camshaft bearings: 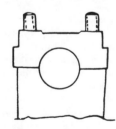 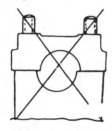	If excessive wear is indicated, or if the engine is being completely rebuilt, camshaft bearings should be replaced. Lubricate the bearing shells, journals and the faces of the bearing caps. Install the caps in the proper order. Note the off-center bearing installation and that the numbers on the cap are not always on the same side.

Note the off-center installation of the bearing caps

Procedure	Method

Finish hone the cylinders:

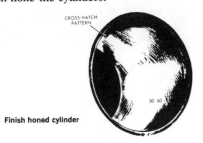

Finish honed cylinder

Chuck a flexible drive hone into a power drill, and insert it into the cylinder. Start the hone, and move it up and down in the cylinder at a rate which will produce approximately a 60° cross-hatch pattern (see illustration). **NOTE:** *Do not extend the hone below the cylinder bore.* After developing the pattern, remove the hone and re-check piston fit. Wash the cylinders with a detergent and water solution to remove abrasive dust, dry, and wipe several times with a rag soaked in engine oil.

Check piston ring end-gap:

Checking ring end-gap

Compress the piston rings to be used in a cylinder, one at a time, into that cylinder, and press them approximately 1″ below the deck with an inverted piston. Using feeler gauges, measure the ring end-gap, and compare to specifications. Pull the ring out of the cylinder and file the ends with a fine file to obtain proper clearance. **CAUTION:** *If inadequate ring end-gap is utilized, ring breakage will result.*

Install the piston rings:

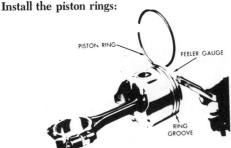

Checking ring side clearance

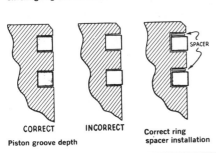

CORRECT   INCORRECT
Piston groove depth

Correct ring spacer installation

Inspect the ring grooves in the piston for excessive wear or taper. If necessary, recut the groove(s) for use with an overwidth ring or a standard ring and spacer. If the groove is worn uniformly, overwidth rings, or standard rings and spacers may be installed without recutting. Roll the outside of the ring around the groove to check for burrs or deposits. If any are found, remove with a fine file. Hold the ring in the groove, and measure side clearance. If necessary, correct as indicated above. **NOTE:** *Always install any additional spacers above the piston ring.* The ring groove must be deep enough to allow the ring to seat below the lands (see illustration). In many cases, a "go-no-go" depth gauge will be provided with the piston rings. Shallow grooves may be corrected by recutting, while deep grooves require some type of filler or expander behind the piston. Consult the piston ring supplier concerning the suggested method. Install the rings on the piston, lowest ring first, using a ring expander. **NOTE:** *Position the ring markings as specified by the manufacturer (see car section).*

Install the camshaft:

Liberally lubricate the camshaft lobes and journals, and slide the camshaft into the block. **CAUTION:** *Exercise extreme care to avoid damaging the bearings when inserting the camshaft.* Install and tighten the camshaft thrust plate retaining bolts.

Procedure	Method
Check camshaft end-play:	* Mount a dial indicator stand so that the stem of the dial indicator rests on the nose of the camshaft, parallel to the camshaft axis. Push the camshaft as far in as possible and zero the gauge. Move the camshaft outward to determine the amount of camshaft end-play. If the end-play is not within tolerance, install shims behind the thrust plate, or reposition the camshaft gear and retest.

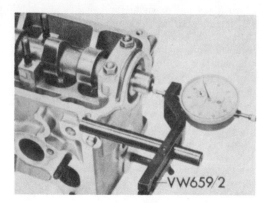

Checking camshaft end-play with a
dial indicator

Install the rear main seal (where applicable):	Position the block with the bearing saddles facing upward. Lay the rear main seal in its groove and press it lightly into its seat. Place a piece of pipe the same diameter as the crankshaft journal into the saddle, and firmly seat the seal. Hold the pipe in position, and trim the ends of the seal flush if required.

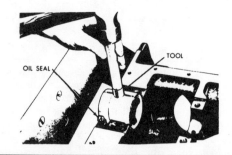

Seating the rear
main seal

Install the crankshaft:	Thoroughly clean the main bearing saddles and caps. Place the upper halves of the bearing inserts on the saddles and press into position. **NOTE:** *Ensure that the oil holes align.* Press the corresponding bearing inserts into the main bearing caps. Lubricate the upper main bearings, and lay the crankshaft in position. Place a strip of Plastigage on each of the crankshaft journals, install the main caps, and torque to specifications. Remove the main caps, and compare the Plastigage to the scale on the Plastigage envelope. If clearances are within tolerances, remove the Plastigage, turn the crankshaft 90°, wipe off all oil and retest. If all clearances are correct, remove all Plastigage, thoroughly lubricate the main caps and bearing journals, and install the main caps. If clearances are not within tolerance, the upper bearing inserts may be removed, without removing the crankshaft, using a bearing roll out pin (see illustration). Roll in a bearing that will provide proper clearance, and retest. Torque all main caps, excluding the thrust bearing cap, to specifications. Tighten the thrust bearing cap finger tight. To properly align the thrust bearing, pry the crankshaft the extent of its axial travel several

Removal and installation of upper bearing insert using a
roll-out pin (© Buick Div. G.M. Corp.)

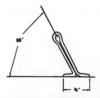

Home made bearing roll-out pin

Procedure	Method

times, the last movement held toward the front of the engine, and torque the thrust bearing cap to specifications. Determine the crankshaft end-play (see below), and bring within tolerance with thrust washers.

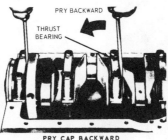

PRY CRANKSHAFT FORWARD   PRY CAP BACKWARD   TIGHTEN CAP

Aligning the thrust bearing

Measure crankshaft end-play:

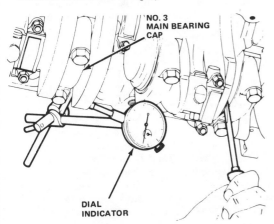

Checking crankshaft end-play with a dial indicator

Mount a dial indicator stand on the front of the block, with the dial indicator stem resting on the nose of the crankshaft, parallel to the crankshaft axis. Pry the crankshaft the extent of its travel rearward, and zero the indicator. Pry the crankshaft forward and record crankshaft end-play. **NOTE:** *Crankshaft end-play also may be measured at the thrust bearing, using feeler gauges (see illustration).*

Checking crankshaft end-play with a feeler gauge

Install the pistons:

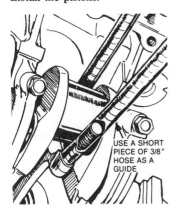

Tubing used as guide when installing a piston

Press the upper connecting rod bearing halves into the connecting rods, and the lower halves into the connecting rod caps. Position the piston ring gaps according to specifications (see car section), and lubricate the pistons. Install a ring compresser on a piston, and press two long (8″) pieces of plastic tubing over the rod bolts. Using the plastic tubes as a guide, press the pistons into the bores and onto the crankshaft with a wooden hammer handle. After seating the rod on the crankshaft journal, remove the tubes and install the cap finger tight. Install the remaining pistons in the same manner. Invert the engine and check the bearing clearance at two points (90° apart) on each journal with Plastigage. **NOTE:** *Do not turn the crankshaft with Plastigage installed.* If clearance is within tolerances, remove *all* Plastigage, thoroughly lubricate the journals, and torque the

Procedure	Method

Installing a piston

rod caps to specifications. If clearance is not within specifications, install different thickness bearing inserts and recheck. **CAUTION:** *Never shim or file the connecting rods or caps.* Always install plastic tube sleeves over the rod bolts when the caps are not installed, to protect the crankshaft journals.

Check connecting rod side clearance:

Checking connecting rod side clearance

Determine the clearance between the sides of the connecting rods and the crankshaft, using feeler gauges. If clearance is below the minimum tolerance, the rod may be machined to provide adequate clearance. If clearance is excessive, substitute an unworn rod, and recheck. If clearance is still outside specifications, the crankshaft must be welded and reground, or replaced.

Inspect the timing chain:

Visually inspect the timing chain for broken or loose links, and replace the chain if any are found. If the chain will flex sideways, it must be replaced. Install the timing chain as specified. **NOTE:** *If the original timing chain is to be reused, install it in its original position.*

Completing the Rebuilding Process

Following the above procedures, complete the rebuilding process as follows:

Fill the oil pump with oil, to prevent cavitating (sucking air) on initial engine start up. Install the oil pump and the pickup tube on the engine. Coat the oil pan gasket as necessary, and install the gasket and the oil pan. Mount the flywheel and the crankshaft vibrational damper or pulley on the crankshaft. **NOTE:** *Always use new bolts when installing the flywheel.* Inspect the clutch shaft pilot bushing in the crankshaft. If the bushing is excessively worn, remove it with an expanding puller and a slide hammer, and tap a new bushing into place.

Position the engine, cylinder head side up. Lubricate the lifters, and install them into their bores. Install the cylinder head, and torque it as specified in the car section. Insert the pushrods (where applicable), and install the rocker shaft(s) (if so equipped) or position the rocker arms on the pushrods. If solid lift-

ers are utilized, adjust the valves to the "cold" specifications.

Mount the intake and exhaust manifolds, the carburetor(s), the distributor and spark plugs. Adjust the point gap and the static ignition timing. Mount all accessories and install the engine in the car. Fill the radiator with coolant, and the crankcase with high quality engine oil.

Break-in Procedure

Start the engine, and allow it to run at low speed for a few minutes, while checking for leaks. Stop the engine, check the oil level, and fill as necessary. Restart the engine, and fill the cooling system to capacity. Check the point dwell angle and adjust the ignition timing and the valves. Run the engine at low to medium speed (800–2500 rpm) for approximately ½ hour, and retorque the cylinder head bolts. Road test the car, and check again for leaks.

Follow the manufacturer's recommended engine break-in procedure and maintenance schedule for new engines.

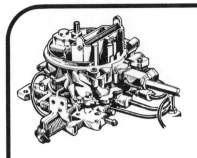

4

Emission Controls and Fuel System

EMISSION CONTROLS

Crankcase Ventilation

The purpose of the crankcase ventilation system is twofold. It keeps harmful vapor by-products of combustion from escaping into the atmosphere and prevents the building of crankcase pressure which can lead to oil leaking. Crankcase vapors are recirculated from the camshaft cover through a hose to the air cleaner. Here they are mixed with the air/fuel mixture and burned in the combusion chamber.

> NOTE: *1978 cars have no crankcase ventilation valve.*

SERVICE

Service the crankcase ventilation valve at the interval suggested in Chapter 1. Remove the crankcase ventilation valve, which is connected to the camshaft cover, and clean it in solvent. At every tune-up, examine the hoses for clogging or deterioration. Clean or replace the hoses as necessary.

Evaporative Emission Control System

This system prevents the escape of raw fuel vapors (unburned hydrocarbons or HC) into the atmosphere. The system consists of a sealed carburetor, unvented fuel tank filler cap, fuel tank expansion chamber, an activated charcoal filter canister and connector hoses. Fuel vapors which reach the filter deposit hydrocarbons on the surface of the charcoal filter element. Fresh air enters the filter when the engine is running and forces the hydrocarbons to the air cleaner where they join the air/fuel mixture and are burned.

SERVICE

Maintenance of the system consists of checking the condition of the various connector hoses and the charcoal filter. The charcoal filter should be replaced at 50,000 mile intervals.

Dual Diaphragm Distributor

The purpose of the dual diaphragm distributor is to improve exhaust emissions during one of the engine's dirtier operating modes, idling. The distributor has a vacuum retard diaphragm, in addition to a vacuum advance diaphragm.

A temperature valve shuts off vacuum from carburetor when coolant temperature is below 130°.

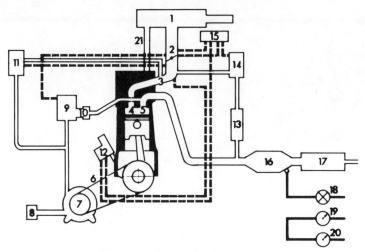

1. Air cleaner
2. Carburetor
3. Intake manifold
4. Intake port
5. Exhaust port
6. Air pump belt
7. Air pump
8. Air pump air filter
9. Diverter valve
10. Pressure valve
11. Anti-backfire valve
12. Distributor
13. EGR filter
14. EGR valve
15. Temperature valve
16. Catalytic converter
17. Muffler
18. Converter temperature light
19. EGR system indicator light
20. Converter indicator light
21. Crankcase ventilation line

Emission control systems schematic

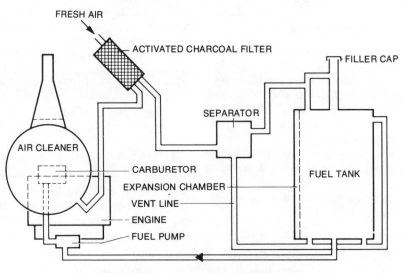

Evaporative emission control system

TESTING

Advance Diaphragm

1. Connect a timing light to the engine. Check the ignition timing as described in Chapter 2.

2. Remove the retard hose from the distributor and plug it. Increase the engine speed. The ignition timing should advance. if it doesn't, then the vacuum unit is faulty and must be replaced.

Temperature Valve

1. Remove the temperature valve and place the threaded portion in hot water.

2. Create a vacuum by sucking on the angled connection.

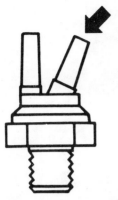

Checking distributor advance temperature valve

3. The valve must be open above approximately 130° F.

Exhaust Gas Recirculation

To reduce NO_x emissions, metered amounts of cooled exhaust gases are added to the air/fuel mixture. The recirculated exhaust gas lowers the peak flame temperature during combustion to cut the output of oxides of nitrogen. Exhaust gas from the manifold passes through a filter where it is cleaned. The EGR valve controls the amount of this exhaust gas which is allowed into the intake manifold.

1975 MODELS

1975 models have an EGR filter and a 2-stage EGR valve. The first stage is controlled by

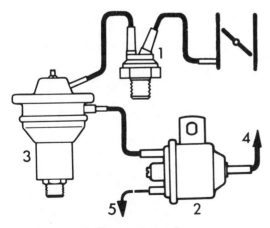

1. Temperature valve
2. Two-way valve
3. EGR valve
4. To brake booster
5. To micro switch

EGR operation—1975

the temperature valve. The second stage is controlled by the micro-switch on the carburetor throttle valve. The switch opens the valve when the throttle valve is open between 30°–67° (manual transmission) or 23°–63° (automatic transmission).

1976 MODELS

The EGR filter was discontinued on 1976 models but the 2-stage EGR valve was retained. On Federal vehicles, only the first stage is connected; California vehicles use both stages.

First stage EGR is controlled by engine vacuum and coolant temperature. The EGR valve is open above approximately 120° F. coolant temperature and below approximately 80° F. At idle and during full throttle acceleration (engine hot), there is no EGR since the engine vacuum is too low to open the valve.

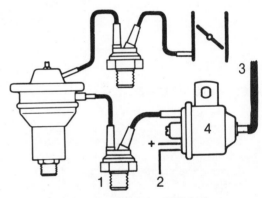

1. Temperature valve for EGR 2nd stage
2. To micro switch on throttle valve
3. Vacuum hose to brake booster
4. Two way valve

EGR operation—1976 and later

The second stage is controlled by temperature, engine vacuum and micro-switch on the carburetor throttle valve. Vacuum is always present at the second stage and the valve is opened at about 120° F. coolant temperature. When the throttle valve opens between 25° and 67°, the micro-switch activates the 2-way valve and allows engine vacuum to reach the second stage.

1977 AND LATER MODELS

The EGR valve on fuel injected models is controlled by a temperature valve and a vacuum amplifier. The valve is located at the front of the intake manifold.

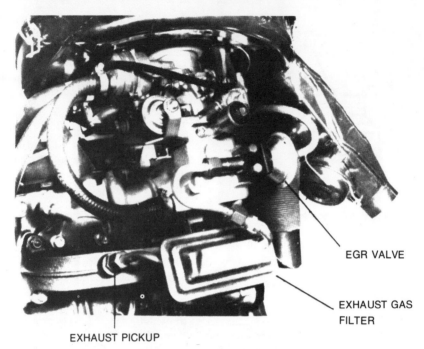

EGR VALVE

EXHAUST GAS
FILTER

EXHAUST PICKUP

EGR system components

TESTING

EGR Valve (1975–76)

1. Disconnect the vacuum line from the EGR valve.

2. Disconnect the vacuum hose from the distributor vacuum unit and extend hose.

3. Start the engine and allow it to idle.

4. Connect the line from the anti-backfire valve to the EGR valve. The engine should stumble or stall.

5. If the idle stays even, the EGR line is clogged or the EGR valve is defective, or the filter is clogged.

EGR Valve (1977 and Later)

Be sure the vacuum lines are not leaking. Replace any that are leaking or cracked.

1. Warm the engine to normal operating temperature.

2. Run the engine at idle.

3. Remove the vacuum hose from the EGR valve.

4. Connect the line from the brake booster to the EGR valve (this can be done by installing a Tee in the vacuum line to the retard side of the distributor diaphragm and running a separate hose from there to the EGR valve.

5. If the engine speed does not change, the EGR valve is clogged or damaged.

EGR Temperature Valve (1975–76)

1. Remove the temperature valve and place the threaded portion in hot water.

2. Create a vacuum by sucking on the angled connection. The valve should be closed below approximately 120° F.

EGR Temperature Valve (1977 and Later)

Warm the engine to normal operating temperature.

1. With the engine at idle, attach a vacuum gauge between the EGR temperature control valve and the EGR valve. The valve

Checking EGR temperature valve (1977 and later)

Checking EGR deceleration valve (1977 and later)

should be replaced if the gauge shows less than 2 in./Hg.

EGR Deceleration Valve (1977 and Later)

1. Remove the hose from the deceleration valve. Plug the hose.
2. Run the engine for a few seconds at 3000 rpm.
3. Snap the throttle valve closed.
4. With your finger, check for section at the hose connection.
5. Remove the hose from the connector.
6. Run the engine at about 3000 rpm. No suction should be felt.

EGR Vacuum Amplifier (1977 and Later)

1. Run the engine at idle.
2. Connect a vacuum gauge between the vacuum amplifier and the throttle valve port.
3. The gauge should read 0.2–0.3 in./Hg. If not, check the throttle plate for correct position or check the port for obstruction.
4. Connect a vacuum gauge between the vacuum amplifier and the temperature valve.
5. Replace the vacuum amplifier if the gauge reads less than 2 in./hg.

MAINTENANCE

The only maintenance is to replace the EGR filter (1975 models only) and to reset the EGR elapsed mileage switch

Resetting the Elapsed Mileage Switch

The EGR reminder light in the speedometer should light up every 15,000 miles as a reminder for maintenance.

To rest the light switch, press the white button (arrow). The speedometer light should go out.

Reset the EGR light switch

Filter Replacement

1. Disconnect the filter EGR line fittings.
2. Remove the filter and discard.
3. Install the new filter into the EGR lines and securely tighten fittings.

REMOVAL AND INSTALLATION

EGR Valve

1. Disconnect the vacuum hose from the EGR valve.
2. Unbolt the EGR line fitting on the opposite side of the valve.
3. Remove the two retaining bolts and lift the EGR valve from the intake manifold.
4. Install the EGR valve in the reverse order of removal. Use a new gasket at the intake manifold.

Air Injection

The air injection system, or air pump, is installed on all models. This system includes a belt-driven air pump, filter, check valve, anti-backfire valve or gulp valve, and connecting hoses and air lines. The system reduces exhaust emissions by pumping fresh air to the exhaust manifold where it combines with the hot exhaust gas to burn away excess hydrocarbons and reduce carbon monoxide.

There is no air injection at high rpm, when the engine vacuum opens the diverter valve venting air pump output to the outside, nor when catalytic converter temperature rises above about 1900° F. The catalytic converter temperature sensor opens a two-way valve, allowing vacuum to reach the diverter valve, venting air pump output to the outside.

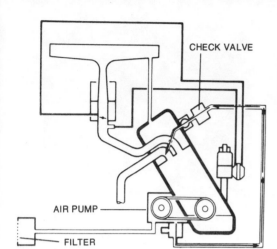

Air injection system schematic

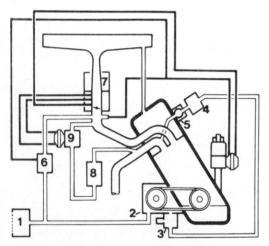

1. Air pump filter
2. Air pump
3. Relief valve
4. Check valve
5. Air manifold
6. Anti-backfire valve
7. Carburetor
8. EGR filter
9. EGR valve

Air injection and EGR systems schematic

MAINTENANCE

Required maintenance on the air pump consists of visually checking the pump, control valves, hoses and lines every 10,000 miles. Clean the air pump filter element at this interval. The filter element should be replaced every 20,000 miles or two years.

TESTING AND SERVICE

Air Pump and Hoses

1. Disconnect the hose from the check valve and plug the valve opening.
2. With the engine idling, check for air flow from the hose. If no air flows from the

Checking air pump and hoses

hose, the hoses are kinked or damaged, the diverter valve is defective or the air pump is defective (it cannot be repaired, only replaced).

Diverter Valve

1. Disconnect the vacuum hose from the F connection.
2. Disconnect the hose from the S connection and connect it to F.
3. With the engine idling, if no air comes from the muffler on the diverter valve the hoses are kinked or damaged or the air pump is defective. If air flows, the diverter valve is OK.

Two-Way Valve

1. Idle the engine and pull the electrical lead from the two-way valve.
2. Ground the valve and connect a test wire directly from the battery to the valve.
3. Increase the engine rpm and check for air output at the diverter valve.
4. If no air flows from the diverter valve, the vacuum line is kinked or disconnected or the diverter valve is bad. If air flows, the two-way valve is OK.

Checking diverter valve (see text)

Anti-Backfire Valve

A defective antibackfire valve could be indicated by the engine backfiring while, coasting.

Checking anti-backfire valve

1. Disconnect the hose from the valve.
2. Start the engine and run it briefly at higher than normal fast idle.
3. Snap the throttle valve closed. As the throttle snaps shut, suction should be felt at the valve for about 1–3 seconds. If not, the vacuum hose is kinked or blocked, the hose between manifold and valve is kinked or blocked or the valve is defective.

Catalytic Converter

All models are equipped with a catalytic converter located in the exhaust system. This device contains noble metals which act as catalysts to cause a reaction to convert hydrocarbons and carbon monoxide into harmless water and carbon dioxide. All service to the converter should be performed by your authorized dealer. It is mandatory that only lead-free gasoline be used in cars equipped with the converter.

Overheating of the catalytic converter is indicated by the CAT light in the speedometer flickering. This can temporarily be caused by a straining engine (trailer pulling, driving on steep grades, etc.) or high speed driving at high temperatures. Either easing the load or slowing down will stop the light from flickering.

More permanent causes include:
Misfiring (faulty or worn plugs),
Faulty ignition timing,
CO value too high,

EGR not shutting off, or
Defective temperature sensor in converter.

Symptoms of a faulty converter include poor engine output, drop in the idle speed or continually stalling engine, rattle in the exhaust system (ceramic insert broken or loose) and high CO reading.

REMOVAL AND INSTALLATION

The converter is unbolted and removed from the car after disconnecting the temperature sensor.

Hold the converter up to a strong light and look through both ends, checking for blockages. If the converter is blocked, replace it.

RESETTING THE CAT WARNING LIGHT

The CAT warning light in the speedometer should come on at 50,000 mile intervals to remind you to have the converter serviced.

The light can be reset by pushing the button marked CAT on the switch. The light on the speedometer should go out.

NOTE: *Vehicles equipped with the Solex 34 PICT-5 carburetor have no "CAT" warning light.*

Reset the catalytic converter elapsed mileage odometer

FUEL SYSTEM

Mechanical Fuel Pump

CLEANING

The filter screen can be removed from the pump and cleaned.

1. Remove the center screw.

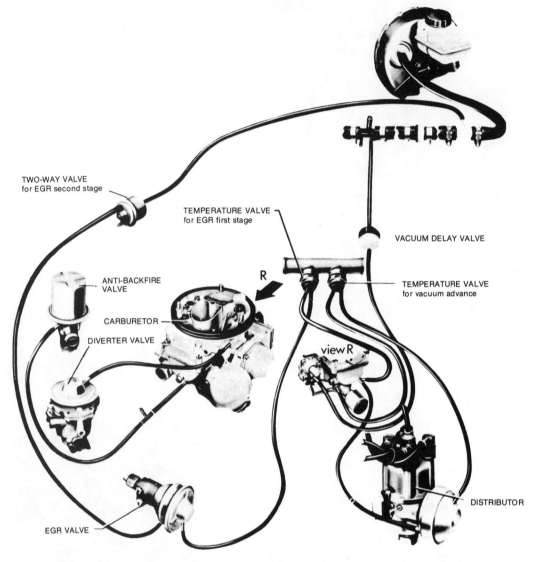

TWO-WAY VALVE
for EGR second stage

TEMPERATURE VALVE
for EGR first stage

VACUUM DELAY VALVE

ANTI-BACKFIRE
VALVE

R

TEMPERATURE VALVE
for vacuum advance

CARBURETOR

DIVERTER VALVE

view R

DISTRIBUTOR

EGR VALVE

Note

Diverter valve vents air pump output to outside at
high rpm. On some 1975 models, diverter valve is
connected to an additional two-way valve

Emission control hoses—1975

2. Remove the screen and gasket. Clean
the screen in a safe solvent.

3. Replace the screen.

4. Install a new gasket and replace the
cover.

NOTE: *Make sure that the depression in
the pump cover engages the projection on
the body of the pump.*

REMOVAL AND INSTALLATION

The fuel pump cannot be repaired and must
be replaced when defective.

1. Disconnect and plug both fuel lines.

2. Remove the two socket head retaining
bolts.

3. Remove the fuel pump and its plastic
flange.

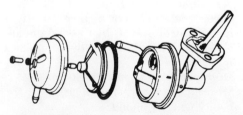

Exploded view of fuel pump showing filter screen

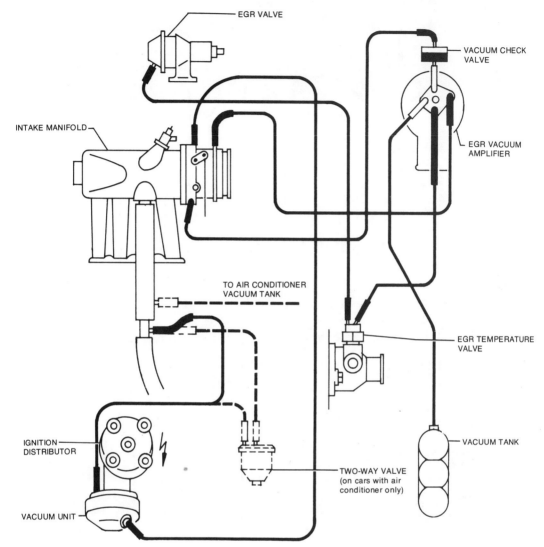

Emission control hoses—1976–77 with CIS California automatic transmission

4. Replace the pump in the reverse order of removal. Use a new flange seal.

Electric Fuel Pump

Electric fuel pumps are used on all fuel injected models.

REMOVAL AND INSTALLATION

The right rear wheel must be removed.

1. Remove the gas tank filler cap to release the pressure.
2. Clean all fuel line connections thoroughly.
3. Disconnect the fuel lines from the gas tank and the fuel accumulator.
4. Disconnect the electrical connector.
5. Remove the fuel pump.

Fuel pump mounting

6. Install the new fuel pump in the reverse order of removal. Make sure that new seal washers are installed on the fuel discharge line.

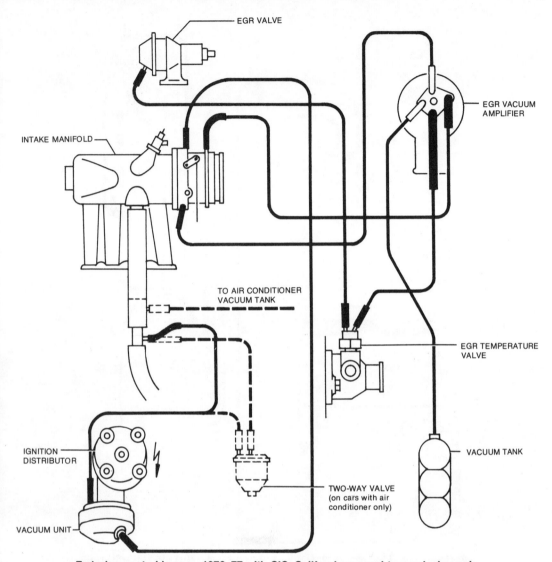

EGR VALVE

EGR VACUUM AMPLIFIER

INTAKE MANIFOLD

TO AIR CONDITIONER VACUUM TANK

EGR TEMPERATURE VALVE

IGNITION DISTRIBUTOR

VACUUM TANK

TWO-WAY VALVE
(on cars with air conditioner only)

VACUUM UNIT

Emission control hoses—1976–77 with CIS, California manual transmission only

Carburetor

The Rabbit and Scirocco carburetor is a Zenith 32/32-2B2 two-barrel. The secondary throat is operated by vacuum. A few 1979 models may use a Solex 34 PICT-5 carburetor.

REMOVAL AND INSTALLATION

NOTE: *1976 models use a new type carburetor gasket that is not interchangeable with the old style.*

1. Remove the air cleaner.
2. Disconnect the fuel line, being careful not to spill any fuel on the hot engine components.
3. Drain some of the coolant and then disconnect the choke hoses.
4. Disconnect the distributor and EGR valve vacuum lines.

OLD TYPE (1975)
PT. NO. 055 129 281A

NEW TYPE (1976)
PT. NO. 049 129 281

New and old style carburetor gaskets are not interchangeable

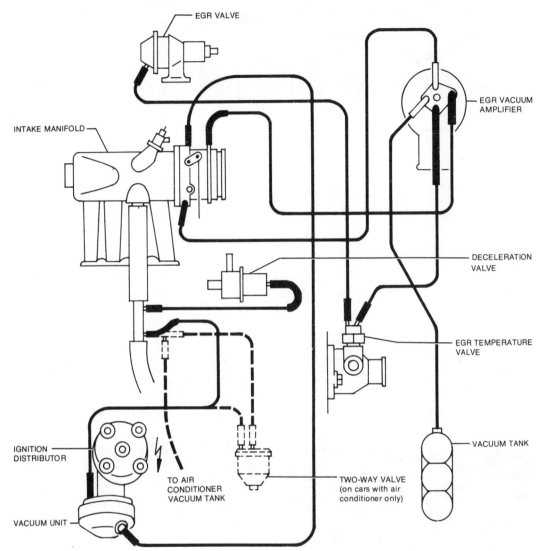

Emission control hoses—1976–77 with CIS, manual transmission

5. Disconnect the electrical lead for the idle cut-off valve.

6. Remove the clip which secures the throttle linkeage to the carburetor. Detach the linkage, being careful not to lose any washers or bushings.

7. Unbolt the carburetor from the manifold and remove it.

8. Use a new gasket when replacing the carburetor. Don't overtighten the nuts.

ZENITH 32/32 2B2 CARBURETOR ADJUSTMENTS

Throttle Gap Adjustment

1975 MODELS

This adjustment is made with the carburetor removed.

1. Close the choke valve fully.

2. Use a drill to check the primary throttle valve opening. Insert the drill between the lower edge of the throttle valve and the inner side of the carburetor bore. The gap should be 0.018-0.020 in.

3. Adjust the gap by turning the linkage screw (b).

1976 MODELS

On these models it is not necessary to remove the carburetor. The engine must be at normal operating temperature.

1. Set the ignition timing.

2. Disconnect and plug the hose from the choke pull-down unit.

3. Open the throttle valve slightly and close the choke valve.

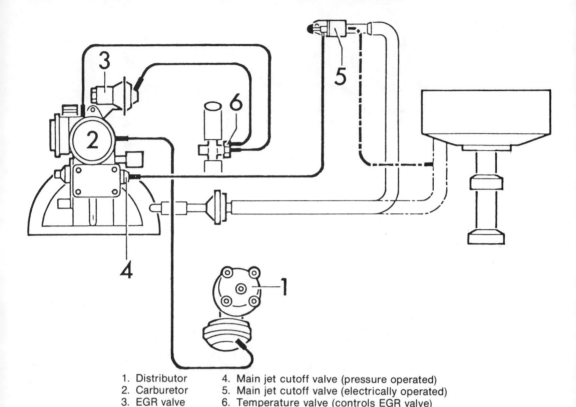

1. Distributor
2. Carburetor
3. EGR valve
4. Main jet cutoff valve (pressure operated)
5. Main jet cutoff valve (electrically operated)
6. Temperature valve (controls EGR valve)

Emission control hoses—1977–78 with Solex 34 PICT-5 carburetor

Throttle gap adjustment 1975 Zenith 32/32-2B2

4. Close the throttle valve; the choke valve should be fully open again.

5. Set the stop screw of the fast idle cam on the highest step. Start the engine.

6. Adjust the speed with the screw (arrow) to: 3150–3250 manual transmission or 3350–3450 automatic transmission.

Choke Gap Adjustment

1. Remove the automatic choke cover.

2. Close the choke valve and push the choke rod to the stop (arrow).

Throttle gap adjustment 1976 Zenith 32/32-2B2

Checking choke gap—1975 Zenith 32/32-2B2

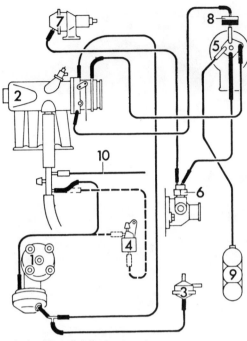

1. Ignition distributor
2. Intake manifold
3. Charcoal filter check valve
4. Two-way valve (cars with air conditioner only)
5. EGR vacuum amplifier
6. EGR temperature valve
7. EGR valve
8. Vacuum check valve
9. Vacuum tank
10. Vacuum hose to air conditioner

Emission control hoses—1978 automatic transmission with CIS

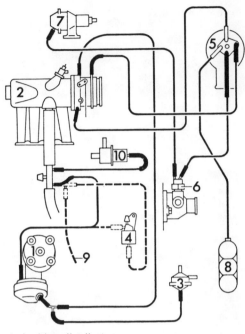

1. Ignition distributor
2. Intake manifold
3. Charcoal filter check valve
4. Two-way valve (cars with air conditioner only)
5. EGR vacuum amplifier
6. EGR temperature valve
7. EGR valve
8. Vacuum tank
9. Vacuum hose to air conditioner
10. Deceleration valve

Emission control hoses—1978 manual transmission, CIS except California

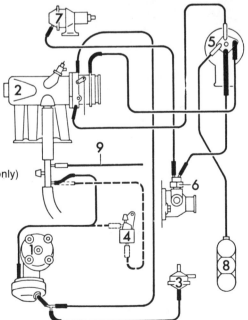

1. Ignition distributor
2. Intake manifold
3. Charcoal filter check valve
4. Two-way valve (cars with air conditioner only)
5. EGR vacuum amplifier
6. EGR temperature valve
7. EGR valve
8. Vacuum tank
9. Vacuum hose to air conditioner

Emission control hoses—1978 manual transmission, CIS, California only

Choke gap adjustment—1975 Zenith 32/32-2B2

Choke gap adjustment—1976 Zenith 32/32-2B2

Automatic choke adjustment—1975–76 Zenith 32/32-2B2

Automatic choke temperature switch adjustment—Zenith 32/32-2B2

3. Hold the choke in position with a rubber band (a).

4. Push the choke lever (b) down slightly to equalize the clearances.

5. Check the choke gap between the edge of the carburetor wall and the edge of the valve with a drill. It should be:

1975—0.17–0.19 in. with vacuum delay valve

—0.15–0.17 in. without vacuum delay valve

1976—0.14 in primary activated

—0.20 in. secondary activated

6. Adjust the gap by turning the screw on the choke vacuum unit in to decrease the gap or out to increase the gap.

Automatic Choke

Align the mark on the automatic choke cover with the mark on the carburetor.

Automatic Choke Temperature Switch

The temperature switch must be removed from the carburetor and checked with an ohmmeter. Connect an ohmmeter across the 2 blades. It should read 0 ohms below 107° F. and infinity above 136° F.

FLOAT LEVEL ADJUSTMENT

The carburetor must be removed.

1. Remove the top cover of the carburetor.

2. Drain any remaining fuel from the float bowls and then invert the carburetor.

3. Measure the distance between the float and the top cover gasket surface. This distance should be 1.08–1.12 in. for the primary

Checking float level

float and 1.16–1.20 in. for the secondary float.

4. Adjust the float level by bending the float arm. Be careful not to push in on the needle, as its tip can be deformed.

THROTTLE LINKAGE ADJUSTMENT

Throttle linkage adjustments are not normally required. However, it is a good idea to make sure that the throttle valve(s) in the carburetor open all the way when the accelerator pedal is held in the wide-open position. Only the primary throttle valve will open on the 32/32-2B2 carburetor; the secondary throttle is vacuum-operated.

SOLEX 34 PICT-5 CARBURETOR ADJUSTMENTS

Throttle Valve Basic Adjustment

You need a vacuum gauge to set the throttle valve. The stop screw (1) is set at the factory, and should not be moved. If the screw is accidentally turned, proceed as follows. Make no adjustment at screw (2).

Basic throttle valve adjustment—Solex 34 PICT-5

1. Run the engine at idle.
2. Remove the vacuum advance hose at the carburetor and connect a vacuum gauge.
3. Remove the plastic screw cap and turn the stop screw in until the gauge indicates vacuum.
4. Turn the stop screw out until the the gauge indicates no vacuum. Turn the screw an additional ¼ turn and install the plastic cap.
5. Adjust the idle and CO.

Choke Valve Adjustment

1. Remove the cover from the automatic choke and fully close the choke.

Choke valve adjusting—Solex 34 PICT-5

2. Push the choke rod in the direction of the arrow and check the gap between the choke valve and the air horn wall. It should be 0.11–0.13 in.
3. Adjust the gap with the adjusting screw (2).
4. Reassemble the choke cover. There is an index mark on the choice housing and another on the choke cover.

Fast Idle Adjustment

The engine should be at normal operating temperature.

1. Run the engine with the screw on the 3rd step of the fast idle cam. The speed should be 2350–2450 rpm. Adjust this speed with the adjusting screw.
2. Stop the engine. Open the choke valve fully and check the gap between the adjusting screw and fast idle cam. It should be 0.008 in.

Altitude Correction

Cars that are generally operated above 3600 feet may require altitude correction, which is

Fast idle adjustment—Solex 34 PICT-5

Adjust fast idle gap—Solex 34 PICT-5

Altitude adjustment—Solex 34 PICT-5

made by backing out the 2 screws (arrows) until they are flush with the carburetor body. Adjust the idle and CO content.

OVERHAUL

Efficient carburetion depends greatly on careful cleaning and inspection during overhaul since dirt, gum, water, or varnish in or on the carburetor parts are often responsible for poor performance.

Overhaul your carburetor in a clean, dust-free area. Carefully disassemble the carburetor, referring often to the exploded views. Keep all similar and lookalike parts segregated during disassembly and cleaning to avoid accidental interchange during assembly. Make a note of all jet sizes.

When the carburetor is disassembled, wash all parts (except diaphragms, electric choke units, pump plunger, and any other plastic, leather, fiber, or rubber parts) in clean carburetor solvent. Do not leave parts in the solvent any longer than is necessary to sufficiently loosen the deposits. Excessive cleaning may remove the special finish from the float bowl and choke valve bodies, leav-

ing these parts unfit for service. Rinse all parts in clean solvent and blow them dry with compressed air or allow them to air dry. Wipe clean all cork, plastic, leather, and fiber parts with a clean, lint-free cloth.

Blow out all passages and jets with compressed air and be sure that there are no restrictions or blockages. Never use wire or similar tools to clean jets, fuel passages, or air bleeds. Clean all jets and valves separately to avoid accidental interchange.

Check all parts for wear or damage. If wear or damage is found, replace the defective parts. Especially check the following:

1. Check the float needle and seat for wear. If wear is found, replace the complete assembly.

2. Check the float hinge pin for wear and the float(s) for dents or distortion. Replace the float if fuel has leaked into it.

3. Check the throttle and choke shaft bores for wear or an out-of-round condition. Damage or wear to the throttle arm, shaft, or shaft bore will often require replacement of the throttle body. These parts require a close tolerance of fit; wear may allow air leakage, which could adversely affect starting and idling.

NOTE: *Throttle shafts and bushings are not included in overhaul kits. They can be purchased separately.*

4. Inspect the idle mixture adjusting needles for burrs or grooves. Any such condition requires replacement of the needle, since you will not be able to obtain a satisfactory idle.

5. Test the accelerator pump check valves. They should pass air one way but not the other. Test for proper seating by blowing and sucking on the valve. Replace the valve if necessary. If the valve is satisfactory, wash the valve again to remove breath moisture.

6. Check the bowl cover for warped surfaces with a straightedge.

7. Closely inspect the valves and seats for wear and damage, replacing as necessary.

8. After the carburetor is assembled, check the choke valve for freedom of operation.

Carburetor overhaul kits are recommended for each overhaul. These kits contain all gaskets and new parts to replace those that deteriorate most rapidly. Failure to replace all parts supplied with the kit (especially gaskets) can result in poor performance later.

Some carburetor manufacturers supply overhaul kits of three basic types: minor re-

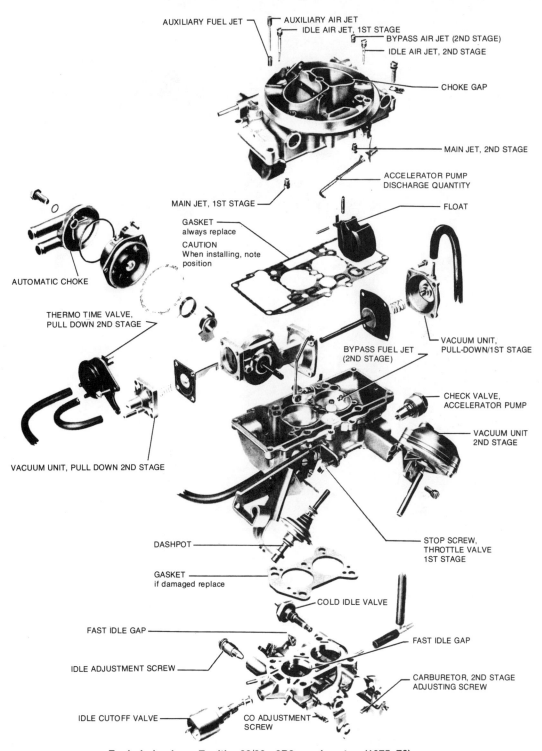

AUXILIARY FUEL JET

AUXILIARY AIR JET

IDLE AIR JET, 1ST STAGE

BYPASS AIR JET (2ND STAGE)

IDLE AIR JET, 2ND STAGE

CHOKE GAP

MAIN JET, 2ND STAGE

ACCELERATOR PUMP
DISCHARGE QUANTITY

MAIN JET, 1ST STAGE

FLOAT

GASKET
always replace

CAUTION
When installing, note
position

AUTOMATIC CHOKE

THERMO TIME VALVE,
PULL DOWN 2ND STAGE

VACUUM UNIT,
PULL-DOWN/1ST STAGE

BYPASS FUEL JET
(2ND STAGE)

CHECK VALVE,
ACCELERATOR PUMP

VACUUM UNIT
2ND STAGE

VACUUM UNIT, PULL DOWN 2ND STAGE

DASHPOT

STOP SCREW,
THROTTLE VALVE
1ST STAGE

GASKET
if damaged replace

COLD IDLE VALVE

FAST IDLE GAP

FAST IDLE GAP

IDLE ADJUSTMENT SCREW

CARBURETOR, 2ND STAGE
ADJUSTING SCREW

IDLE CUTOFF VALVE

CO ADJUSTMENT
SCREW

Exploded view—Zenith 32/32 2B2 carburetor (1975–76)

pair; major repair; and gasket kits. Basically,
they contain the following:

Minor Repair Kits:
   All gaskets
   Float needle valve

Volume control screw
All diaphragms
Spring for the pump diaphragm
Major Repair Kits:
   All jets and gaskets

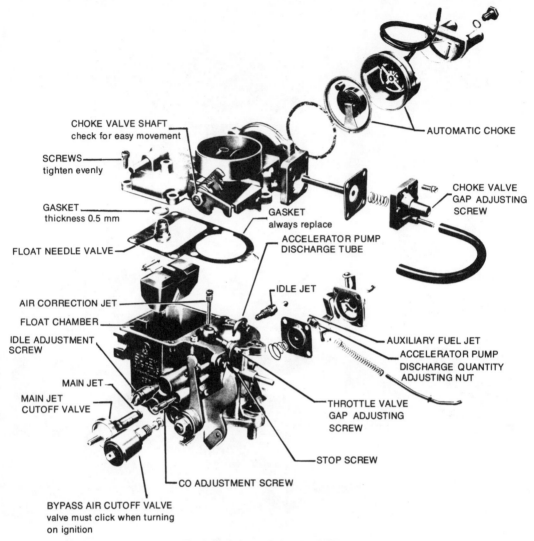

CHOKE VALVE SHAFT
check for easy movement

SCREWS
tighten evenly

GASKET
thickness 0.5 mm

FLOAT NEEDLE VALVE

AIR CORRECTION JET

FLOAT CHAMBER

IDLE ADJUSTMENT
SCREW

MAIN JET

MAIN JET
CUTOFF VALVE

BYPASS AIR CUTOFF VALVE
valve must click when turning
on ignition

AUTOMATIC CHOKE

CHOKE VALVE
GAP ADJUSTING
SCREW

GASKET
always replace

ACCELERATOR PUMP
DISCHARGE TUBE

IDLE JET

AUXILIARY FUEL JET

ACCELERATOR PUMP
DISCHARGE QUANTITY
ADJUSTING NUT

THROTTLE VALVE
GAP ADJUSTING
SCREW

STOP SCREW

CO ADJUSTMENT SCREW

Exploded view—Solex 34 PICT-5

All diaphragms
Float needle valve
Volume control screw
Pump ball valve
Float
Complete intermediate rod
Intermediate pump lever
Some cover hold-down screws and washers
Gasket Kits:
    All gaskets
After cleaning and checking all components, reassemble the carburetor, using new parts and referring to the exploded view. When reassembling, make sure that all screws and jets are tight in their seats, but do not overtighten, as the tips will be distorted. Tighten all screws gradually, in rotation. Do not tighten needle valves into their seats; uneven jetting will result. Always use new gas-

kets. Be sure to adjust the float level when reassembling.

CIS Fuel Injection

CIS SENSOR PLATE HEIGHT ADJUSTMENT

The height adjustment of the sensor plate must be checked under fuel pressure. You will also need a bridging adaptor (US 4480/3).

1. Install a pressure gauge in the line between the fuel distributor and control pressure regulator.

2. Remove the rubber elbow from the air flow sensor housing.

3. Remove the fuel pump relay from the fuse panel and install a bridging adaptor (US 4480/3).

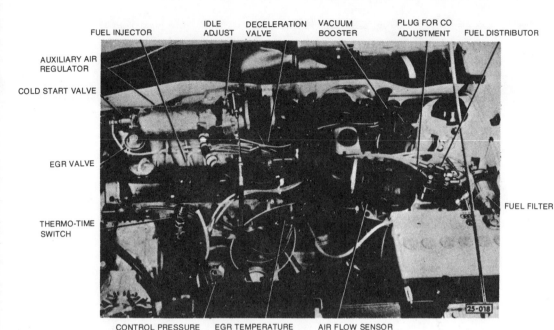

FUEL INJECTOR — IDLE ADJUST — DECELERATION VALVE — VACUUM BOOSTER — PLUG FOR CO ADJUSTMENT — FUEL DISTRIBUTOR

AUXILIARY AIR REGULATOR

COLD START VALVE

EGR VALVE

FUEL FILTER

THERMO-TIME SWITCH

CONTROL PRESSURE REGULATOR — EGR TEMPERATURE CONTROL VALVE — AIR FLOW SENSOR

CIS fuel injection components

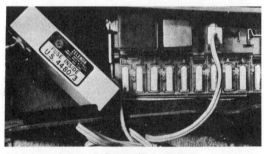

Bridging adaptor (US 4480/3) installed

4. Switch the adaptor ON and wait until pressure reads 49–54 psi.

5. Switch the bridging adaptor OFF; the pressure should fall to 28–37 psi.

6. The upper edge of the sensor plate must be even with the bottom of the air cone

taper or no more than 0.020 in. below the bottom of the taper.

7. Bend the clip to adjust the height.

8. Recheck the pressure readings after adjusting.

9. Remove the pressure gauge, reconnect the fuel lines and install the fuel pump reply.

THERMO-TIME SWITCH TEST

NOTE: *To properly perform the following tests, the engine must be cold with the water temperature below 95° F. (35° C.).*

1. Disconnect the cold start valve on the end of the intake manifold.

2. Connect a test light across the cold start valve terminals.

3. Connect a jumper wire from the 1 terminal on the ignition coil to ground.

CIS sensor plate adjustment

Thermotime switch (arrow)

Cold-start valve (arrow)

4. Operate the starter. If the test light fails to light after 8 seconds, the thermotime switch is defective and should be replaced.

COLD START VALVE TEST

Disconnect the cold start valve

NOTE: *Do not remove the fuel line from the cold start valve.*

2. Remove the cold start valve from the manifold and point the nozzle into a measuring container.

3. Connect a jumper wire from one terminal of the cold start valve to terminal 15 on the ignition coil.

4. Connect a second jumper wire from the other cold start valve terminal to ground.

5. Remove the fuel pump relay and bridge the relay plate terminals L13 and L14 with a fused (8 amp) jumper wire.

6. Turn the ignition switch ON and observe the fuel spray pattern from the cold start valve. The spray pattern from the nozzle must be cone-shaped and steady. If not replace the valve.

7. Turn the ignition switch off.

8. Wipe the nozzle dry with clean rag and check for leakage. If drops form within one minute, the valve is defective and must be replaced.

AUXILIARY AIR REGULATOR TEST

NOTE: *The engine must be cold to perform this test.*

1. Remove and plug the hose from the auxiliary air regulator.

2. Observe gate valve with a mirror. The valve must be open. If the valve is not open, replace the regulator.

3. Idle the engine for 5 minutes. Again check the gate valve, it should be closed. If

the valve did not close, replace the auxiliary air regulator.

CONTROL PRESSURE REGULATOR TEST

The system is under considerable constant pressure. The only practical test that should be attempted by the owner is one using an ohmmeter.

Be sure the engine is at normal operating temperature. There should be no loose fuel fittings or other fire hazards when the electrical connections are disengaged.

1. Remove the electrical connector from the control pressure regulator.

2. Turn the ignition ON.

3. Check the voltage supply with a voltmeter. There should be a minimum of 11.5 volts available at the regulator.

4. Connect an ohmmeter across the terminals of the regulator socket. Resistance should be approximately 20 ohms.

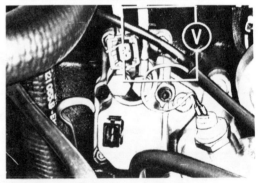

Checking control pressure regulator

FUEL INJECTOR TEST

1. Remove the injector but leave it connected to the fuel line.

2. Point the injector into a measuring container.

3. Remove the fuel pump relay and bridge the relay plate terminials L13 and L14 with a fused (8 amp) jumper wire.

4. Remove the air duct from the air flow sensor.

5. Turn the ignition switch ON.

6. Lift the air flow sensor plate with a magnet and observe the injector nozzle spray pattern. The spray pattern must be cone shaped and even, if not replace the injector.

7. Turn the ignition OFF and hold the injector horizontally; it should not drip.

8. Moisten the rubber seals on the injectors with fuel before installing.

9. Press the injectors firmly into place.

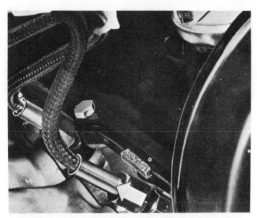

Removing fuel injector (gasoline engine)

CHECKING THE FUEL PUMP

The CIS fuel injection system uses an electric fuel pump located at the right rear of the car.

If the fuel pump is malfunctioning, check the following.

1. Operate the starter and listen at the right rear of the vehicle to see if the pump is running.

2. If it does not run, check the fuse on the front of the fuel pump relay located on the relay plate under the dash.

3. If the fuse is OK, replace the fuel pump relay. If it still does not run, replace the fuel pump.

CHECKING FUEL PUMP OUTPUT

To test the fuel pump output, you'll need a graduated container that will hold at least 1 quart.

1. Check the fuel filter. If it's dirty, replace it.

2. Connect a jumper wire from the #1 terminal of the ignition coil to ground to prevent the engine from starting.

3. Remove the fuel return line and hold it in a container of at least 1 quart capacity.

Checking fuel pump output

Operate the starter for 30 seconds. If delivery is not at least ¾ quart in 30 seconds, replace the pump.

4. Remove the jumper wire and reconnect the fuel line.

FUEL DISTRIBUTOR

Removal and Installation

NOTE: *When removing the fuel distributor be sure the control plunger does not fall out from underneath.*

1. Disconnect the fuel lines.

2. Remove the fuel distributor.

3. If the control plunger has been removed, moisten it with gasoline before installing. The small shoulder on the plunger is inserted first.

Remove fuel distributor retaining screws (arrows)

Diesel Fuel Injection

The diesel fuel system is an extremely complex and sensitive system. Very few repairs or adjustments are possible by the owner. Any service other than that listed here should be referred to an authorized VW dealer or diesel specialist. The injection pump itself is not repairable; it can only be replaced.

Any work done to the diesel fuel injection should be done with absolute cleanliness. Even the smallest specks of dirt will have a disastrous effect on the injection system.

Do not attempt to remove the fuel injectors. They are very delicate and must be removed with a special tool to prevent damage. The fuel in the system is also under tremendous pressure (1700–1850 psi), so it's not wise to loosen any lines with the engine running. Exposing your skin to the spray from the injector at working pressure can cause fuel to penetrate the skin.

CHECKING INJECTION PUMP TIMING

Checking the injection pump timing also involves checking the valve timing. To alter the

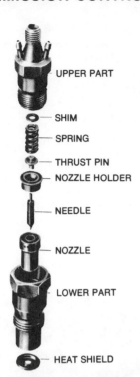

UPPER PART

SHIM

SPRING

THRUST PIN

NOZZLE HOLDER

NEEDLE

NOZZLE

LOWER PART

HEAT SHIELD

Diesel engine fuel injector (do not disassemble)

The ball pin on the pump lever must be aligned with the mark

Accelerator cable adjustment

injection pump timing, the camshaft gear must be removed and repositioned. This also changes the valve timing. Special tool (VW 210) is necessary to properly tension the injection pump drive belt on the diesel engine.

1. Set the engine at TDC on No. 1 cylinder. In this position, the TDC mark on the flywheel should be aligned with boss on the bell housing and both valves of No. 1 cylinder should be closed.

2. The marks on the pump and mounting plate should also be aligned.

3. If the valve timing is incorrect, set the valve timing as detailed in Chapter 3.

ACCELERATOR CABLE ADJUSTMENT

The ball pin on the pump lever should be pointing up and be aligned with the mark in the slot. The accelerator cable should be attached at the upper hole in the bracket. With the pedal in the full throttle position, adjust the cable so that the pump lever contacts the stop with no binding or strain.

COLD START CABLE ADJUSTMENT

When the cold start knob on the dash is pulled out, the fuel injection pump timing is advanced 2.5°. This improves cold starting and running until the engine warms up.

1. Insert the washer on the cable.

Checking injection pump timing

Cold start cable adjustment

2. Insert the cable in the bracket with the rubber bushing. Install the cable in the pin.

3. Install the lockwasher.

4. Move the lever to the zero position (direction of arrow). Pull the inner cable tight and tighten the clamp screw.

CHECKING GLOW PLUGS CURRENT SUPPLY

1. Connect a test light between No. 4 cylinder glow plug and ground.

2. Turn the key to the heat position. The test light should light up.

Checking glow plug

3. If not, check the glow plug relay, ignition switch, or fuse box relay plate.

CHECKING GLOW PLUGS

Make this check after establishing that there is current to the glow plugs.

1. Remove the wire and glow plug bus bar.

2. Connect the test light between the battery positive terminal and each glow plug in turn.

3. If the light lights, the glow plug is OK. If not, the glow plug is defective and must be replaced.

Checking glow plug current supply

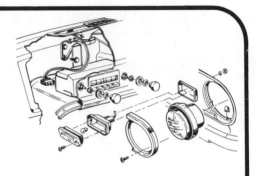

5

Chassis Electrical

HEATER UNIT

The heater core and blower are contained in the heater assembly which is removed and disassembled to service either component. The heater assembly is located in the passenger compartment under the center of the dash.

NOTE: *From chassis no. 171 819 741, the Rabbit uses a slightly different fresh air housing.*

REMOVAL AND INSTALLATION

1. Disconnect the battery ground cable.
2. Drain the cooling system.
3. Remove the windshield washer container from its mounts. Remove the ignition coil.
4. Disconnect the two hoses from the heater core connections at the firewall.
5. Unplug the electrical connector.
6. Remove the heater control knobs on the dash.
7. Remove the two retaining screws and remove the controls from the dash complete with brackets.
8. Pull the cable connection off the electric motor.
9. Disconnect the cable from the lever on the round knob.
10. Using the screwdriver, pry the retain-

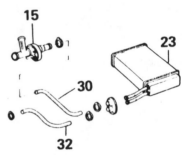

Heater core (23), hoses (30 and 32), and heater control valve (15)

ing clip off the fresh air housing [the front portion of the heater].

11. Remove the fresh air housing complete with the controls.

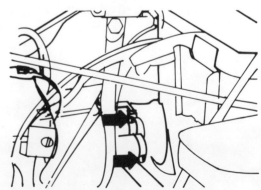

Heater hose connections at firewall

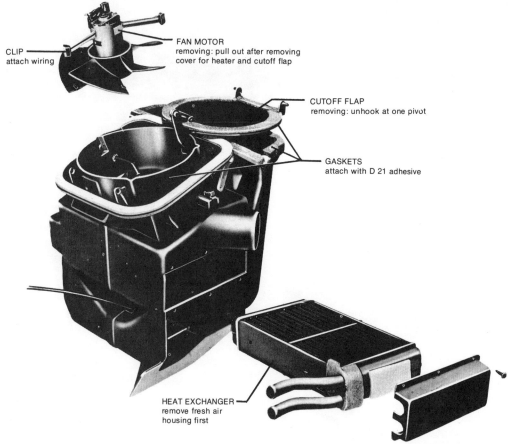

CLIP
attach wiring

FAN MOTOR
removing: pull out after removing
cover for heater and cutoff flap

CUTOFF FLAP
removing: unhook at one pivot

GASKETS
attach with D 21 adhesive

HEAT EXCHANGER
remove fresh air
housing first

Heat exchanger and fan motor

12. Detach the left and right air hoses.

13. Remove the heater-to-dash panel mounting screws and lower the heater assembly.

14. Pull out the two pins and remove the heater cover. Unscrew and remove the fan motor.

15. Remove the six screws retaining the heater core cover and lift out the core.

16. Installation is the reverse of removal. Refill the cooling system. When installing the new type of housing in cars with the old fresh air/heater, use 2 clamps and make hole by cutting along the line (w). Clip the connections and seal any gaps. Up to and including 1976 models, when installing the new control flap in the old housing, slide the Bowden Cable eye over the shaft and cut off the shaft. On 1977 and later models slide the cable eye over the shaft.

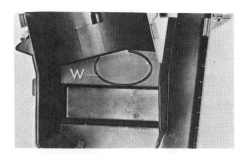

Cut a hole along line (W)

Use sealer at joint (arrow)

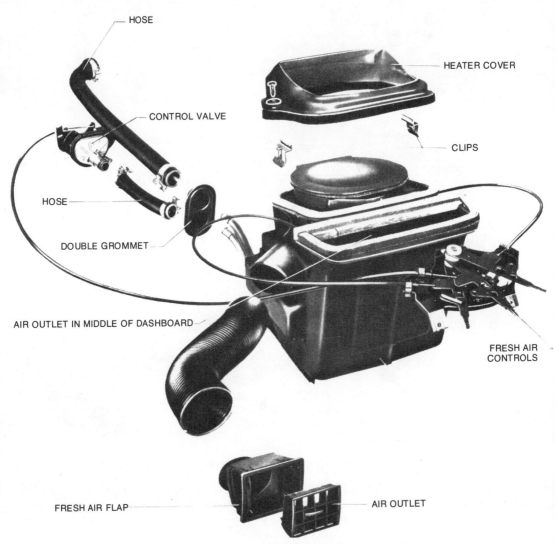

HOSE

HEATER COVER

CONTROL VALVE

CLIPS

HOSE

DOUBLE GROMMET

AIR OUTLET IN MIDDLE OF DASHBOARD

FRESH AIR CONTROLS

FRESH AIR FLAP

AIR OUTLET

Exploded view of heater assembly cables and hoses

On 1977 and later models, slide cable over shaft (1). On 1976 and earlier models, slide the cable over shaft (2). Cut off shaft (1)

RADIO

NOTE: *The radio is a dealer installed option.*

REMOVAL AND INSTALLATION

1. Remove the knobs from the radio.
2. Remove the nuts from the radio control shafts.
3. Detach the antenna lead from the jack on the radio case.

CAUTION: *Never operate the radio without a speaker; severe damage to the output transistor will result. If the speaker must be replaced, use a speaker of the correct impedance (ohms) or else the output transistors will be damaged and require replacement*

4. Detach the power and speaker leads.

5. Remove the radio support nuts and bolts.

6. Withdraw the radio from beneath the dashboard.

7. Installation is performed in the reverse order of removal.

WINDSHIELD WIPERS

Wiper Refill

REPLACEMENT

To replace the rubber blade inserts:

1. Pull the wiper arms up off the windshield.

2. Using a pair of pliers, squeeze the two steel inserts at the open end of the blade.

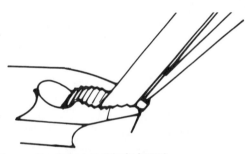

Squeezing the wiper blade insert

3. Pull the insert of the rubber filler.

4. Remove the rubber filler.

5. Insert the new rubber filler making sure that the retainers engage the recesses in the second grooves.

6. Slide the metal inserts into the upper grooves of the rubber blade so that the notch in the insert faces the rubber. Engage the projections in grooves on both sides.

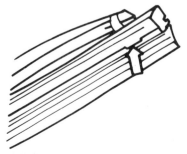

Notch in blade insert

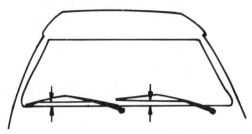

Blade-to-molding distance should be 1⅜ in. for the Rabbit driver's side and 1 in. on the Scirocco; passenger's side should be 2½ in. on the Rabbit and 1³/₁₆ in. on the Scirocco.

Arms

REMOVAL AND INSTALLATION

1. Lift the blade and arm up off the windshield.

2. Simultaneously push the arm down and lift the smaller end cap up [see the illustration].

3. Remove the retaining nut and lift the arm off the shaft.

4. Install the arm in the reverse order of removal. When properly installed, the blades should be as shown.

Front Motor

REMOVAL AND INSTALLATION

When removing the wiper motor, leave the mounting frame in place. Do not remove the wiper drive crank from the motor shaft—if it must be removed for any reason, matchmark the shaft, motor, and crank for reinstallation.

1. Access is with the hood open. Disconnect the battery ground cable.

2. Detach the connecting rods from the motor crank arm only.

3. Pull off the wiring plug.

4. Remove the 4 mounting bolts. You may have to energize the motor for access to the top bolt.

5. Remove the motor. Reverse the procedure for installation.

Rear Motor

REMOVAL AND INSTALLATION

There are 2 kinds of rear wiper motors used on Rabbits. Up until 1976, a gear housing with smooth cover plate was used; later models use a ribbed gear housing. Parts are different and cannot be combined, except that a new style wiper motor bracket can be installed on earlier models. The Scirocco uses the same motor as the corresponding Rabbit,

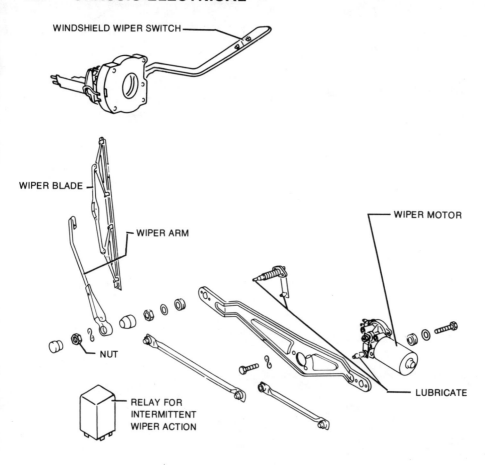

WINDSHIELD WIPER SWITCH

WIPER BLADE

WIPER ARM

WIPER MOTOR

NUT

RELAY FOR INTERMITTENT WIPER ACTION

LUBRICATE

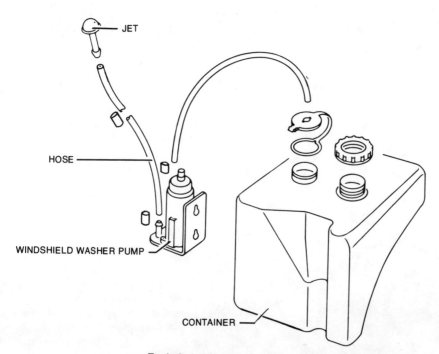

JET

HOSE

WINDSHIELD WASHER PUMP

CONTAINER

Exploded view of front wiper motor and linkage

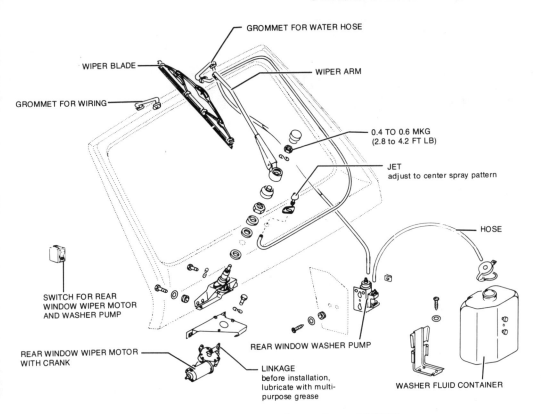

Exploded view of rear wiper motor and linkage

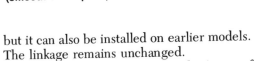

Rear wiper motor used through 1976 models (smooth cover plate)

Rear wiper motor used 1977 and later models (ribbed cover plate and different linkage)

but it can also be installed on earlier models. The linkage remains unchanged.

NOTE: *Do not interchange the wires of terminal 53 and 53a on the switch. Damage to the motor diode will result.*

INSTRUMENT CLUSTER

REMOVAL AND INSTALLATION

1. Disconnect the battery ground cable.
2. Remove the fresh air controls trim plate.

3. Remove the radio or glove box.
4. Unscrew the speedometer drive cable from the back of the speedometer. Detach the electrical plug.

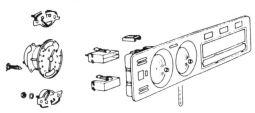

Exploded view of instrument cluster

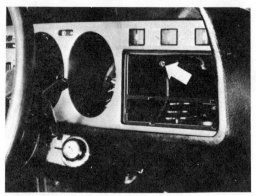

Instrument cluster attaching screw inside glove compartment

5. Remove the attaching screw inside the radio/glove box opening.

6. Remove the instrument cluster. Reverse the procedure for installation.

SPEEDOMETER CABLE

The speedometer cable should not be kinked or greased. When installing the Scirocco speedometer cable, attach the cable to the bracket so the speedometer cable will not contact the clutch cable.

1. Unscrew the speedometer cable from the rear of the instrument cluster and from the EGR elapsed mileage counter.

2. Unsnap the rubber grommets from the dash panel support and the firewall.

3. Pull the speedometer cable through the holes.

4. The other end of the cable is attached to the EGR counter and transaxle.

5. Installation is the reverse of removal.

The speedometer cable should not be kinked or greased. When installing the Scirocco speedometer cable, attach it to the bracket (see Instrument Cluster Removal and Installation) to avoid the speedometer cable contacting the clutch cable.

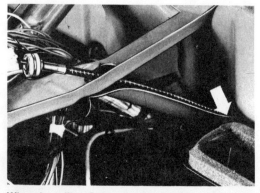

When installing Scirocco speedometer cable, attach the cable to the bracket (arrow)

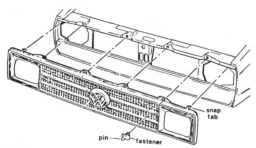

Grille and retaining pins used on Westmoreland Rabbits

HEADLIGHT

REMOVAL AND INSTALLATION

1. Remove the grille. On Westmoreland Rabbit's (those made in the U.S., with square headlamps), the radiator grille is retained by 2 snap-tabs and 4 fasteners. Use a nail or small punch to remove the pins. New fasteners (Part No. 171 853 695 A) are needed to install the grille.

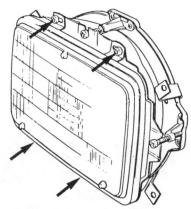

Remove the 4 screws (arrows) holding the trim ring on Westmoreland Rabbits. Do not disturb the headlight aiming screws (top and right side).

Remove the grille retaining screws

There are 4 grille retaining screws on each side (large black arrows). After removing the grille, remove the headlight bezel screws (A). Don't disturb the headlight aiming screws (B)

2. Remove the three headlight retaining ring screws.

NOTE: *Do not disturb the two headlight aiming screws or it will be necessary to reaim the headlights.*

3. Remove headlight retaining ring.

4. Pull the headlight out of the housing and unplug the multi-connector.

5. Replace the new bulb in the reverse order of removal. Make sure that the three

Bulb Chart

Bulb	1975–77	1978
High beam (Scirocco)	4001	4001
Low/high beam (Scirocco)	4000	4000
Headlight (Rabbit)	6014	6014
Front turn/parking light	1034	1034
Side marker	57	1816
Rear turn signal	1073	1073
Stoplight	1073	1073
Taillight	67	67
Back-up light	1073	1073
License light	57	1816
Interior light	211	211
Trunk light (Scirocco)	211	211

lugs on the bulb engage the slots in the housing.

FUSES AND RELAYS

All fuses and relays are located in the lower left dashboard, protected by a clear plastic cover. Use VW ceramic type fuses. VW recommends that relays be replaced by your dealer.

Fuses

Fuses are listed according to numbers on the fuse box cover.

Fuse No.	Protected Circuit	Fuse Rating (amp)
S1	Low beam (left)	8
S2	Low beam (right)	8
S3	High beam (left) and high beam warning light	8
S4	High beam (right)	8
S5	Rear window defroster	16①
S6	Stop lights; hazard flasher	8
S7	Interior light, cigarette lighter, clock	8
S8	Turn signals (including indicator light)	8
S9	Back-up lights and horn	8
S10	Blower motor	16②
S11	Windshield wiper/washer; rear washer pump motor	8
S12	License plate light	8
S13	Parking light (right), tail light (right), side marker light (right)	8
S14	Parking light (left), tail light (left), side marker light (left)	8
S15	Radiator fan	16③
S20⑤	Electric fuel pump	16④
S30 (in line under the dash)	Rear windshield wiper	8

① 1975–8 amp
② 1975–76—8 amp
③ 1975—vacant
④ 1977–78 and 1976 special edition Scirocco only
⑤ This may be marked S31 on 1978 models
NOTE: *If S5 or S10 has an 8 amp (white) fuse it can be replaced by a 16 amp (pink) fuse as later production models.*

WIRING DIAGRAMS

NOTE: *Wiring diagrams have been left out of this book. As cars have become more complex, and available with longer and longer option lists, wiring diagrams have grown in size and complexity also. It has become virtually impossible to provide a readable reproduction in a reasonable number of pages.*

6

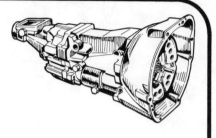

Clutch and Transaxle

MANUAL TRANSAXLE

TRANSAXLE REMOVAL AND INSTALLATION

The engine and transaxle may be removed together as explained under "Engine Removal and Installation" or the transaxle may be removed alone, as explained here.

1. Disconnect the battery ground cable.
2. Support the left end of the engine at the lifting eye.
3. Remove the left transmission mount bolts (between the transmission and the firewall and ground strap.)
4. Turn the engine until the lug on the flywheel (to the left of the TDC mark) aligns

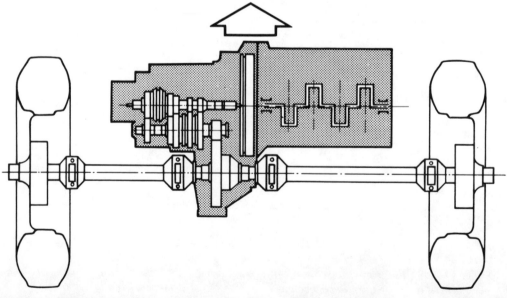

Cutaway showing the transaxle arrangement. The differential is located behind the transmission section of the transaxle.

Remove the shift linkage from the selector shaft lever (9a) and relay lever (9b)

with the flywheel timing pointer. The transmission/engine must be in this position to be separated

5. Detach the speedometer drive cable, backup light wire, and clutch cable.

6. Remove the engine to transmission bolts.

7. Disconnect the shift linkage.

8. Detach the transmission ground strap.

9. Remove the starter.

10. Remove the engine mounting support near the starter.

11. Remove the rear transmission mount.

12. Unbolt and wire up the drive-shafts.

13. From underneath, remove the bolts for the large cover plate, but don't remove it. Unbolt the small cover plate on the firewall side of the engine. Remove the engine to transmission nut immediately below the small plate.

14. Press the transmission off the dowels and remove it from below the car.

To install the transaxle:

15. The recess in the flywheel edge must be at 3:00 o'clock (facing the left end of the engine). Tighten the engine to transmission bolts to 47 ft lbs. Tighten the engine mounting support bolts to 47 ft lbs. Tighten the driveshaft bolts to 32 ft lbs.

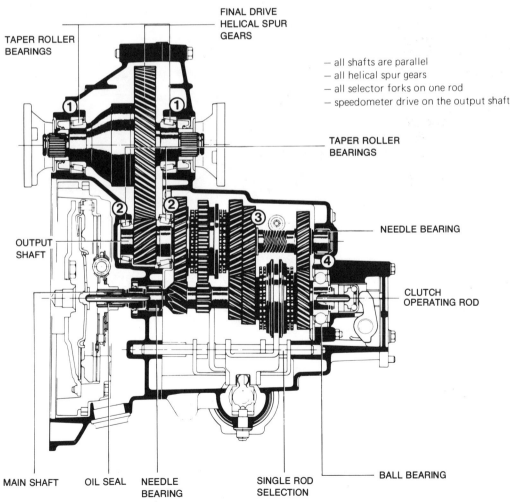

Cross-section of the transaxle. 1, 2, 3, and 4 are adjustment shims.

16. Check the adjustment of the shift linkage.

SHIFT LINKAGE ADJUSTMENT

1. Adjust the long rod over the left drive-shaft coupling to a length of 6.42–6.50 in.

2. Adjust the short angled rod that attaches to the final drive housing to a length of 1.18–1.25 in.

3. Make the lower part of the floorshift lever vertical (in the side to side plane) in the first gear position by loosening the bearing plate that supports the end of the long shift rod that connects to the bottom of the floor-

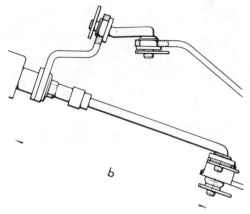

Adjust the gearshift linkage (B) to 6.42–6.50 in.

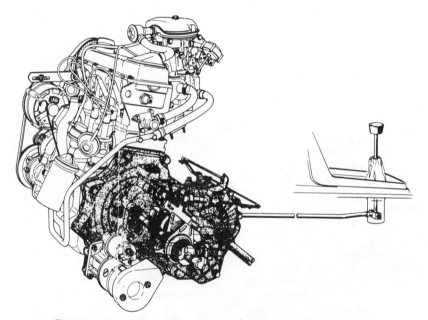

Phantom view of transaxle showing positioning of shift linkage

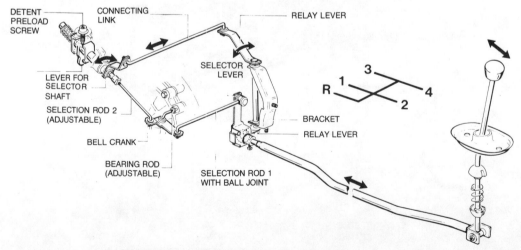

DETENT PRELOAD SCREW

CONNECTING LINK

RELAY LEVER

LEVER FOR SELECTOR SHAFT

SELECTOR LEVER

SELECTION ROD 2 (ADJUSTABLE)

BELL CRANK

BEARING ROD (ADJUSTABLE)

BRACKET

RELAY LEVER

SELECTION ROD 1 WITH BALL JOINT

R 1 3 4 2

Shift linkage—adjustment is made at selection rod 2

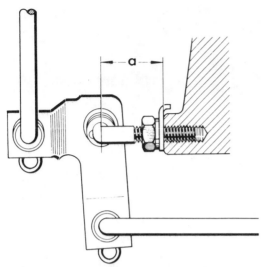

Adjust the relay lever (A) to 1.18–1.25 in.

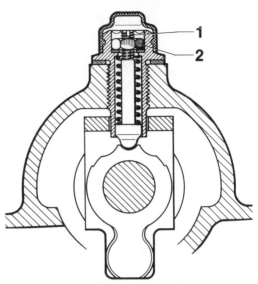

On 1975 models turn the plunger (1) until the nut (2) starts to move

shift lever. Tighten the mounting nuts when the lever is vertical.

4. Make the lower part of the floorshift lever vertical (in the fore and aft plane) in the Neutral position by pulling up the boot and loosening the two lever plate bolts. Move the plate until the lever is vertical.

5. If, after complete adjustment, the linkage is still spongy or jams, check the selector shaft lockbolt adjustment.

Adjusting gearshift lever

SELECTOR SHAFT LOCKBOLT ADJUSTMENT

Make this adjustment after linkage adjustment, if the linkage still feels spongy or jams. There are 2 kinds of lockbolts; those with plastic caps (1975) or those with lockrings (1976 and later).

1975 MODELS

1. Remove the linkage from the selector shaft lever and put the transmission in Neutral.

2. Turn the slotted plunger until the plunger hits bottom. The nut will start to move out.

3. From here, turn the plunger back ¼ turn and install the plastic cap.

4. Reconnect the linkage.

1976 AND LATER MODELS

1. Disconnect the shift linkage and put the transmission in Neutral.

2. Loosen the locknut and turn the adjusting sleeve in until the lockring lifts off the sleeve.

3. Turn the adjusting sleeve back until the lockring just contacts the sleeve. Tighten the locknut.

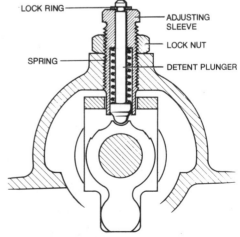

On 1976 and later models, loosen the locknut and turn the adjusting sleeve

4. Turn the shaft slightly. The lockring should lift as soon as the shaft is turned.

5. Reconnect the linkage.

BACK-UP LIGHT SWITCH

On earlier models, the back-up light switch is located inside the transmission housing and operated by a lug on the reverse gear shift fork. On later models the switch is located externally on a bracket, operated by the selector shaft lever. Externally mounted switches can be adjusted by moving or bending the bracket.

CLUTCH

PEDAL FREE-PLAY ADJUSTMENT

Clutch pedal free-play should be ⅝ in. Pedal free-play is the distance the pedal can be

Clutch pedal free-play adjustment

depressed before the linkage starts to act on the throwout bearing.

1. Adjust the clutch pedal free-play by loosening the two nuts on the cable. The

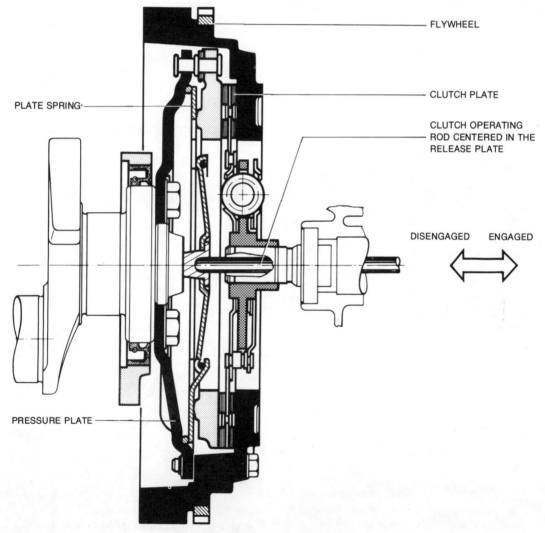

Cutaway view of the clutch

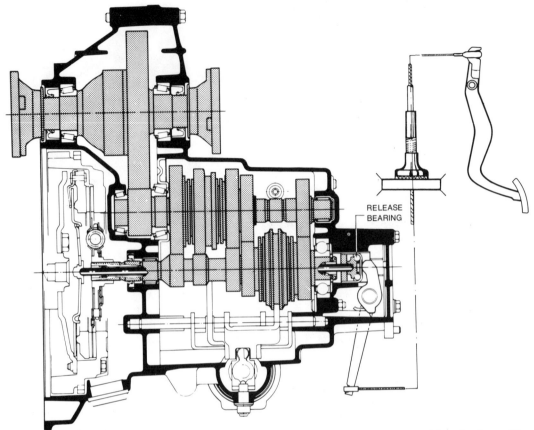

When the clutch pedal is depressed, the cable and lever push the throwout (release) bearing toward the clutch. The operating rod is pushed, which in turn disengages the clutch.

cable adjustment point is on the front of the transmission.

2. After obtaining the correct free-play, tighten the adjusting nuts.

REMOVAL AND INSTALLATION

These cars use a type of clutch more common to motorcycles than to cars. The pressure plate is bolted to the flywheel and the flywheel bolted to the pressure plate; in other words, these two parts have switched places. The clutch release lever and bearing are in the left end of the transmission. The clutch is actuated by a release rod which passes through a hollow transmission shaft. The throwout bearing is in the transaxle and lubricated with transmission oil.

1. Remove the transmission.

2. Attach a toothed flywheel holder and gradually loosen the flywheel to pressure plate bolts one or two turns at a time in a crisscross pattern to prevent distortion.

3. Remove the flywheel and the clutch disc.

NOTE: *If replacing the flywheel, the new one has only a TDC mark. Additional timing marks must be cut into the flywheel as shown.*

4. Use a screwdriver to remove the release plate retaining ring. Remove the release plate.

A timing notch must be cut into new flywheels. A = 5/8 in. (7½° BTDC) and B = 9/32 in. (3° ATDC)

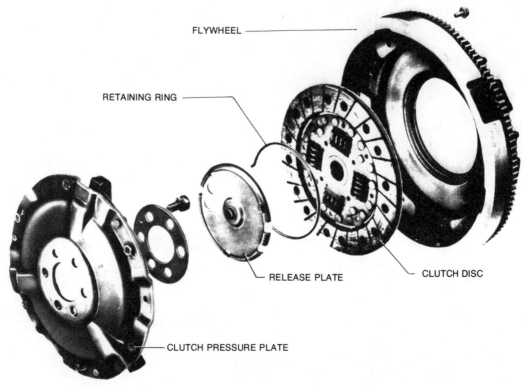

FLYWHEEL

RETAINING RING

RELEASE PLATE

CLUTCH DISC

CLUTCH PRESSURE PLATE

Exploded view of the flywheel/clutch assembly

5. Lock the pressure plate in place and unbolt it from the crankshaft. Loosen the bolts one or two turns at a time in a crisscross pattern to prevent distortion.

6. On installation, use new bolts to attach the pressure plate to the crankshaft. Use a thread locking compound and torque the bolts in a diagonal pattern to 54 ft lbs.

7. Lubricate the clutch disc splines, release plate contact surface, and pushrod socket with multi-purpose grease. Install the release plate, retaining ring, and clutch disc.

8. Use a dummy shaft to align the clutch disc.

9. Install the flywheel, tightening the bolts one or two turns at a time in a crisscross pattern to prevent distortion. Torque the bolts to 14 ft lbs.

10. Replace the transmission. Adjust the clutch free-play.

AUTOMATIC TRANSMISSION

TRANSAXLE REMOVAL AND INSTALLATION

The engine and transaxle may be removed together as explained under "Engine Re-moval and Installation" or the transaxle may be removed alone, as explained here.

1. Disconnect both battery cables.

2. Disconnect the speedometer cable at the transmission.

3. Support the left end of the engine at the lifting eye. Attach a hoist to the transaxle.

4. Unbolt the rear transmission carrier from the body then from the transaxle. Un-bolt the left side carrier from the body.

5. Unbolt the right driveshaft and wire it up.

6. Remove the starter. The third bolt is between the engine and the starter.

7. Remove the transmission protection plate and converter cover plate. 1976 and later models use 1. mm bolts. If a new plate is installed on cars with old transmission housing, use flat washers with the old 8 mm bolts. Remove the torque converter.

8. Shift into P and disconnect the floor-shift linkage at the transmission.

9. Remove the accelerator and carbu-retor cable bracket at the transmission.

10. Unbolt the left side transmission car-rier from the transmission.

11. Unbolt the front transmission mount from the transmission.

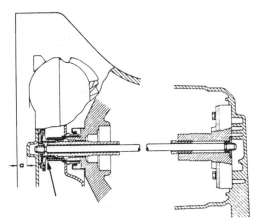

When attaching transmission to engine, be sure torque converter is seated on the one-way clutch support (arrow). When converter is properly seated, A = 1–3/16 in.

12. Unbolt the bottom of the engine from the transmission. Lift the transaxle slightly, swing the left driveshaft up, remove the rest of the bolts, pull the transmission off the mounting dowels, and lower the transaxle out of the car. Secure the converter so it doesn't fall out.

CAUTION: *Don't tilt the torque converter.*

To install the transaxle:

13. Push the transmission onto the mounting dowels and install two bolts. Be sure the torque converter is fully seated on the clutch support. The distance "A" should be 1³/₁₆ in. Lift the unit until the left driveshaft can be installed and install the rest of the bolts. Torque them to 39 ft lbs. Align the transmission the left mount must be in the center of the body mount. Dimension x on both sides should be equal.

14. Tighten the front transmission mount bolts to 39 ft lbs. Install the left side transmission carrier to the transmission.

15. Connect the accelerator and carbu-

Align the engine/transmission mount. Dimension X must be equal

retor cable bracket. Connect the floor-shift linkage.

16. Tighten the torque converter to drive plate bolts to 22 ft lbs. Torque the driveshaft bolts to 32 ft lbs.

17. Connect the speedometer cable and the battery cables.

PAN REMOVAL AND INSTALLATION, STRAINER SERVICE

NOTE: *As of transmission No 09096 a new, cleanable oil filter is used which requires a deeper oil pan. Also beginning with transmission number EQ-15 106, the drain plug was no longer installed in the oil pan.*

1. Remove the drain plug and let the fluid drain into a pan. If the pan has no drain plug, loosen the pan bolts until a corner of the pan can be lowered to drain the fluid.

2. Remove the pan bolts and take off the pan.

3. Discard the old gasket and clean the pan out. Be very careful not to get any threads or lint from rags into the pan.

4. The manufacturer says that the filter needn't be replaced unless the fluid is very dirty and burnt smelling. When replacing the strainer be carefull, the specified torque for the strainer screws is 2 ft lbs.

NOTE: *Beginning with Transmission number 13 03 8, there is an additional strainer under the valve body. When installing it, be sure it fits into the locating lug of the transfer plate.*

5. Replace the pan with a new gasket and tighten the bolts, in a criss-cross pattern, to 14 ft lbs.

6. Using a long-necked funnel, pour in 2½ qts of Dexron automatic transmission fluid through the dipstick tube. Start the engine and shift through all the transmission ranges with the car stationary. Check the level on the dipstick with the lever in Neutral. It should be up to the lower end of the dipstick. Drive the car until it is warmed up and re-check the level.

LINKAGE ADJUSTMENT

Check the cable adjustment as follows:

1. Run the engine at 1,000–1,200 rpm with the parking brake on.

2. Select Reverse—a drop in engine speed should be noticed.

3. Select Park—engine speed should increase. Pull the shift lever against Reverse, the engine speed shouldn't drop.

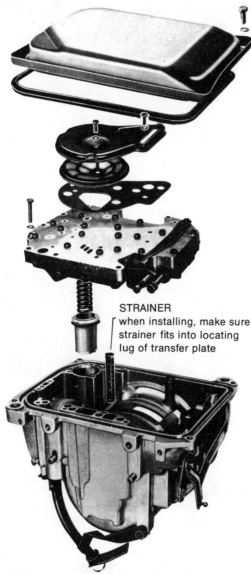

STRAINER
when installing, make sure
strainer fits into locating
lug of transfer plate

Beginning with transmission 13 03 8, an additional strainer is used beneath the valve body. It cannot be installed on earlier models.

4. Move the shift lever to Neutral—an increase in engine speed should be noticed.

5. Shift the lever into Drive—a noticeable drop in engine speed should result.

6. Shift into 1—the lever must engage without having to overcome any resistance.

7. To adjust the cable—Shift into Park. Loosen the cable clamp at the transmission end of the cable.

8. Press the transmission lever all the way to the left.

9. Hold the lever in place and tighten the cable clamp.

TRANSMISSION CABLE ADJUSTMENT

1. Make sure that the throttle is closed, the choke is off, and the fast idle cam is inoperative. Detach the cable end at the transmission.

2. Press the lever at the transmission end of the cable toward the cable.

3. You should be able to insert the cable end into the transmission lever without moving the lever.

4. Adjust the cable length to correct

SECOND GEAR (REAR BAND ADJUSTMENT)

NOTE: *The transmission must be horizontal when band adjustments are performed. You should have an in/LB torque wrench to properly perform this adjustment.*

1. Tighten the second gear band adjusting screw to 7.2 ft lb [86 in. lb].

2. Loosen the screw and tighten it again to 3.6 ft lb (43 in. lb).

3. Turn the screw out 2½ turns and then tighten the locknut.

NEUTRAL START SWITCH

The combination neutral start and backup light switch is mounted inside the shifter housing. The starter should operate in park or neutral only. To adjust:

1. Remove the cover and shift into park.

2. Loosen the clamp nut.

3. Push the shift lever to the left and tighten the clamp nut.

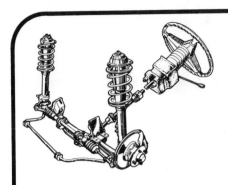

7

Suspension and Steering

FRONT SUSPENSION

The front suspension is a simple strut design. It consists of a lower control arm, ball joint, and suspension strut. In a MacPherson strut design, such as this, the shock absorber strut serves as a locating member of the suspension as well as a damper. A shock absorber insert is located inside the body of the strut. A concentric coil spring is the springing medium.

Ball Joint

The maximum allowable play (up and down) is 0.010 in.

REMOVAL AND INSTALLATION

1. Jack up the front of the car and support it on stands.
2. Matchmark the ball joint-to-control arm position.
3. Remove the retaining bolt and nut.
4. Pry the lower control arm and ball joint down and out of the strut.
5. Drill out the rivets and enlarge the holes to 9/32 in.
6. Remove the ball joint assembly.
7. Bolt new ball joint in place. Tighten the bolts to 18 ft lbs. Tighten the retaining bolt for the ball joint stud to 21 ft lbs.

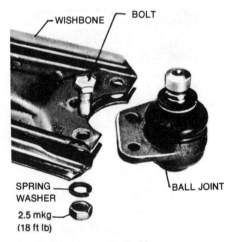

Service ball joints are bolted in

Shock Absorbers
TESTING

The function of a shock absorber is to dampen harsh spring movement and provide a means of dissipating the motion of the wheels so that the shocks encountered by the wheels are not totally transmitted to the body and, therefore, to you and your passengers. As the wheel moves up and down, the shock absorber shortens and lengthens, thereby imposing a restraint on movement by its hydraulic action.

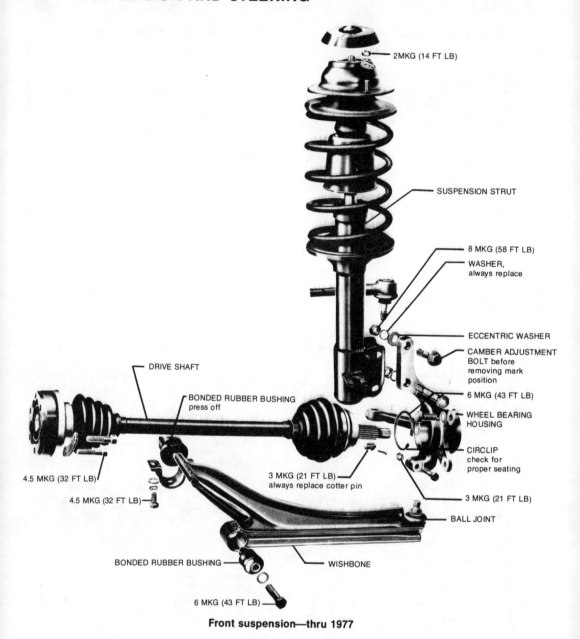

2MKG (14 FT LB)

SUSPENSION STRUT

8 MKG (58 FT LB)

WASHER, always replace

ECCENTRIC WASHER

CAMBER ADJUSTMENT BOLT before removing mark position

6 MKG (43 FT LB)

WHEEL BEARING HOUSING

CIRCLIP check for proper seating

DRIVE SHAFT

BONDED RUBBER BUSHING press off

3 MKG (21 FT LB) always replace cotter pin

3 MKG (21 FT LB)

BALL JOINT

4.5 MKG (32 FT LB)

4.5 MKG (32 FT LB)

BONDED RUBBER BUSHING

WISHBONE

6 MKG (43 FT LB)

Front suspension—thru 1977

A simple way to see if your shock absorbers are functioning correctly is to push one corner of the car down a few times. This will compress the spring on that side of the car as well as the shock absorber. If the shock absorber is functioning properly, it will control the spring's tendency to remain in motion. Thus the car will level itself almost instantly when you release the downward pressure. If the car continues to bounce up and down several times, the shock absorber is worn out and should be replaced. Examine the strut body for heavy oil streaking, which would in-

dicate shock leakage. Replace a leaky shock absorber.

REMOVAL AND INSTALLATION

Since the shock absorber cartridge is contained within the strut assembly, it's necessary to remove the strut and then the coil spring in order to remove the shock. A special VW tool is needed to remove the shock absorber retainer, so we recommend removing the strut yourself and then taking the assembly to a dealer or spring shop to have the spring compressed and removed and the new

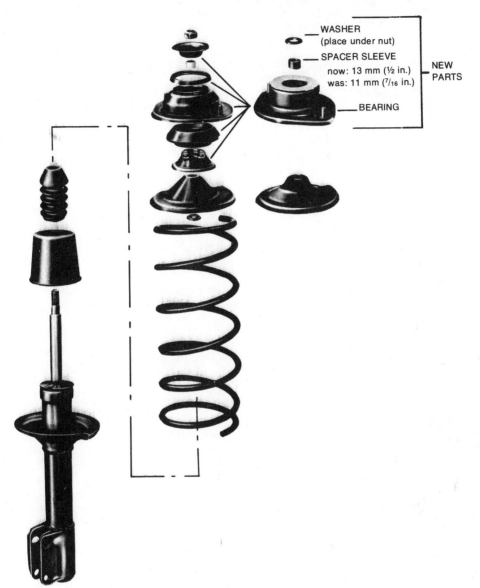

WASHER
(place under nut)

SPACER SLEEVE
now: 13 mm (½ in.)
was: 11 mm (⁷/₁₆ in.)

NEW
PARTS

BEARING

A modified front strut is used on 1978 and later models

shock absorber cartridge installed. Strut removal and installation is the major labor charge here, so you'll save that part of the expense and avoid the danger of compressing the spring.

Strut

REMOVAL AND INSTALLATION

1. With the car on the ground, remove the front axle nut. Loosen the wheel bolts.
2. Raise and support the front of the car. Remove the wheels.
3. Remove the brake caliper from the strut and hang it with wire. Detach the brake line clips from the strut.

4. At the tie-rod end, remove the cotter pin, back off the castellated nut, and pull the end off the strut with a puller.
5. Loosen the stabilizer bar bushings and detach the end from the strut being removed.
6. Remove the ball joint as described above.
7. Pull the axle driveshaft from the strut.
8. Remove the upper strut-to-fender retaining nuts.
9. Pull the strut assembly down and out of the car.
10. Installation is the reverse of removal. The axle nut is tightened to 180–216 ft lbs, lower control arm-to-strut 16 ft lbs, caliper-

to-strut 44 ft lbs and stabilizer to control arm 7 ft lbs.

COIL SPRING AND SHOCK ABSORBER SERVICE

Due to the necessity of using a spring compressor, these procedures are best left to a dealer or spring shop. To remove the spring, the strut must be mounted in a large vise, the spring compressed, the retaining nut and cover removed, and the spring slowly released. A special tool is needed to remove the shock absorber retainer, after which the shock absorber is easily removed. Assembly is the reverse of removal.

Axle Shaft

REMOVAL AND INSTALLATION

Axle shafts are retained to the transaxle by allen bolts. If the right shaft is being removed, disconnect the exhaust pipe and transaxle bracket. The axle shaft nut requires 180–215 ft. lbs torque.

1. Remove the axle shaft nut.
2. Remove the allen head bolts retaining the axle shaft to the transaxle.
3. Pull the axle shaft out and up and place it on top of the transaxle.
4. Turn the steering wheel all the way to the side of the shaft being removed. Pull the axle shaft from the steering knuckle.
5. Installation is the reverse of removal. The axle nut is tightened to 180–215 ft. lbs.

Front End Alignment

NOTE: *When checking wheel alignment, the car must be empty, tire pressure correct and on a level surface.*

CAMBER ADJUSTMENT

Camber angle is the number of degrees which the centerline of the wheel is inclined from the vertical. Camber reduces loading of the outer wheel bearing and improves the tire contact patch while cornering.

Camber is adjusted by loosening the nuts of the two bolts holding the top of the wheel bearing housing to the bottom of the strut, and turning the top eccentric bolt. The range of adjustment is 2°.

CASTER

Caster angle is the number of degrees in which a line drawn through the steering knuckle pivots is inclined from the vertical,

Top eccentric bolt provides camber adjustment

toward the front or rear of the car. Positive caster improves directional stability and decreases susceptibility to croswinds or road surface deviations. Other than the replacement of damaged suspension components, caster is not adjustable.

TOE-OUT

The front wheels on the Rabbit and Scirocco are set with a slight toe-in, rather than toe-out as on most front wheel drive cars. Most front wheel drive cars are set with toe-out to counteract the tendency of the driving wheels to toe-in excessively. Due to the design of the front suspension, toe-out is not necessary. Toe-in is the amount, measured in inches, that the wheels are closer together at the front than at the rear. Toe-in is checked with the wheels straight-ahead. One toe-rod linkage is adjustable. Loosen the nuts and clamps and adjust the length of the tie-rod for correct toe-in.

Toe-in is checked with the wheels straight-ahead. Only the right tie-rod is adjustable, but replacement left tie-rods are adjustable. Replacement left tie-rods should be set to the same length as the original. Toe-in should be adjusted only with the right tie-rod. If the steering wheel is crooked, remove and align it.

REAR SUSPENSION

The rear suspension consists of individual trailing arms connected by a cross-chassis torsion beam. Each wheel is suspended by a coil spring mounted over a shock absorber strut unit. The torsion beam acts as a rear stabilizer bar, twisting to resist body roll.

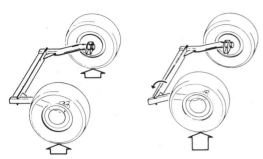

Suspension struts absorb the movement when both wheels move the same amount. When just one wheel moves, the torsion beam twists and acts as a stabilizer.

Shock Absorbers

REMOVAL AND INSTALLATION

The complete rear shock absorber strut must be removed from the car for shock absorber replacement. The same recommendation as the front shock replacement applies here. That is, to remove the strut yourself and then have the shock absorber replaced at a dealer or spring shop. This avoids the danger of compressing the spring yourself or having to purchase a spring compressing tool for a one time use.

1. Disconnect the strut from the body at the top.

2. Remove the through-bolt and nut at the bottom of the strut.

3. Remove the strut from the car.

4. Installation is the reverse of removal. Tighten the lower nut to 32 ft lbs.

Stub Axle

REMOVAL AND INSTALLATION

1. Remove the grease cap.

2. Remove the cotter pin, nutlock, adjusting nut, spacer, wheel bearing and brake drum.

3. Detach the brake line and plug it.

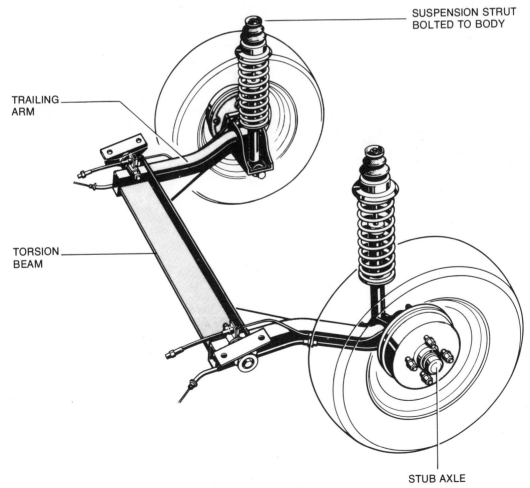

SUSPENSION STRUT BOLTED TO BODY

TRAILING ARM

TORSION BEAM

STUB AXLE

Rear suspension

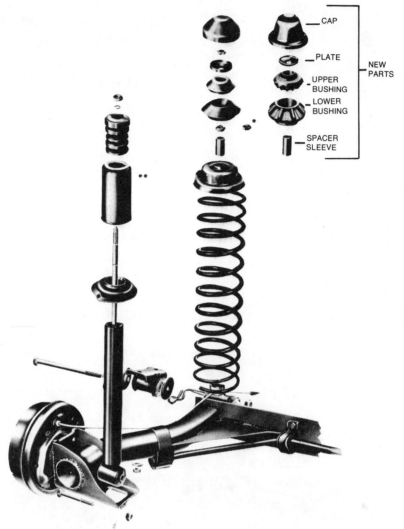

CAP

PLATE

UPPER
BUSHING

LOWER
BUSHING

SPACER
SLEEVE

NEW
PARTS

A modified rear strut is used on 1978 and later models

4. Remove the brake backing plate complete with brake asssembly.

5. Unbolt and remove the stub axle.

6. Installation is the reverse of removal. Always replace the spring washer with a new one and bleed the brakes. Pack the bearings and adjust the bearing end-play.

Wheel Bearing Adjustment

The wheel bearings are correctly adjusted when the thrust washer can be moved slightly with a screwdriver under finger pressure. Do not twist the screwdriver or lever it. Install a new cotter pin.

Rear wheel bearing adjustment

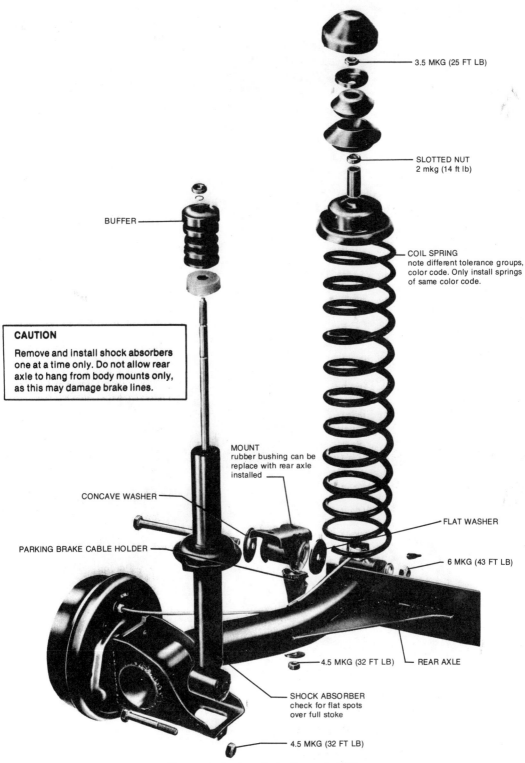

3.5 MKG (25 FT LB)

SLOTTED NUT
2 mkg (14 ft lb)

COIL SPRING
note different tolerance groups,
color code. Only install springs
of same color code.

BUFFER

CAUTION

Remove and install shock absorbers
one at a time only. Do not allow rear
axle to hang from body mounts only,
as this may damage brake lines.

MOUNT
rubber bushing can be
replace with rear axle
installed

CONCAVE WASHER

FLAT WASHER

PARKING BRAKE CABLE HOLDER

6 MKG (43 FT LB)

4.5 MKG (32 FT LB)

REAR AXLE

SHOCK ABSORBER
check for flat spots
over full stoke

4.5 MKG (32 FT LB)

Rear suspension strut—through 1977

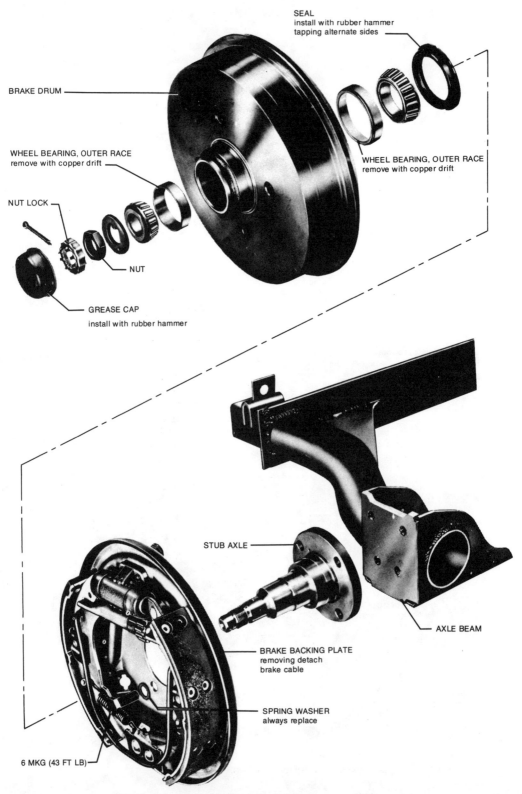

SEAL
install with rubber hammer
tapping alternate sides

BRAKE DRUM

WHEEL BEARING, OUTER RACE
remove with copper drift

WHEEL BEARING, OUTER RACE
remove with copper drift

NUT LOCK

NUT

GREASE CAP
install with rubber hammer

STUB AXLE

AXLE BEAM

BRAKE BACKING PLATE
removing detach
brake cable

SPRING WASHER
always replace

6 MKG (43 FT LB)

Stub axle removal

Wheel Alignment Specifications

| Year | Model | Caster ① | | Camber ① | | Toe-in ① (in.) | Steering Axis Inclination (deg) |
		Range (deg)	Preferred Setting (deg)	Range (deg)	Preferred Setting (deg)		
1975–78	All	1°20′P–2°20′P	1°50′P	10′N–50′P	20′P	30′N–5′N	

P—Positive
N—Negative
① Rear wheel caster, camber, toe-in not adjustable
  Front wheel caster is not adjustable

STEERING

The Rabbit and Scirocco are equipped with rack and pinion steering. The tie-rods are end-mounted. One tie-rod is adjustable. No maintenance is required on the rack and pinion.

Steering Wheel

REMOVAL AND INSTALLATION

1. Grasp the center cover pad and pull it from the wheel.
2. Loosen and remove the steering shaft nut.
3. Pull the wheel off the shaft.
4. Disconnect the horn wire.

5. Replace the wheel in the reverse order of removal. Tighten the nut to 36 ft lbs. With the front wheels straight ahead, the cancelling lug on the steering wheel points left.

Turn Signal Switch

1. Disconnect the battery ground cable.
2. Remove the steering wheel.
3. Remove the switch retaining screws.
4. Pry the switch housing off the column.
5. Disconnect the electrical plugs at the back of the switch.
6. Remove the switch housing.
7. Replace in the reverse order of removal.

NOTE: *Tap spacer sleeve into column*

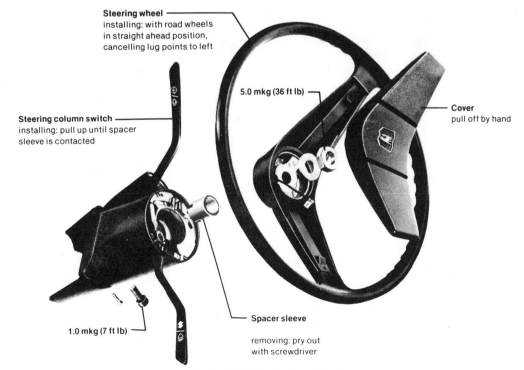

Steering wheel
installing: with road wheels in straight ahead position, cancelling lug points to left

5.0 mkg (36 ft lb)

Cover
pull off by hand

Steering column switch
installing: pull up until spacer sleeve is contacted

1.0 mkg (7 ft lb)

Spacer sleeve
removing: pry out with screwdriver

Typical Rabbit steering wheel

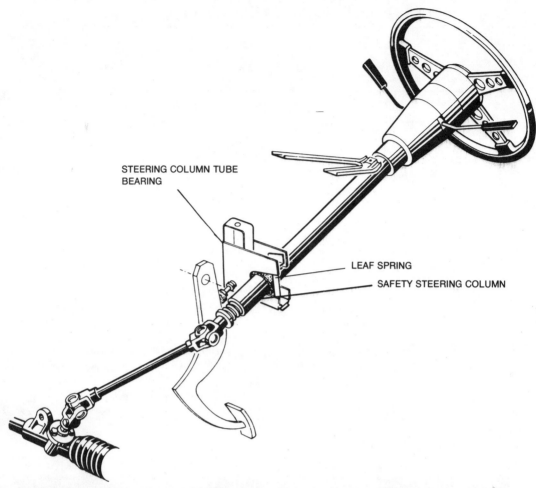

STEERING COLUMN TUBE
BEARING

LEAF SPRING

SAFETY STEERING COLUMN

Safety steering column. On manual transmission models, the column would disengage the leaf spring and pivot to the right on impact. On automatic transmission cars, the column swings to the side and telescopes in on impact.

(carefully) until there is 0.08–0.16 in. clearance between the wheel and the hub.

Ignition Switch and Steering Lock

REMOVAL AND INSTALLATION

NOTE: *The lock itself cannot be removed, only the cylinder. The acces hole for removing the lock cylinder may be missing. Before the lock cylinder can be removed, drill a hole according to following dimensions:*

a = .472 in. (12 mm)

b = .393 in. (10 mm)Drill the hole ⅛ in. deep.

Remove the steering wheel and turn signal switch. Remove the steering column shaft covers.

The lock is clamped to the steering column

with special bolts whose heads shear off on installation. These must be drilled out in order to remove the switch.

On replacement, make sure that the lock tang is ligned with the slot in the steering column.

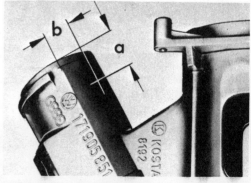

Lock cylinder removal—see text

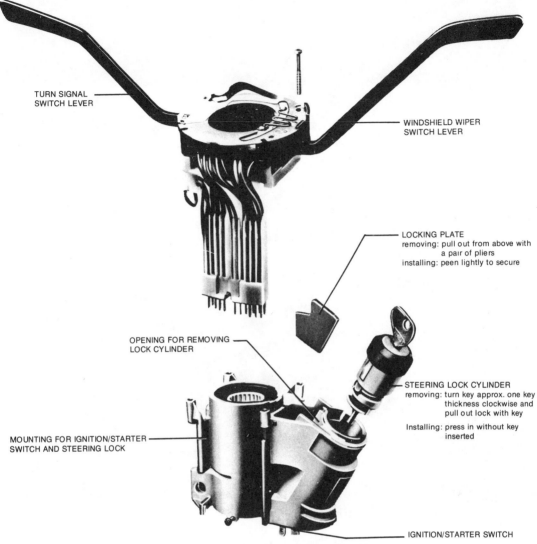

TURN SIGNAL
SWITCH LEVER

WINDSHIELD WIPER
SWITCH LEVER

LOCKING PLATE
removing: pull out from above with
a pair of pliers
installing: peen lightly to secure

OPENING FOR REMOVING
LOCK CYLINDER

STEERING LOCK CYLINDER
removing: turn key approx. one key
thickness clockwise and
pull out lock with key

Installing: press in without key
inserted

MOUNTING FOR IGNITION/STARTER
SWITCH AND STEERING LOCK

IGNITION/STARTER SWITCH

Steering lock/ignition switch—1975–76

Steering Gear

The steering rack should be installed with equal distances between housing on both sides. Tie-rods should also have an equal distance on both sides.

1. Disconnect the steering shaft U-joint and wire it out of the way.

2. Disconnect the tie rods at the steering rack and wire them out of the way.

Right side tie-rod adjustment

3. Remove the steering rack and drive.

4. Install the steering rack and drive and torque the attaching hardware to 14 ft. lbs.

5. Tighten the steering gear adjusting screw until it touches the thrust washer. Tighten the lock nut.

6. Install the steering shaft.

7. Check the front end alignment.

Steering Linkage

TIE-ROD REMOVAL AND INSTALLATION

1. Center the steering rack.

2. Remove the cotter pin and nut from the tie rod end.

TURN SIGNAL
SWITCH LEVER

WINDSHIELD WIPER
SWITCH LEVER

WEDGE
remove for inter-
mittent wiper operation

HEADLIGHT DIMMER SWITCH

STEERING LOCK
CYLINDER

MOUNTING FOR IGNITION/
STARTER SWITCH AND
STEERING LOCK
lock part/bearing
cannot be removed

IGNITION/STARTER SWITCH
removing:
pull steering column switch off
column. Remove set screw

Steering lock/ignition switch—1978 and later

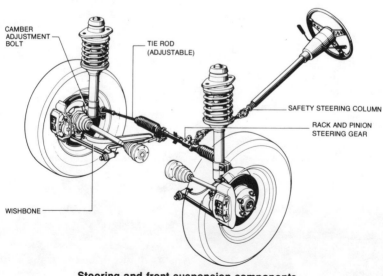

CAMBER
ADJUSTMENT
BOLT

TIE ROD
(ADJUSTABLE)

SAFETY STEERING COLUMN

RACK AND PINION
STEERING GEAR

WISHBONE

Steering and front suspension components

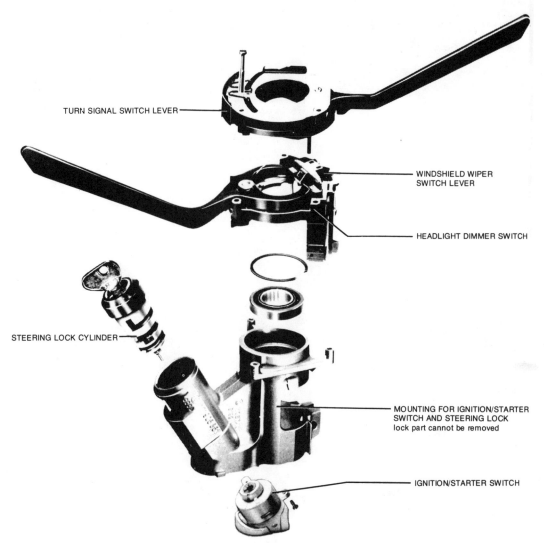

TURN SIGNAL SWITCH LEVER

WINDSHIELD WIPER
SWITCH LEVER

HEADLIGHT DIMMER SWITCH

STEERING LOCK CYLINDER

MOUNTING FOR IGNITION/STARTER
SWITCH AND STEERING LOCK
lock part cannot be removed

IGNITION/STARTER SWITCH

Steering lock/ignition switch—1977

3. Disconnect the tie rod from the steering rack.

4. If the right side tie rod is being replaced, adjust it to 15 in. (c) as illustrated.

5. Adjust the steering rack and tie rods as outlined in steps 5 and 6 of the Rabbit and Scirocco "Steering Gear Removal and Installation".

8

Brakes

BRAKE SYSTEM

The base equipment Rabbit is equipped with drum brakes. The optional Rabbit and all Sciroccos are equipped with front disc brakes and rear drum brakes. The braking system converts a tremendous amount of mechanical energy (forward motion of your car) into

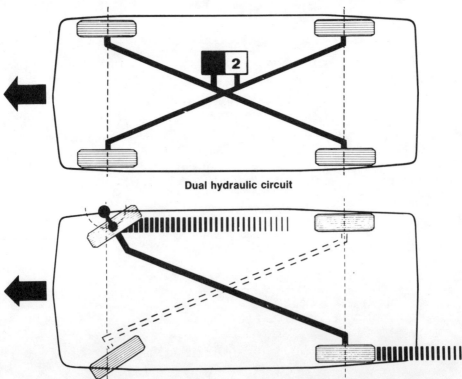

Dual hydraulic circuit

One front and one rear brake remain operational when one system fails

Brake Specifications
All measurements given are (in.) unless noted

Year	Model	Lug Nut Torque (ft/lb)	Master Cylinder Bore	Brake Disc		Brake Drum			Minimum Lining Thickness	
				Minimum Thickness	Maximum Run-Out	Diameter	Max. Machine O/S	Max. Wear Limit	Front	Rear
1975–78	All	65	0.82	0.41 ①	0.004	9.059–9.067 (front)	9.087 (front)	9.106 (front)	②	0.097 (riveted) 0.059 (bonded)
						7.086 (rear)	7.105 (rear)	7.125 (rear)		

NOTE: *Minimum lining thickness is as recommended by the manufacturer. Because of variations in state inspection regulations, the minimum allowable thickness may be different than recommended by the manufacturer.*
① New thickness—0.472 in. (stamped in disc)
   Do not remove more than 0.02 in. per side
② Drum brakes—Lining thickness w/o backing plate—0.157 in.
      Wear limit w/o backing plate—0.039 in.
      Lining thickness including backing plate—0.294 in.
      Wear limit including backing plate—0.176 in.

some other form of energy, in this case heat. When the brake pads (front) and linings (rear) come into contact with the discs and drums, the resultant friction stops the car by converting the mechanical energy into heat energy. This conversion takes place each time you step on the brake pedal.

Adjustment

The front disc brakes require no adjustment, as disc brakes automatically adjust themselves to compensate for pad wear. The drum brakes must be periodically adjusted, or whenever free travel is one third or more of the total pedal travel.
1. Raise the rear of the car. Place the jack

Drum brake adjustment

under the center of the torsion bar/axle. The jack pad should be at least 4 in. square, otherwise you may damage the axle.
2. Block the front wheels and release the parking brake. Step on the brake pedal hard to center the linings.
3. Remove the rubber plug from the rear of the backing plate on each wheel.
4. Insert a brake adjusting tool or wide-bladed screwdriver and turn the adjuster wheel until the brakes drag as you turn the tire/wheel.
5. Turn the adjuster in the opposite direction and back it off two notches.
6. Repeat on the other wheel.
7. Lower the car and road-test. Readjust, if necessary.

Wheel Bearings

NOTE: *For rear wheel bearing adjustment, see Suspension and Steering, Chapter 7.*
There is no front wheel bearing adjustment. The bearing is pressed into the steering knuckle. The axle nut torque of 167 ft lbs (tightened with the wheels on the ground) is all that is necessary.

HYDRAULIC SYSTEM

The hydraulic system is a dual circuit type which has the advantage of retaining 50%

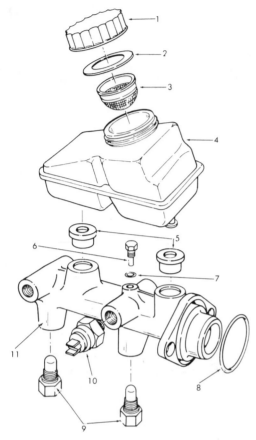

1. Reservoir cap
2. Washer
3. Filter screen
4. Reservoir
5. Master cylinder plugs
6. Stop screw
7. Stop screw seal
8. Master cylinder seal
9. Residual pressure valves
10. Warning light sender unit
11. Brake master cylinder housing

Master cylinder body and reservoir

braking effectiveness in the event of failure in one system. The circuits are arranged so that you always have one front and one rear brake for a more controlled emergency stop. The right front and left rear are one circuit; the left front and right rear the second circuit. The dual master cylinder is attached to the brake booster which is in turn bolted to the firewall. The booster uses intake manifold vacuum to provide pedal assist. The booster is used because the front discs require more effort than drum brakes.

The brake pedal/booster assembly is linked to the master cylinder by a pushrod and yoke. Since brake fluid cannot be compressed (liquids are not compressible), step-

ping on the brake pedal causes the master cylinder pistons to transmit hydraulic pressure to the brake unit at each wheel. This pressure is transmitted through the brake lines.

The brake failure unit is a hydraulic valve/electrical switch will alert you of brake problems via the warning light on the dashboard. A piston inside the switch is kept centered by one brake system's pressure on one side and the other system's pressure on the opposite side. Should a failure occur in one system, the piston would go to the "Bad" side and complete an electrical circuit to the warning lamp. This switch also functions as a parking brake reminder light and will go out when the brake is released.

Master Cylinder
REMOVAL AND INSTALLATION

1. To prevent brake fluid from spilling out and damaging the paint, place a protective cover over the fender.

2. Disconnect and plug the brake lines.

3. Disconnect the electrical plug from the sending unit for the brake failure switch.

4. Remove the two master cylinder mounting nuts.

5. Lift the master cylinder and reservoir out of the engine compartment being careful not to spill any fluid on the fender. Empty out and discard the brake fluid.

CAUTION: *Do not depress the brake pedal while the master cylinder is removed.*

6. Position the master cylinder and reservoir assembly onto the studs for the booster and install the washers and nuts. Tighten the nuts to no more than 10 ft lbs.

7. Remove the plugs and connect the brake lines.

8. Bleed the entire brake system as explained further on in this chapter.

OVERHAUL

Purchase a genuine VW overhaul kit and sufficient brake fluid before starting this procedure.

1. Remove the master cylinder from the booster.

2. Firmly mount the master cylinder in a vise. Use clean rags to protect the cylinder from the vise jaws.

3. Grasp the plastic reservoir and pull it out of the rubber plugs. Remove the plugs.

4. Remove the stop-screw from the

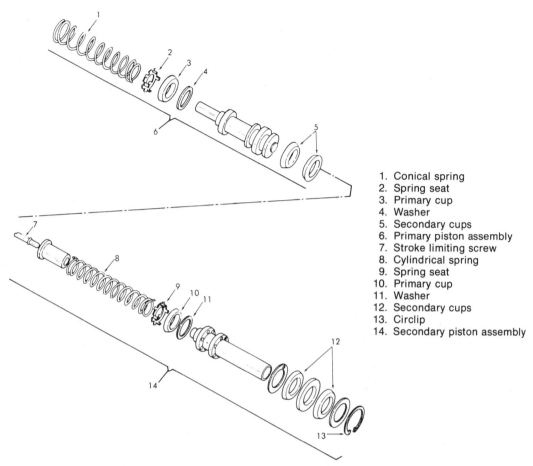

1. Conical spring
2. Spring seat
3. Primary cup
4. Washer
5. Secondary cups
6. Primary piston assembly
7. Stroke limiting screw
8. Cylindrical spring
9. Spring seat
10. Primary cup
11. Washer
12. Secondary cups
13. Circlip
14. Secondary piston assembly

Exploded view of master cylinder components (vehicles with brake booster)

center of the cylinder. Discard the stop screw seal, a new one is in the kit.

5. At the end of the master cylinder is a snap-ring (circlip); remove it, using snap-ring pliers.

6. Shake out the secondary piston assembly. If the primary piston remains lodged in the bore, it can be forced by applying conpressed air to the open brake line fitting.

7. Disassemble the secondary piston. The two secondary rings will be replaced with those in the rebuilding kit. Save the washers and spacers.

8. Carefully clamp the secondary piston, slightly compress the spring and screw out the stroke limiting bolt.

9. Remove the secondary piston stop sleeve bolt, spring, spring seat, and support washer.

10. Replace all parts with those supplied in the overhaul kit.

11. Clean all metal parts in denatured alchol and dry them with compressed air.

12. Check every part you are reusing. Pay close attention to the cylinder bores. If there is any scoring or rust, have the master cylinder honed or replace it.

13. Lightly coat the bores and cups with brake fluid. Assemble the cylinder components in the exact sequence shown in the illustration.

14. Install the primary piston assembly, notice that the primary spring is conically shaped. Be sure that you aren't using the secondary spring.

NOTE: *Since April 1977, the primary clip and piston seal (in Teves master cylinders) have number of small grooves on the lips. The new version have a groove (B) and chamfer (A) and can be installed in place of earlier versions, identified by a silver strip around the seal.*

15. Using a plastic rod or other nonmetallic tool, push the primary piston assembly into the housing until the stop bolt (with a new seal) can be screwed in and tightened.

16. Assemble the secondary piston. Fasten the spring, spring seat, primary cup, and

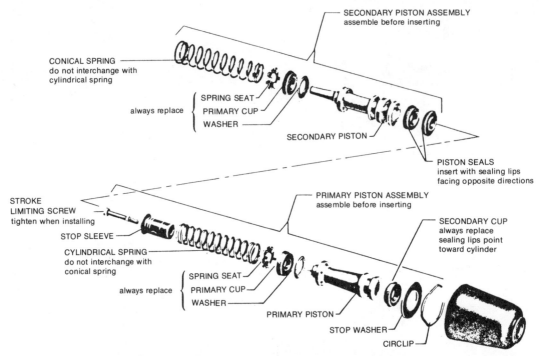

Exploded view of master cylinder without brake booster

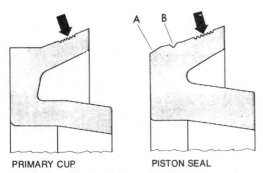

PRIMARY CUP   PISTON SEAL

On Teves master cylinder, the primary cup has a number of grooves and the identification of the piston seal has been changed (A = chamfer, B = groove)

stop sleeve to the piston with the stroke limiting bolt.

17. Assemble the remaining master cylinder components in the reverse order of disassembly. Ensure that the snap-ring is fully seated and that the piston caps are properly positioned. Install the secondary piston with master cylinder opening facing down.

18. Install and tighten the brake failure warning sending unit.

Bleeding

Anytime a brake line has been disconnected the hydraulic system should be bled. The brakes should also be bled when the pedal travel becomes unusually long ("soft pedal") or the car pulls to one side during braking. The proper bleeding sequence is: right rear wheel, left rear wheel, right front caliper, and left front caliper. You'll need a helper to pump the brake pedal while you open the bleeder valves.

NOTE: *If the system has been drained, first refill it with fresh brake fluid. Following the above sequence, open each bleeder valve by ½ to ¾ of a turn and pump the brake pedal until fluid runs out of the valve. Proceed with the bleeding as outlined below.*

1. Remove the bleeder valve dust cover and install a rubber bleeder hose.

2. Insert the other end of the hose into a container about ⅓ full of brake fluid.

3. Have an assistant pump the brake pedal several times until the pedal pressure increases.

4. Hold the pedal under pressure and then start to open the bleeder valve about ½ to ¾ of a turn. At this point, have your assistant depress the pedal all the way and then quickly close the valve. The helper should allow the pedal to return slowly

NOTE: *Keep a close check on the brake fluid in the reservoir and top it up as necessary throughout the bleeding process.*

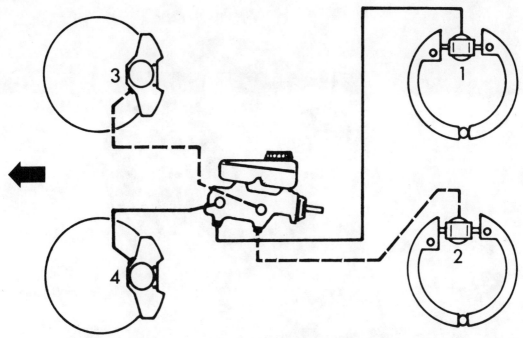

Proper brake bleeding sequence

5. Keep repeating this procedure until no more air bubbles can be seen coming from the hose in the brake fluid.

6. Remove the bleeder hose and install the dust cover.

7. Continue the bleeding at each wheel in sequence.

NOTE: *Don't splash any brake fluid on the paintwork. Brake fluid is very corrosive and will eat paint away. Any fluid accidentally spilled on the body should be immediately flushed off with water.*

FRONT DISC BRAKES

The Rabbit and Scirocco use single piston, floating caliper disc brakes. In this design, the single piston forces one pad against the rotating brake disc. Counter pressure forces against the floating frame and the frame then pushes the second pad into the disc. The advantages of the floating caliper are, better heat dissipation, simpler repairs, fewer leaks, and less sensitivity to variance in disc thickness and parallelism.

Brake Pads

REMOVAL AND INSTALLATION

Brake pads should be replaced when there is no visible clearance between the pads and the cross-spring or when they are worn to a thickness of ¼ in. (6mm).

NOTE: *Most models are equipped with brake pad wear indicators. When the pad is worn, a lug on the pad contacts the disc causing a pulsation in the brake pedal.*

1. Jack up the front of the car and support it on stands. Remove the wheels.

2. Pry the clip out of both retaining pins.

3. While pressing down on the cross-spring, push the pad retaining pins out with a drift or small screwdriver.

4. Reference mark positions of the brake pads if they are being reused.

5. Remove the cross-spring from the caliper.

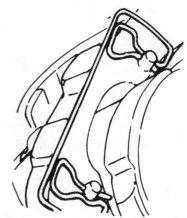

Retaining clip

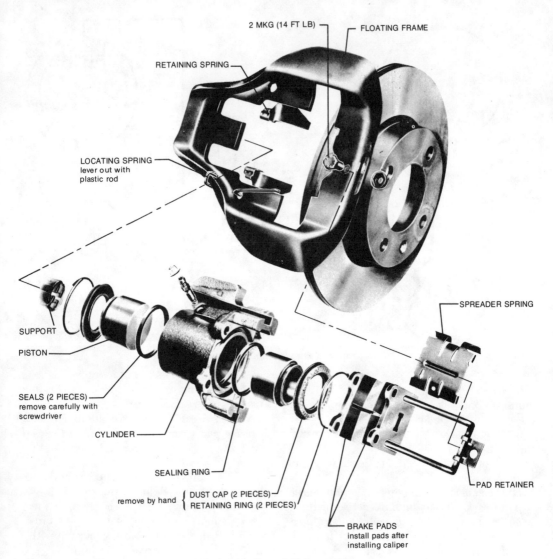

2 MKG (14 FT LB)

FLOATING FRAME

RETAINING SPRING

LOCATING SPRING
lever out with
plastic rod

SUPPORT

PISTON

SEALS (2 PIECES)
remove carefully with
screwdriver

CYLINDER

SEALING RING

remove by hand { DUST CAP (2 PIECES)
RETAINING RING (2 PIECES)

SPREADER SPRING

PAD RETAINER

BRAKE PADS
install pads after
installing caliper

Exploded view of Girling caliper

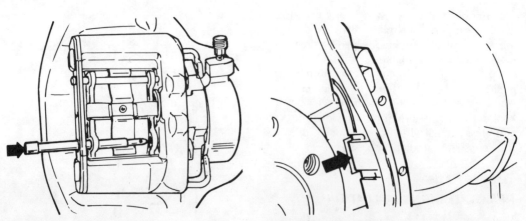

Removing retaining pins

Outer brake pad notch

6. Remove the inner brake pad. VW has a special tool for this purpose, but by using a small drift or punch you can pry the pad out of the caliper until it can be gripped by a pair of pliers and removed.

7. The outer brake pad is positioned in a notch. Use a flat, smooth piece of hardwood or metal to press the floating caliper frame and piston cylinder outward.

8. Grip the outer pad and remove it. Press the piston back into the cylinder with a flat piece of wood or metal.

9. Siphon out about half of the brake fluid in the reservoir to prevent it from overflowing when the piston is pushed in and new thicker pads are inserted.

10. Check that the piston is at the proper 20° angle. Make a gauge out of stiff cardboard.

11. Install the brake pads into the caliper. NOTE: *Replace used pads in the side of the caliper from which they were removed. When installing new pads always replace the pads on the opposite wheel at the same time.*

12. Position the cross-spring in the caliper and then carefully tap the pad retaining pins

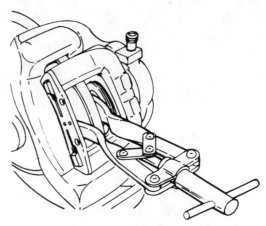

Pressing the piston in for pad installation

into place with a small hammer. Install the pin clip.

Calipers
REMOVAL AND INSTALLATION

1. Jack up the front of the car and support it on stands.

2. Remove the brake pads as outlined above.

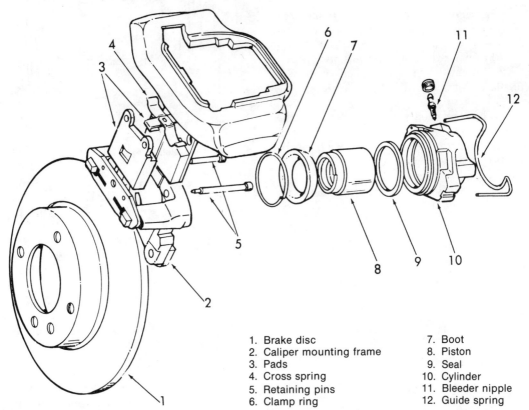

1. Brake disc
2. Caliper mounting frame
3. Pads
4. Cross spring
5. Retaining pins
6. Clamp ring
7. Boot
8. Piston
9. Seal
10. Cylinder
11. Bleeder nipple
12. Guide spring

Exploded view of the Teves caliper. Two types of calipers (Teves and Girling) are used. Both are very similar.

Checking piston positioning

3. If you are removing the caliper for overhaul, disconnect and plug the brake line at the caliper. If not, do not remove the hose—hang it by a wire.

4. Remove the two caliper-to-strut retaining bolts and remove the caliper.

5. Install the caliper using the reverse of the removal procedure. Tighten the two retaining bolts to 43 ft lbs.

6. Bleed the brakes.

OVERHAUL

NOTE: *Purchase a genuine VW overhaul kit and sufficient brake fluid before starting.*

1. Remove the caliper as outlined above.

2. Mount the caliper in a soft-jawed vise or place cloths over the jaws to protect the caliper.

3. Pry the fixed mounting frame off the floating frame.

4. Separate the caliper cylinder from the floating frame by prying it and the guide spring off the frame. Use a brass drift to lightly tap on the cylinder and place a piece of wood under the piston to protect it.

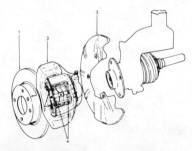

1. Brake disc   4. Brake pads
2. Retaining pins   5. Splash shield
3. Brake caliper

Caliper and disc mounting

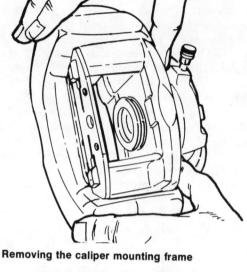

Removing the caliper mounting frame

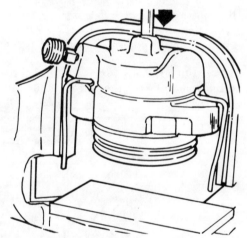

Removing the caliper cylinder

5. Using pliers remove the piston clamp ring. Remove and discard the rubber dust cover, a new one is supplied with the rebuilding kit.

6. Remove the piston from the cylinder. If it is stubborn, remove the bleeder screw and blow it out with compressed air.

CAUTION: *Hold the piston over a block of wood when doing this as the piston will fly out with considerable force.*

7. When the piston pops out of the caliper, remove the rubber seal with a wood or plastic pin to avoid damaging the seal groove.

8. Clean all metal parts in denatured alcohol. Never use a mineral based solvent such as gasoline, kerosene, acetone or the like. These solvents deteriorate rubber parts. Inspect the pistons and their bores. They

must be free of scoring and pitting. Replace the cylinder if there is any damage.

9. Discard all rubber parts. The caliper rebuilding kit includes new boots and seals which should be used as the caliper is reassembled.

10. Lightly coat the cylinder bore, piston, and seal with brake assembly paste or fresh brake fluid.

11. Using a vice, install the piston into the cylinder.

12. Position the guide spring in the groove of the brake cylinder and, using a brass drift, install the cylinder on the floating frame.

13. Place the mounting frame in the guide spring and slip it onto the floating frame. The fixed frame has two grooves which position it over the raised ribs of the floating frame.

14. Install pads, caliper, and bleed the brakes.

Brake Disc

INSPECTION AND CHECKING

Brake discs may be checked for lateral runout while installed on the car. This check will require a dial indicator gauge and stand to mount it on the caliper. VW has a special tool for this purpose which mounts the dial indicator to the caliper, but it can also be mounted on the shaft of a C-clamp attached to the outside of the caliper.

1. Remove the wheel and reinstall the wheel bolts (tightened to 65 ft lbs) to retain the disc to the hub.

2. Mount the dial indicator securely to the caliper. The feeler should touch the disc about ½ in. below the outer edge.

3. Rotate the disc and observe the gauge. Radial run-out (wobble) must not exceed 0.004 in. (0.1 mm). A disc which exceeds this specification must be replaced or refinished.

4. Brake discs which have excessive radial run-out, sharp ridges, or scoring can be refinished. First grinding must be done on both sides of the disc to prevent squeaking and vibrating. Discs which have only light grooves and are otherwise acceptable can be used without refinishing.

The standard disc is 0.47 in. (12 mm) thick. It should not be ground to less than 0.39 in. (11 mm).

REMOVAL AND INSTALLATION

1. Loosen the wheel bolts. Remove the hub cap.

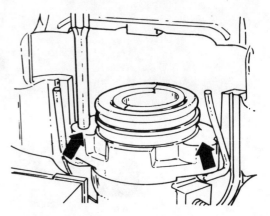

Installing the cylinder

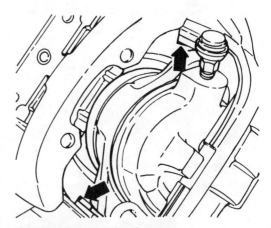

Installing the mounting frame

2. Jack up the front of the car and place it on stands. Remove the wheel(s).

3. Remove the caliper as outlined above.

4. Remove the disc-to-hub retaining screw.

5. Grip the disc with both hands and give it a sharp pull to remove it. A stubborn disc should be removed with a puller. Never strike the disc with a hammer.

6. The disc is installed in the reverse order of removal. Don't forget to install the retaining screw. Install the caliper and bleed the brakes.

7. Install the wheel and lower the car. Tighten the wheel bolts diagonally to 65 ft lbs. This is doubly important because the bolts not only retain the wheels, but attach the disc to the hub.

DRUM BRAKES

NOTE: *The following information applies to both front and rear brakes.*

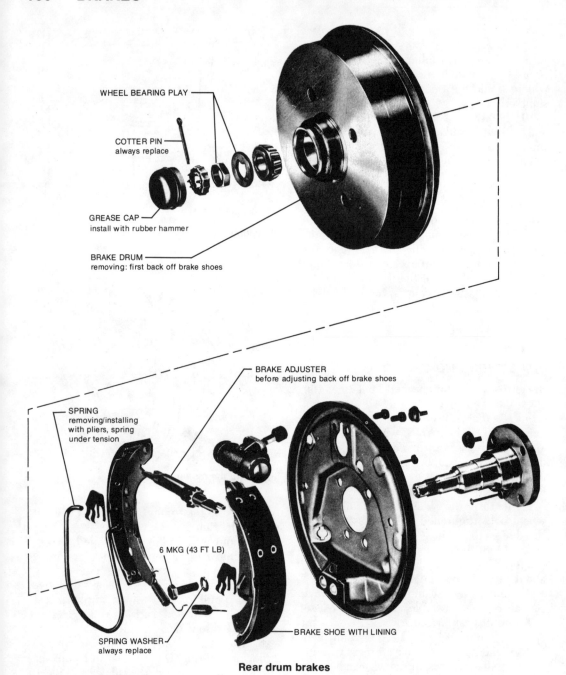

WHEEL BEARING PLAY

COTTER PIN
always replace

GREASE CAP
install with rubber hammer

BRAKE DRUM
removing: first back off brake shoes

BRAKE ADJUSTER
before adjusting back off brake shoes

SPRING
removing/installing
with pliers, spring
under tension

6 MKG (43 FT LB)

SPRING WASHER
always replace

BRAKE SHOE WITH LINING

Rear drum brakes

Brake Drums

REMOVAL AND INSTALLATION

1. Loosen the wheel bolts.
2. Jack up the rear of the car and support it on stands. Remove the wheel(s).
3. Pry off the hub cap.
4. Remove and discard the cotter pin.
5. Remove the castellated nut, hex nut, and washers.

6. Pull off the brake drum. Be careful not to lose the inner race of the outer bearing.

NOTE: *If the brake drum is stubborn, remove the rubber cover at the backing plate and back off the brake adjuster with an adjusting tool or wide-bladed screwdriver. If this doesn't work, use a puller. Never heat the drum or beat on it with a hammer.*

7. Check the brake drum for any cracks,

scores, grooves, or an out-of-round condition. Replace a drum which shows cracking. Smooth light scoring with fine emery cloth. If scoring is extensive have the drum turned. Never have a drum turned more than 0.03 in.

8. The stub axle bearings in the brake drum must be pressed out for replacement. Take the drum(s) to a competent machinist to have them removed. Always use new seals on reassembly.

9. After greasing the bearings and installing them in the drum with new seals, place the drum onto the stub axle.

10. Install the washer and the hex nut. Tighten the nut and then loosen it. Retighten the nut slightly so that the washer between the nut and the bearing can just be moved with a screwdriver (refer to the illustration). Correct bearing play is 0.0012–.0027 in in (0.03–.03mm).

11. Install the castellated nut and insert a new cotter pin. Fill the hub cap with grease and install it.

12. Install the wheel and lower the car.

Brake Shoes

REMOVAL AND INSTALLATION

NOTE: *Only do one side at a time. This way, you will always have one side intact as a reference.*

1. Remove the brake drum.

2. Using pliers, disconnect the lower spring.

3. Disconnect the anchor spring and pins from each shoe.

4. Detach the parking brake cable by pressing back the spring with needlenose pliers and then disconnecting the cable at the lever.

5. Remove the second lower spring.

6. Raise up brake shoe from the bottom and remove the adjusting mechanism.

7. Lift the brake shoes and remove the upper springs. Remove both brake shoes.

8. Clean and inspect all brake parts. Spray solvents are available for brake cleaning which do not affect linings. Do not spray rubber parts with solvent.

9. Check the wheel cylinders for boot condition and leaking.

10. Inspect the replacement shoes for nicks or burrs, lubricate the backing plate contact points with Lubriplate®, lubricate the brake cable, lever and adjuster, and then assemble.

11. Reverse the removal procedure for assembly. When completed, install the drum and make an initial adjustment by turning the adapter wheel until a slight drag is felt between the shoes and drum, and back off about ¼ turn. Complete adjustment as described earlier in this chapter.

Wheel Cylinders

REMOVAL AND INSTALLATION

1. Remove the brake shoes.

2. Loosen the brake line on the rear of the cylinder, but do not pull the line away from the cylinder or it may bend.

3. Remove the bolts and lockwashers that attach the wheel cylinder to the backing plate and remove the cylinder.

4. Position the new wheel cylinder on the backing plate and install the cylinder attaching bolts and lockwashers.

5. Attach the metal brake line or rubber hose by reversing the procedure given in step two or three.

6. Install the brakes and bleed the brake system.

OVERHAUL

1. Remove the brakes.

2. Place a bucket or some old newspapers under the brake backing plate to catch the brake fluid that will run out of the wheel cylinder.

3. Remove the boots from the ends of the wheel cylinders.

4. Push one piston toward the center of the cylinder to force the opposite piston and

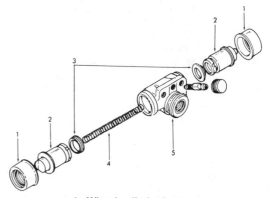

1. Wheel cylinder boot
2. Piston
3. Cup
4. Wheel cylinder spring
5. Wheel cylinder housing

Exploded view of brake cylinder

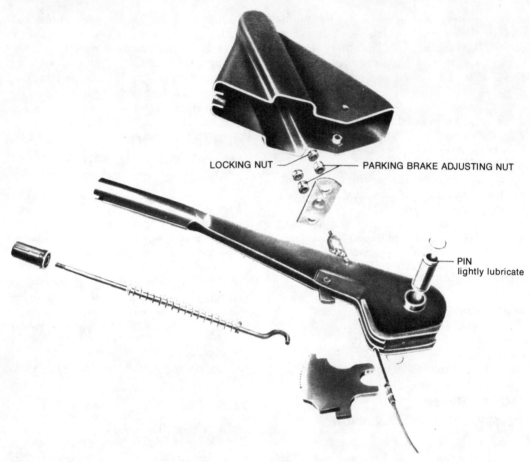

LOCKING NUT — PARKING BRAKE ADJUSTING NUT

PIN
lightly lubricate

Parking brake handle assembly

cup out the other end of the cylinder. Reach in the open end of the cylinder and push the spring, cup, and piston out of the cylinder.

5. Remove the bleeder screw from the rear of the cylinder, on the back of the backing plate.

6. Inspect the inside of the wheel cylinder. If it is scored in any way, the cylinder must be honed with a wheel cylinder hone or fine emery paper, and finished with crocus cloth if emery paper is used. If the inside of the cylinder is excessively worn, the cylinder will have to be replaced, as only 0.003 in. of material can be removed from the cylinder walls. Whenever honing or cleaning wheel cylinders, keep a small amount of brake fluid in the cylinder to serve as a lubricant.

7. Clean any foreign matter from the pistons. The sides of the pistons must be smooth for the wheel cylinders to operate properly.

8. Clean the cylinder bore with alcohol and a lint-free rag. Pull the rag through the bore several times to remove all foreign matter and dry the cylinder.

9. Install the bleeder screw and the return spring in the cylinder.

10. Coat new cylinder cups with new brake fluid and install them in the cylinder. Make sure that they are square in the bore or they will leak.

11. Install the pistons in the cylinder after coating them with new brake fluid.

12. Coat the insides of the boots with new brake fluid and install them on the cylinder. Install and bleed the brakes.

PARKING BRAKE

The parking brake activates the rear brake shoes through a cable attached to the lever between the seats.

Cable
ADJUSTMENT

Parking brake adjustment is made at the cable end nuts on top of the handbrake lever.

1. Block the front wheels. Jack up the rear

Adjusting parking brake handle assembly

of the car high enough for you to slide under. Support the car with a jackstand.

2. Apply the parking brake so that the lever is on the second notch.

3. Slide directly under the passenger compartment.

4. Tighten the compensator nut until both rear wheels can just be turned by hand.

5. Release the parking brake lever and check that both wheels can be easily turned.

6. Lubricate the compensator with chassis grease.

9

Body

The list of tools and equipment you may need to fix minor body damage ranges from very basic hand tools to a wide assortment of specialized body tools. Most minor scratches, dings and rust holes can be fixed using an electric drill, wire wheel or grinder attachment, half-round plastic file, sanding block, various grades of sandpaper (#120, which is coarse through #600, which is fine, in both wet and dry types), auto body plastic, primer, touch-up paint, spreaders, newspaper and masking tape. If you intend to try straightening any dents, you'll probably also need a slide hammer (dent puller).

Most auto body repair kits contain all the materials you need to do the job right in the kit. So, if you have a small rust spot or dent you want to fix, check the contents of the kit before you run out and buy any additional tools.

ALIGNING BODY PANELS

Doors

There are several methods of adjusting doors. Your vehicle will probably use one of those illustrated.

Whenever a door is removed and is to be reinstalled, you should matchmark the position of the hinges on the door pillars. The holes of the hinges and/or the hinge attaching points are usually oversize to permit alignment of doors. The striker plate is also moveable, through oversize holes, permitting up-and-down, in-and-out and fore-and-aft movement. Fore-and-aft movement is made by adding or subtracting shims from behind the striker and pillar post. The striker should be adjusted so that the door closes fully and remains closed, yet enters the lock freely.

DOOR HINGES

Don't try to cover up poor door adjustment with a striker plate adjustment. The gap on each side of the door should be equal and uniform and there should be no metal-to-metal contact as the door is opened or closed.

1. Determine which hinge bolts must be loosened to move the door in the desired direction.

2. Loosen the hinge bolt(s) just enough to allow the door to be moved with a padded pry bar.

3. Move the door a small amount and check the fit, after tightening the bolts. Be sure that there is no bind or interference with adjacent panels.

4. Repeat this until the door is properly positioned, and tighten all the bolts securely.

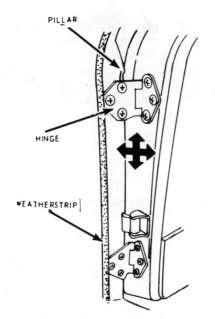

Door hinge adjustment

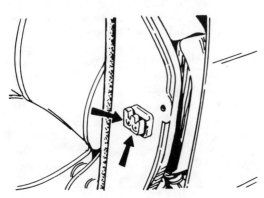

Move the door striker as indicated by arrows

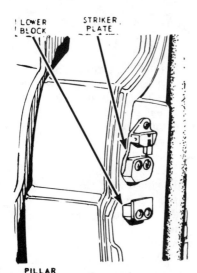

Striker plate and lower block

Hood, Trunk or Tailgate

As with doors, the outline of hinges should be scribed before removal. The hood and trunk can be aligned by loosening the hinge bolts in their slotted mounting holes and moving the hood or trunk lid as necessary. The hood and trunk have adjustable catch locations to regulate lock engagement bumpers at the front and/or rear of the hood provide a vertical adjustment and the hood lockpin can be adjusted for proper engagement.

The tailgate on the station wagon can be adjusted by loosening the hinge bolts in their slotted mounting holes and moving the tailgate on its hinges. The latchplate and

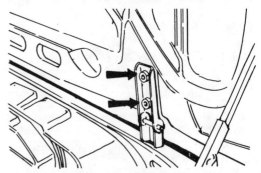

Loosen the hinge boots to permit fore-and-aft and horizontal adjustment

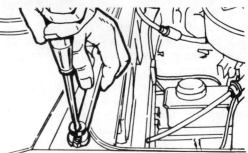

The hood is adjusted vertically by stop-screws at the front and/or rear

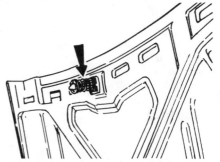

The hood pin can be adjusted for proper lock engagement

latch striker at the bottom of the tailgate opening can be adjusted to stop rattle. An adjustable bumper is located on each side.

RUST, UNDERCOATING, AND RUSTPROOFING

Rust

About the only technical information the average backyard mechanic needs to know about rust is that it is an electro-chemical process that works from **the inside out** on unprotected ferrous metals such as steel and iron. Salt, pollution, humidity—these things and more create and promote the formation of rust. You can't stop rust once it starts. Once rust has started on a fender or a body panel, the only sure way to stop it is to replace the part.

It's a lot easier to prevent rust than to remove it, especially if you have a new car and most late model cars are pretty well rustproofed when the leave the factory. In the early seventies, it seemed like cars were rusting out faster than you could pay them off and Detroit (and the imports) realized that this is not exactly the way you build customer loyalty.

Undercoating

Contrary to what most people think, the primary purpose of undercoating is not to prevent rust, but to deaden noise that might otherwise be transmitted to the car's interior. Since cars are pretty quiet these days anyway, dealers are only too willing to promote undercoating as a rust preventative. Undercoating will of course, prevent some rust, but only if applied when the car is brand-new. In any case, undercoating doesn't provide the protection that a good rustproofing does. If you do decide to undercoat your car and it's not brand-new, you have a big clean-up job ahead of you. It's a good idea to have the underside of the car professionally steam-cleaned and save yourself a lot of work. Spraying undercoat on dirty or rusty parts is only going to make things worse, since the undercoat will trap any rust causing agents.

Rustproofing

The best thing you can do for a new or nearly new car is to have it properly rust-proofed. There are two ways you can go about this. You can do it yourself, or you can have one of the big rustproofing companies do it for you. Naturally, it's going to cost you a lot more to have a big company do it, but it's worth it if your car is new or nearly new. If you own an older car that you plan to hang onto for a while, then doing it yourself might be the best idea. Professional rust-proofing isn't cheap ($100–$250), but it's definitely worth it if your car is new. The rustproofing companies won't guarantee their jobs on cars that are over three months old or have more than about 3000 miles on them because they feel the corrosion process may have already begun.

If you have an older car that hasn't started to rust yet, the best idea might be to purchase one of the do-it-yourself rustproofing kits that are available, and do the job yourself.

Drain Holes

Rusty rocker panels are a common problem on nearly every car, but they can be prevented by simply drilling some holes in your rocker panels to let the water out, or keeping the ones that are already there clean and unclogged. Most cars these days have a series of holes in the rocker panels to prevent moisture collection there, but they frequently become clogged up. Just use a small screwdriver or penknife to keep them clean. If your car doesn't have drain holes, it's a simple matter to drill a couple of holes in each panel.

Repairing Minor Body Damage

Unless your car just rolled off the showroom floor, chances are it has a few minor scratches or dings in it somewhere, or a small rust spot you've been meaning to fix. You just haven't been able to decide whether or not you can really do the job. Well, if the damage is anything like that presented here, there are a number of auto body repair kits that contain everything you need to repair minor scratches, dents, and rust spots. Even rust holes can be repaired if you use the correct kit. If you're unsure of your ability, start out with a small scratch. Once you've mastered small scratches and dings, you can work your way up to the more complicated repairs. When doing rust repairs, remember that unless all the rust is removed, it's going to come back in a year or less. Just sanding the rust down and applying some paint won't work.

Repairing Minor Surface Rust and Scratches

1. Just about everybody has a minor rust spot or scratches on their car. Spots such as these can be easily repaired in an hour or two. You'll need some sandpaper, masking tape, primer, and a can of touch-up paint.

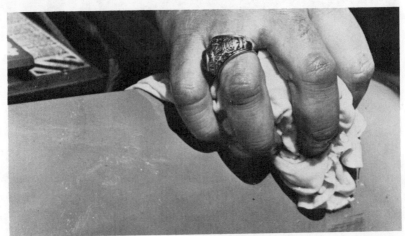

2. The first step is to wash the area down to remove all traces of dirt and road grime. If the car has been frequently waxed, you should wipe it with thinner or some other wax remover so that the paint will stick.

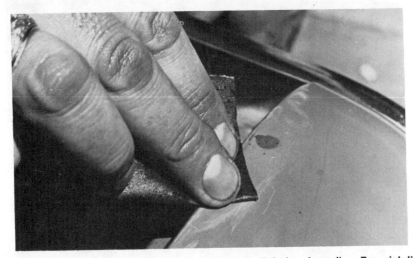

3. Small rust spots and scratches like these will only require light hand sanding. For a job like this, you can start with about grade 320 sandpaper and then use a 400 grit for the final sanding.

4. Once you've sanded the area with 320 paper, wet a piece of 400 paper and sand it lightly. Wet sanding will feather the edges of the surrounding paint into the area to be painted. For large areas, you could use a sanding block, but it's not really necessary for a small job like this.

5. The area should look like this once you're finished sanding. Wipe off any water and run the palm of your hand over the sanded area with your eyes closed. You shouldn't be able to feel any bumps or ridges anywhere. Make sure you have sanded a couple of inches back in each direction so you'll get good paint adhesion.

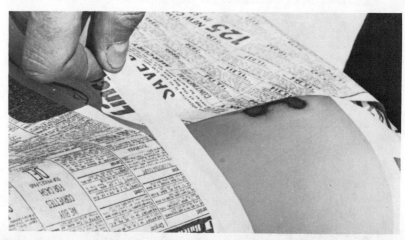

6. Once you have the area sanded to your satisfaction, mask the surrounding area with masking tape and newspaper. Be sure to cover any chrome or trim that might get sprayed. You'll have to mask far enough back from the damaged area to allow for overspray. If you mask right around the sanded spots, you'll end up with a series of lines marking the painted area.

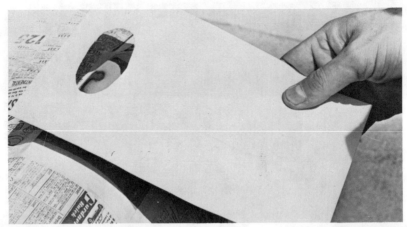

7. You can avoid a lot of excess overspray by cutting a hole in a piece of cardboard that approximately matches the area you are going to paint. Hold the cardboard steady over the area as you spray the primer on. If you haven't painted before, it's a good idea to practice on something before you try painting your car. Don't hold the paint can in one spot. Keep it moving and you'll avoid runs and sags.

8. The primered area should look like this when you have finished. It's better to spray several light coats than one heavy coat. Let the primer dry for several minutes between coats. Make sure you've covered all the bare metal.

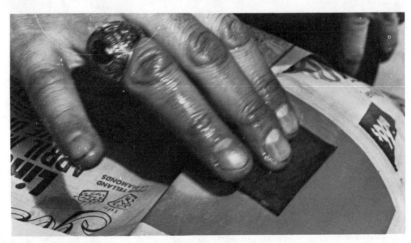

9. After the primer has dried, sand the area with wet 400 paper, wash it off and let it dry. Your final coat goes on next, so make sure the area is clean and dry.

10. Spray the touch-up paint on using the cardboard again. Make the first coat a very light coat (known as a fog coat). Remember to keep the paint can moving smoothly at about 8–12 inches from the surface.

11. Once you've finished painting, let the paint dry for about 15 minutes before you remove the masking tape and newspaper.

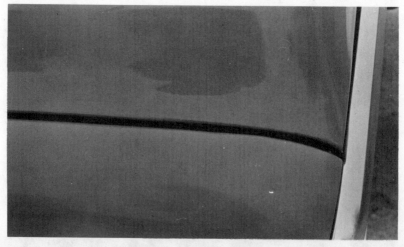

12. Let the paint dry for several days before you rub it out lightly with rubbing compound, and the finished job should be indistinguishable from the rest of the car. Don't rub hard or you'll cut through the paint.

Repairing Rust Holes With Fiberglass

1. The job we've picked here isn't an easy one mainly because of the location. The compound curves make the work trickier than if the surface were flat.

2. You'll need a drill and a wire brush for the first step, which is the removal of all the paint and rust from the rusted-out area.

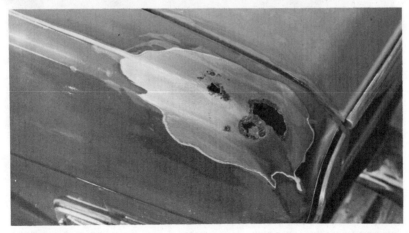

3. When you've finished grinding, the area to be repaired should look like this. Grind the paint back several inches in each direction to ensure that the patch will adhere to the metal. Remove all the damaged metal or the rust will return.

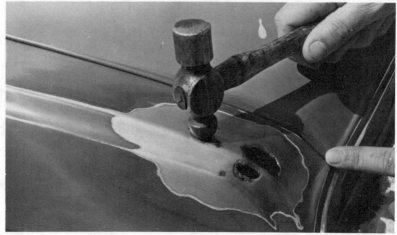

4. Tap the edges of the holes inward with a ballpeen hammer to allow for the thickness of the fiberglass material. Tap lightly so that you don't destroy any contours.

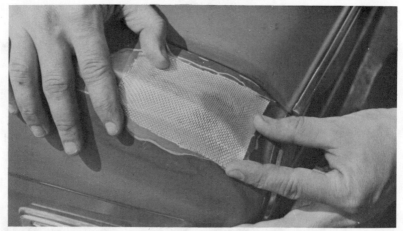

5. Follow the directions of the kit you purchase carefully. With fiberglass repair kits, the first step is generally to cut one or two pieces of fiberglass to cover the hole. Quite often, the procedure is to cut one patch the size of the prepared area and one patch the size of the hole.

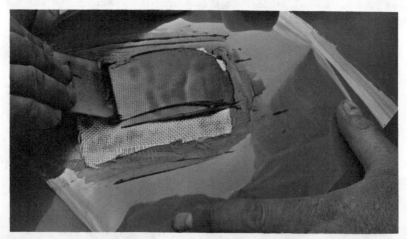

6. Mix the fiberglass material and the patching compound together following the directions supplied with the kit. With this particular kit, a layer type process is used, with the entire mixture being prepared on a piece of plastic film known as a release sheet. Keep in mind that not all kits work this way. Be careful when you mix the catalyst with the resin, as too much catalyst will harden the mixture before you can apply it.

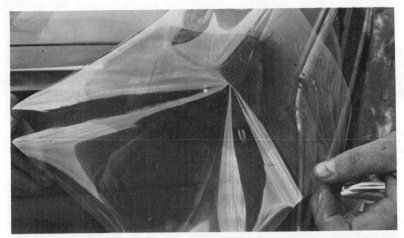

7. Spread the material on the damaged area using the release sheet. This process is essentially meant for smooth flat areas, and as a result, the release sheet would not adhere to the surface properly on our test car. If this happens to you, you'll probably have to remove the release sheet and spread the fiberglass compound out with your fingers or a small spreader.

8. This is what the fiberglass mixture looked like on our car after it had hardened. Because of the contours, we found it nearly impossible to smooth the mixture with a spreader, so we used our fingers. Unfortunately, it makes for a messy job that requires a lot of sanding. If you're working on a flat surface, you won't have this problem.

9. After the patch has hardened, sand it down to a smooth surface. You'll probably have to start with about grade 100 sandpaper and work your way up to 400 wet paper. If you have a particularly rough surface, you could start with a half-round plastic file.

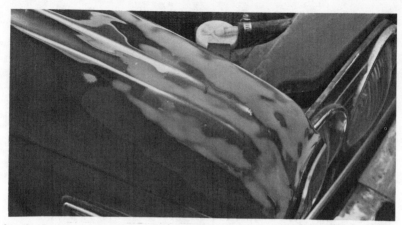

10. This is what the finished product should look like before you apply paint. Many of the kits come with glazing compound to fill in small imperfections left after the initial sanding. You'll probably need some. We did. The entire sanding operation took about an hour. Feather the edges of the repaired area into the surrounding paint carefully. As in any other body job, your hand is the best indicator of what's smooth and what isn't. It doesn't matter if it looks smooth. It's got to feel smooth. Take your time with this step and it will come out right.

11. Once you've smoothed out the repair, mask the entire area carefully, and spray the repair with primer. Keep the spray can moving in steady even strokes, overlap every stroke, and keep the spray can about 8–12 inches from the surface. Apply several coats of primer, letting the primer dry between coats.

12. The finished product (in primer) looks like this. If you were going to just spot paint this area, the next step would be to spray the correct color on the repaired area. This particular car is waiting for a complete paint job.

Appendix

General Conversion Table

Multiply by	To convert	To	
2.54	Inches	Centimeters	.3937
30.48	Feet	Centimeters	.0328
.914	Yards	Meters	1.094
1.609	Miles	Kilometers	.621
.645	Square inches	Square cm.	.155
.836	Square yards	Square meters	1.196
16.39	Cubic inches	Cubic cm.	.061
28.3	Cubic feet	Liters	.0353
.4536	Pounds	Kilograms	2.2045
4.226	Gallons	Liters	.264
.068	Lbs./sq. in. (psi)	Atmospheres	14.7
.138	Foot pounds	Kg. m.	7.23
1.014	H.P. (DIN)	H.P. (SAE)	.9861
——	To obtain	From	Multiply by

Note: 1 cm. equals 10 mm.; 1 mm. equals .0394″.

Conversion—Common Fractions to Decimals and Millimeters

INCHES			INCHES			INCHES		
Common Fractions	Decimal Fractions	Millimeters (approx.)	Common Fractions	Decimal Fractions	Millimeters (approx.)	Common Fractions	Decimal Fractions	Millimeters (approx.)
1/128	.008	0.20	11/32	.344	8.73	43/64	.672	17.07
1/64	.016	0.40	23/64	.359	9.13	11/16	.688	17.46
1/32	.031	0.79	3/8	.375	9.53	45/64	.703	17.86
3/64	.047	1.19	25/64	.391	9.92	23/32	.719	18.26
1/16	.063	1.59	13/32	.406	10.32	47/64	.734	18.65
5/64	.078	1.98	27/64	.422	10.72	3/4	.750	19.05
3/32	.094	2.38	7/16	.438	11.11	49/64	.766	19.45
7/64	.109	2.78	29/64	.453	11.51	25/32	.781	19.84
1/8	.125	3.18	15/32	.469	11.91	51/64	.797	20.24
9/64	.141	3.57	31/64	.484	12.30	13/16	.813	20.64
5/32	.156	3.97	1/2	.500	12.70	53/64	.828	21.03
11/64	.172	4.37	33/64	.516	13.10	27/32	.844	21.43
3/16	.188	4.76	17/32	.531	13.49	55/64	.859	21.83
13/64	.203	5.16	35/64	.547	13.89	7/8	.875	22.23
7/32	.219	5.56	9/16	.563	14.29	57/64	.891	22.62
15/64	.234	5.95	37/64	.578	14.68	29/32	.906	23.02
1/4	.250	6.35	19/32	.594	15.08	59/64	.922	23.42
17/64	.266	6.75	39/64	.609	15.48	15/16	.938	23.81
9/32	.281	7.14	5/8	.625	15.88	61/64	.953	24.21
19/64	.297	7.54	41/64	.641	16.27	31/32	.969	24.61
5/16	.313	7.94	21/32	.656	16.67	63/64	.984	25.00
21/64	.328	8.33						

Conversion—Millimeters to Decimal Inches

mm	inches	mm	inches	mm	inches	mm	inches	mm	inches
1	.039 370	31	1.220 470	61	2.401 570	91	3.582 670	210	8.267 700
2	.078 740	32	1.259 840	62	2.440 940	92	3.622 040	220	8.661 400
3	.118 110	33	1.299 210	63	2.480 310	93	3.661 410	230	9.055 100
4	.157 480	34	1.338 580	64	2.519 680	94	3.700 780	240	9.448 800
5	.196 850	35	1.377 949	65	2.559 050	95	3.740 150	250	9.842 500
6	.236 220	36	1.417 319	66	2.598 420	96	3.779 520	260	10.236 200
7	.275 590	37	1.456 689	67	2.637 790	97	3.818 890	270	10.629 900
8	.314 960	38	1.496 050	68	2.677 160	98	3.858 260	280	11.032 600
9	.354 330	39	1.535 430	69	2.716 530	99	3.897 630	290	11.417 300
10	.393 700	40	1.574 800	70	2.755 900	100	3.937 000	300	11.811 000
11	.433 070	41	1.614 170	71	2.795 270	105	4.133 848	310	12.204 700
12	.472 440	42	1.653 540	72	2.834 640	110	4.330 700	320	12.598 400
13	.511 810	43	1.692 910	73	2.874 010	115	4.527 550	330	12.992 100
14	.551 180	44	1.732 280	74	2.913 380	120	4.724 400	340	13.385 800
15	.590 550	45	1.771 650	75	2.952 750	125	4.921 250	350	13.779 500
16	.629 920	46	1.811 020	76	2.992 120	130	5.118 100	360	14.173 200
17	.669 290	47	1.850 390	77	3.031 490	135	5.314 950	370	14.566 900
18	.708 660	48	1.889 760	78	3.070 860	140	5.511 800	380	14.960 600
19	.748 030	49	1.929 130	79	3.110 230	145	5.708 650	390	15.354 300
20	.787 400	50	1.968 500	80	3.149 600	150	5.905 500	400	15.748 000
21	.826 770	51	2.007 870	81	3.188 970	155	6.102 350	500	19.685 000
22	.866 140	52	2.047 240	82	3.228 340	160	6.299 200	600	23.622 000
23	.905 510	53	2.086 610	83	3.267 710	165	6.496 050	700	27.559 000
24	.944 880	54	2.125 980	84	3.307 080	170	6.692 900	800	31.496 000
25	.984 250	55	2.165 350	85	3.346 450	175	6.889 750	900	35.433 000
26	1.023 620	56	2.204 720	86	3.385 820	180	7.086 600	1000	39.370 000
27	1.062 990	57	2.244 090	87	3.425 190	185	7.283 450	2000	78.740 000
28	1.102 360	58	2.283 460	88	3.464 560	190	7.480 300	3000	118.110 000
29	1.141 730	59	2.322 830	89	3.503 903	195	7.677 150	4000	157.480 000
30	1.181 100	60	2.362 200	90	3.543 300	200	7.874 000	5000	196.850 000

To change decimal millimeters to decimal inches, position the decimal point where desired on either side of the millimeter measurement shown and reset the inches decimal by the same number of digits in the same direction. For example, to convert 0.001 mm to decimal inches, reset the decimal behind the 1 mm (shown on the chart) to 0.001; change the decimal inch equivalent (0.039″ shown) to 0.000039″.

Tap Drill Sizes

National Fine or S.A.E.

Screw & Tap Size	Threads Per Inch	Use Drill Number
No. 5	44	37
No. 6	40	33
No. 8	36	29
No. 10	32	21
No. 12	28	15
¼	28	3
⁵/₁₆	24	1
³/₈	24	Q
⁷/₁₆	20	W
½	20	²⁹/₆₄
⁹/₁₆	18	³³/₆₄
⅝	18	³⁷/₆₄
¾	16	¹¹/₁₆
⅞	14	¹³/₁₆
1⅛	12	1³/₆₄
1¼	12	1¹¹/₆₄
1½	12	1²⁷/₆₄

Tap Drill Sizes

National Coarse or U.S.S.

Screw & Tap Size	Threads Per Inch	Use Drill Number
No. 5	40	39
No. 6	32	36
No. 8	32	29
No. 10	24	25
No. 12	24	17
¼	20	8
⁵/₁₆	18	F
³/₈	16	⁵/₁₆
⁷/₁₆	14	U
½	13	²⁷/₆₄
⁹/₁₆	12	³¹/₆₄
⅝	11	¹⁷/₃₂
¾	10	²¹/₃₂
⅞	9	⁴⁹/₆₄
1	8	⅞
1⅛	7	⁶³/₆₄
1¼	7	1⁷/₆₄
1½	6	1¹¹/₃₂

Decimal Equivalent Size of the Number Drills

Drill No.	Decimal Equivalent	Drill No.	Decimal Equivalent	Drill No.	Decimal Equivalent
80	.0135	53	.0595	26	.1470
79	.0145	52	.0635	25	.1495
78	.0160	51	.0670	24	.1520
77	.0180	50	.0700	23	.1540
76	.0200	49	.0730	22	.1570
75	.0210	48	.0760	21	.1590
74	.0225	47	.0785	20	.1610
73	.0240	46	.0810	19	.1660
72	.0250	45	.0820	18	.1695
71	.0260	44	.0860	17	.1730
70	.0280	43	.0890	16	.1770
69	.0292	42	.0935	15	.1800
68	.0310	41	.0960	14	.1820
67	.0320	40	.0980	13	.1850
66	.0330	39	.0995	12	.1890
65	.0350	38	.1015	11	.1910
64	.0360	37	.1040	10	.1935
63	.0370	36	.1065	9	.1960
62	.0380	35	.1100	8	.1990
61	.0390	34	.1110	7	.2010
60	.0400	33	.1130	6	.2040
59	.0410	32	.1160	5	.2055
58	.0420	31	.1200	4	.2090
57	.0430	30	.1285	3	.2130
56	.0465	29	.1360	2	.2210
55	.0520	28	.1405	1	.2280
54	.0550	27	.1440		

Decimal Equivalent Size of the Letter Drills

Letter Drill	Decimal Equivalent	Letter Drill	Decimal Equivalent	Letter Drill	Decimal Equivalent
A	.234	J	.277	S	.348
B	.238	K	.281	T	.358
C	.242	L	.290	U	.368
D	.246	M	.295	V	.377
E	.250	N	.302	W	.386
F	.257	O	.316	X	.397
G	.261	P	.323	Y	.404
H	.266	Q	.332	Z	.413
I	.272	R	.339		

Anti-Freeze Chart

Temperatures Shown in Degrees Fahrenheit +32 is Freezing

Cooling System Capacity Quarts	*Quarts of ETHYLENE GLYCOL Needed for Protection to Temperatures Shown Below* 1	2	3	4	5	6	7	8	9	10	11	12	13	14
10	+24°	+16°	+ 4°	−12°	−34°	−62°								
11	+25	+18	+ 8	− 6	−23	−47								
12	+26	+19	+10	0	−15	−34	−57°							
13	+27	+21	+13	+ 3	− 9	−25	−45							
14			+15	+ 6	− 5	−18	−34							
15			+16	+ 8	0	−12	−26							
16			+17	+10	+ 2	− 8	−19	−34	−52°					
17			+18	+12	+ 5	− 4	−14	−27	−42					
18			+19	+14	+ 7	0	−10	−21	−34	−50°				
19			+20	+15	+ 9	+ 2	− 7	−16	−28	−42				
20				+16	+10	+ 4	− 3	−12	−22	−34	−48°			
21				+17	+12	+ 6	0	− 9	−17	−28	−41			
22				+18	+13	+ 8	+ 2	− 6	−14	−23	−34	−47°		
23				+19	+14	+ 9	+ 4	− 3	−10	−19	−29	−40		
24				+19	+15	+10	+ 5	0	− 8	−15	−23	−34	−46°	
25				+20	+16	+12	+ 7	+ 1	− 5	−12	−20	−29	−40	−50°
26					+17	+13	+ 8	+ 3	− 3	− 9	−16	−25	−34	−44
27					+18	+14	+ 9	+ 5	− 1	− 7	−13	−21	−29	−39
28					+18	+15	+10	+ 6	+ 1	− 5	−11	−18	−25	−34
29					+19	+16	+12	+ 7	+ 2	− 3	− 8	−15	−22	−29
30					+20	+17	+13	+ 8	+ 4	− 1	− 6	−12	−18	−25

For capacities over 30 quarts divide true capacity by 3. Find quarts Anti-Freeze for the ⅓ and multiply by 3 for quarts to add.

For capacities under 10 quarts multiply true capacity by 3. Find quarts Anti-Freeze for the tripled volume and divide by 3 for quarts to add.

To Increase the Freezing Protection of Anti-Freeze Solutions Already Installed

Cooling System Capacity Quarts	*Number of Quarts of ETHYLENE GLYCOL Anti-Freeze Required to Increase Protection*													
	From +20° F. to					*From +10° F. to*					*From 0° F. to*			
	0°	*−10°*	*−20°*	*−30°*	*−40°*	*0°*	*−10°*	*−20°*	*−30°*	*−40°*	*−10°*	*−20°*	*−30°*	*−40°*
10	1¾	2¼	3	3½	3¾	¾	1½	2¼	2¾	3¼	¾	1½	2	2½
12	2	2¾	3½	4	4½	1	1¾	2½	3¼	3¾	1	1¾	2½	3¼
14	2¼	3¼	4	4¾	5½	1¼	2	3	3¾	4½	1	2	3	3½
16	2½	3½	4½	5¼	6	1¼	2½	3½	4¼	5¼	1¼	2¼	3¼	4
18	3	4	5	6	7	1½	2¾	4	5	5¾	1½	2½	3¾	4¾
20	3¼	4½	5¾	6¾	7½	1¾	3	4¼	5½	6½	1½	2¾	4¼	5¼
22	3½	5	6¼	7¼	8¼	1¾	3¼	4¾	6	7¼	1¾	3¼	4½	5½
24	4	5½	7	8	9	2	3½	5	6½	7½	1¾	3½	5	6
26	4¼	6	7½	8¾	10	2	4	5½	7	8¼	2	3¾	5½	6¾
28	4½	6¼	8	9½	10½	2¼	4¼	6	7½	9	2	4	5¾	7¼
30	5	6¾	8½	10	11½	2½	4½	6½	8	9½	2¼	4¼	6¼	7¾

Test radiator solution with proper hydrometer. Determine from the table the number of quarts of solution to be drawn off from a full cooling system and replace with undiluted anti-freeze, to give the desired increased protection. For example, to increase protection of a 22-quart cooling system containing Ethylene Glycol (permanent type) anti-freeze, from +20° F. to −20° F. will require the replacement of 6¼ quarts of solution with undiluted anti-freeze.

Index

A

Air cleaner, 4
Air conditioning, 9
  Sight glass check, 9
Alternator, 54
Appendix, 175
Automatic transmission, 134
  Adjustment, 135
  Filter service, 135
  Pan removal, 135
  Removal and Installation, 134
Axle, 11
  Fluid recommendations, 11
  Lubricant level, 11
Axle ratios
Axle shafts, 140

B

Back-up lights switch, 132
Ball joints, 136
Battery
  Jump starting, 19
  Maintenance, 13
  Removal, 59
Belt tension, 7
Brakes, 148
  Adjustment, 148
  Bleeding, 154
  Fluid level, 11
  Fluid recommendations, 11
  Front brakes, 155, 159
  Master cylinder, 152
  Parking brake, 162
  Rear brakes, 159
Breaker points, 21
Bulbs
Body Care, 163

C

Camshaft and bearings, 68
Capacities, 13
Carburetor
  Adjustment, 27, 107
  Overhaul, 112
  Replacement, 106
Catalytic converter, 103
Charging system, 54
Chassis lubrication, 18
Clutch, 132
  Adjustment, 132
  Removal and installation, 133
Compression, 42
Connecting rod and bearings, 87
Cooling system, 78
Crankcase ventilation (PCV), 6
Crankshaft, 94
Cylinder head torque sequence, 72

D

Distributor
  Removal and installation, 54
  Breaker points, 21
Drive axle, 128, 134
Dwell angle, 23

E

Electrical
  Chassis, 119
  Engine, 53
Emission controls, 96
Engine, 59
  Camshaft, 68
  Cylinder head, 71
  Cylinder head torque sequence, 72
  Exhaust manifold, 73
  Front cover, 68
  Identification, 3
  Intake manifold, 72
  Oil recommendations, 16
  Piston (positioning) 74
  Rebuilding, 79
  Removal and installation, 62
  Specifications, 59
  Timing belt, 65
  Timing belt cover, 65
  Timing gears, 67
  Tune-up
Evaporative canister, 6
Exhaust manifold, 73

F

Firing order, 54
Fluid level checks, 10
  Battery, 13
  Coolant, 11
  Engine oil, 10
  Master cylinder, 11
  Rear axle, 11
  Steering gear, 13
  Transmission, 10
Fluid recommendations, 16
Front suspension, 136
  Wheel alignment, 140
Front wheel bearing, 151
Fuel injection, 28, 114
  Adjustment, 28, 114
Fuel filter, 14
Fuel pump, 103
Fuel system, 103
Fuses and flashers, 127

H

Headlights, 126
Heater, 119

I

Identification, 3
  Vehicle, 3
  Engine, 3
  Transmission, 4
Idle speed and mixture, 27
Ignition switch, 146
Ignition timing, 23

Instrument cluster, 125
Intake manifold, 72

J

Jacking, 19
Jump starting, 19

L

Light bulb specifications, 127
Lubrication, 16
  Chassis, 18
  Engine, 16

M

Maintenance (routine), 3
  Intervals, 4
Manifolds, 72, 73
Manual transmission, 128
Master cylinder, 152
Model identification, 3

N

Neutral safety switch, 132

O

Oil and fuel recommendations, 16
Oil change, 17
Oil filter (engine), 18
Oil pan, 76
Oil pump, 78
Oil level (engine), 10

P

Parking brake, 162
Piston and rings, 74
  Installation, 74
  Positioning, 74
PCV valve, 6

R

Radiator, 78
Radio, 122
Rear suspension, 140
Rear Main oil seal, 76
Rings (piston), 74
Routine maintenance, 4

S

Shock absorber, 136
  Front, 136
  Rear, 141
Spark plugs, 20
Specifications
  Battery and starter, 59
  Brakes, 151

Capacities, 13
Crankshaft & connecting rod, 60
Fuses, 127
General engine, 59
Light bulb, 127
Piston and ring, 60
Torque, 60
Tune-up, 22
Valve, 60
Wheel alignment, 145
Speedometer cable, 126
Springs
　Front, 140
　Rear, 141
Starter, 56
Steering, 145
　Gear, 147
　Linkage, 147
　Wheel, 145
Stub axle, 141

T

Thermostat, 78
Tie-rod, 147
Tires, 13
Tools & equipment, 2
Torsion bar

Towing, 19
Transmission
　Automatic, 134
　Manual, 128
Troubleshooting, 30
Tune-up, 20
　Procedures, 20
　Specifications, 22
Turn signal switch, 145

V

Valves
　Adjustment, 25
　Service, 81
Vehicle identification, 3

W

Water pump, 78
Wheels, 13
Wheel alignment, 140
Wheel bearings, 142, 151
Wheel cylinders, 161
Windshield wipers, 123
　Arm, 123
　Blade, 123
　Motor, 123